Contents

KU-639-814

Temple life colour section following p.64

Capital cuisine colour section following p.112

Colour maps section following p.224

3

Introduction to

Beijing

Beijing is China at its most dynamic: a vivid metropolis spiked with high-rises, changing and growing at a furious, unfettered pace. Yet this forward-looking capital of the world's newest superpower is also where, for a thousand years, the drama of China's imperial history was played out, with the emperor sitting enthroned at the centre of the Chinese universe. Though Beijing is a very different city today, it still remains spiritually and politically the heart of the nation. Shanghai and Hong Kong may be where the money is, but it's Beijing that pulls the strings, and its lure is irresistible to many Chinese, who come here to fulfil dreams of success in business, politics or the arts.

The Chinese character *chai* (demolish), painted in white on old buildings – and the cranes that skewer the skyline – attest to the speed of change, affecting not just the city's architecture: as China embraces capitalism, social structures are also being revolutionized. The government is as determined as ever to repress dissent, but outside the political arena, just about anything goes these days. Students in the latest street fashions while away their time in Internet cafés, dropouts dye their hair and mosh in punk clubs, bohemians dream up boutiques over frappuccinos. New prosperity is evident everywhere – witness all the Mercedes-driving businessmen and the schoolkids with mobile phones – but not everyone has benefited: migrant day-labourers wait for work outside the stations, and homeless beggars, not long ago a rare sight, are now as common as in Western cities.

The first impression of Beijing, for both foreigners and visiting Chinese, is often of a bewildering vastness, conveyed by the sprawl of uniform apartment

The **Rough Guide** to

written and researched by

Simon Lewis

ROUGH
GUIDES

NEW YORK • LONDON • DELHI

www.roughguides.com

Preparing for the Olympics

The **Beijing Olympics** is about a great deal more than sport. The games are being presented as China's coming out party, showing the world that the new China is a force to be reckoned with, and that Beijing is a worthy capital for a modern superpower.

Accordingly, an awe-inspiring building program is underway. In the far north of the city, along the old imperial axis, where the Yuan dynasty city gates once stood, Herzog and de Meuron's futuristic 90,000-seater **National Olympic Stadium** is being constructed. Its massive external lattice of intertwined beams have earned it the nickname, the "Bird's Nest". Nearby, the **National Swimming Centre** is equally stunning; it's a translucent block swathed in an energy-saving skin that looks like bubble wrap (dubbed the "Water Cube"). The eight-kilometre north–south **pathway** to the Olympic park has been transformed by Albert Speer Junior (the son of Hitler's favourite architect) into a green strip of parkland, playgrounds and walkways. Other regeneration projects include six new subway lines, a light-rail system and a new airport terminal.

If anything is likely to spoil the party, it is the city's appalling **pollution** – Beijing only had sixty clear-sky days in 2006. Around 12 billion dollars has been spent on **green projects**: all the dirtiest factories have been moved, at huge cost, out into the sticks; a 130-kilometre tree belt has been constructed around the city; and there's been mandatory adoption of European emission standards for vehicles. But all these measures to improve air quality have already been cancelled out by the vast increase in **car ownership** – there are now almost three million cars on the streets. In order to cut down on smog, in the months before the Olympics, traffic will be strictly controlled, with more than a million cars banned from entering the city. In order to guarantee at least a few clear days, the clouds over the city will be seeded (via silver iodide-fired from rockets) to force them to rain just before the Games.

buildings in which most of the city's population of twelve million are housed, and the eight-lane freeways that slice it up. It's a perception reinforced on closer acquaintance by the concrete desert of Tian'anmen Square, and the gargantuan buildings of the modern executive around it. The main tourist sights – the Forbidden City, the Summer Palace and the Great Wall – also impress with their scale, while more manageable grandeur is on offer at the city's attractive temples, including the Tibetan-style Yonghe Gong, the Taoist Baiyun Guan, and the astonishing Temple of Heaven, once a centre for imperial rites.

Chinese script

Chinese characters are simplified images of what they represent, and their origins as pictograms can often still be seen, even though they have become highly abstract today. The earliest known examples of Chinese writing are predictions, which were cut into "oracle bones" over three thousand years ago during the Shang dynasty, though the characters must have been in use long before, for these inscriptions already amount to a highly complex writing system. As the characters represent **concepts**, not sounds, written Chinese cuts through the problem of communication in a country with many different dialects. However, learning the writing system is ponderous, taking children an estimated two years longer than with an alphabet. Foreigners learning Mandarin use the modern **pinyin** transliteration system of accented Roman letters – used in this book – to help memorize the sounds. For more, see p.185.

With its sights, history and, by no means least, delicious food (all of China's diverse cuisines can be enjoyed cheaply at the city's numerous restaurants and street stalls), Beijing is a place almost everyone enjoys. But it's essentially a private city, one whose surface, though attractive, is difficult to penetrate. The city's history and unique character are in the details: to find and experience these, check out the little antique markets; the local shopping districts; the smaller, quirkier sights; the *hutongs*, the city's twisted grey stone alleyways that are – as one Chinese guidebook puts it – "fine and numerous as the hairs of a cow"; and the parks, where you'll see Beijingers performing *tai ji* and old men sitting with their caged songbirds. Take advantage, too, of the city's burgeoning nightlife and see just how far the Chinese have gone down the road of what used to be deemed "spiritual pollution". Keep your eyes open, and you'll soon notice that westernization and the rise of a brash consumer society is not the only trend here; just as marked is the revival of older Chinese culture,

▲ Boys playing football, Jingshan Park

▼ Bronze bird statue, Hall of Supremacy

much of it outlawed during the more austere years of communist rule. Witness, for example, the sudden re-emergence of the **teahouse** as a genteel meeting place, and the renewed interest in traditional music and opera and **imperial cuisine** – dishes once enjoyed by the emperors.

What to see

I n the absolute centre of Beijing, **Tian'anmen Square** is the physical and spiritual heart of the city. Some of the most significant sights are very close by, including the **Forbidden City**, two colossal museums, and the formidable buildings of the modern executive, as well as the corpse of Chairman Mao, lying pickled in his sombre mausoleum.

The main tourist sights impress with their scale

The road leading south from here, **Qianmen Dajie**, once the pivot of the ancient city, is now a busy market area that leads to the magnificent **Temple of Heaven**. These days the main axis of the city has shifted to the east–west road, a showcase of grandiose architecture that divides Tian'anmen Square and the Forbidden City. Changing its name every few kilometres along its length, the thoroughfare is generally referred to as **Chang'an Jie**. Westward, this street takes you past the shopping district of **Xidan** to the **Military Museum**, monument to a fast-disappearing overtly communist ethos. To the east, the road zooms past more giant buildings and glamorous shopping districts – notably **Wangfujing**, **Jianguomen** and the **Silk Market** – to the little oasis of calm that is the **Ancient Observatory**, where Jesuit priests used to teach the charting of the heavens.

Once, dark, twisting little alleys – or **hutongs** – formed a web between the grid lines of the major streets; now, almost all have been bulldozed.

▼ Dazhalan street scene

The charming heritage district centred around the Houhai lakes, north of the Forbidden City, is one of the few areas to retain this traditional street plan. Many sights here are remnants of the imperial past, when the area was home to princes, dukes and eunuchs. They might be tricky to navigate, but this is one of the few parts of the city where aimless rambling is rewarded. Easier to track down is **Beihai Park**, the imperial pleasure grounds, just north of the Forbidden City, and the fine **Yonghe Gong**, a popular Lama-ist temple in the northern outskirts.

Beijing's sprawling outskirts are a messy jumble of farmland, housing and industry, but it's here you'll find the most pleasant places to retreat from the city's hectic pace, including the two **summer palaces**, the giant parks of **Badachu** and **Xiangshan**, and the **Tanzhe, Fahai** and **Jietai temples**. Well outside the city – but within the scope of a day-trip – is the **Great Wall**, which winds over lonely ridges only a few hours' drive north of the capital.

A week is long enough to explore the city and its main sights, and get out to the Great Wall. With more time, try to venture further afield: the imperial pleasure complex of **Chengde** is easily accessible from the capital by train and bus.

Chinese Traditional Medicine

Chinese traditional medicine has been used for 2200 years – ever since the semi-mythical Xia king compiled his classic work on medicinal herbs. Around eight thousand "**herbs**" derived from roots, leaves, twigs, fruit and animal parts are used–usually dried or roasted – but sometimes stir-fried. They are generally taken as a bitter and earthy tasting tea.

Diagnosis involves feeling the pulse, examining the tongue and face, and listening to the tone of voice. Infections are believed to be caused by internal imbalances, so the **whole body** is treated, rather than just the symptom. In the treatment of flu, for example, a "cold action" herb would be used to reduce fever, another to induce sweating and so flush out the system, and another as a replenishing tonic.

Just as aspirin is derived from willow bark, many Western drugs come from traditional herbal remedies: artemisin is one such medicine, and is an effective anti-malarial treatment.

With their presentation boxes of ginseng roots and deer antlers, traditional Chinese **pharmacies** are colourful places; a good one to check out in Beijing is Tongrentang on Dazhalan, which also offers on-the-spot diagnosis.

When to go

The best time to visit Beijing is in the **autumn** (Sept–Oct), when it's dry and clement. Next best is the short **spring**, in April and May – it's dry and comfortably warm, though a little windy. Fortunately, the spring dust storms that once plagued the city have lessened of late. In **winter** (Nov–Feb) it gets very cold, down to -20°C (-4°F), and the mean winds that whip off the Mongolian plains feel like they're freezing your ears off. **Summer** (June–Aug) is muggy and hot, with temperatures up to 30°C (86°F) and sometimes beyond.

The run-up to **Chinese New Year** (falling in late Jan or early to mid-Feb) is

Fish painting

◀ The cable car at Simatai

a great time to be in the country: everyone is in festive mood and the city is bedecked with decorations. This isn't a good time to travel around, however, as much of the population is on the move, and transport systems become hopelessly overstretched. It's best to avoid Beijing during the first three days of the festival itself, as everyone is at home with family, and a lot of businesses and sights are closed.

Climate

	°C (°F) Average daily		Rainfall Average daily
	max	min	mm (in)
Jan	1 (34)	-10 (14)	4 (0.2)
Feb	4 (39)	-8 (18)	5 (0.2)
March	11 (52)	-1 (30)	8 (0.3)
April	21 (70)	7 (45)	17 (0.7)
May	27 (81)	13 (55)	35 (1.4)
June	31 (88)	18 (64)	78 (3.1)
July	31 (88)	21 (70)	243 (9.6)
Aug	30 (86)	20 (68)	141 (5.6)
Sept	26 (79)	14 (57)	58 (2.3)
Oct	20 (68)	6 (43)	16 (0.6)
Nov	9 (48)	-2 (28)	11 (0.4)
Dec	3 (37)	-8 (18)	3 (0.1)

20

things not to miss

It's not possible to see everything Beijing has to offer on a short trip – and we don't suggest you try. What follows is a selective taste of the city's highlights: stunning temples, delicious food, fantastic markets and fascinating excursions beyond the city – all arranged in colour-coded categories to help you find the very best things to see and experience. All entries have a page reference to take you straight into the guide, where you can find out more.

01 **Tian'anmen Square** Page **50** • The grandiose heart of communist China, a concrete plain laden with historical resonances.

02
Mao's mausoleum Page 53 • Join the queue of awed peasants shuffling past the pickled corpse of the founder of modern China in his giant tomb.

03 The Botanical Gardens Page 115
• Especially on sunny days in spring, Beijing's botanical gardens offer welcome respite from the city's sombre palette.

04 Houhai Lake Page 94
• Beautiful and serene in the early morning, Houhai Lake is the perfect setting for a lazy cappuccino – then get out on the water in a duck-shaped pedalo.

05 Forbidden City Page 56 •
For five centuries centre of the Chinese universe and private pleasure ground of the emperor, this sumptuous palace complex ranks as the city's main attraction.

06 Temple of Heaven
Page **68** • A gorgeous temple in an elegant park.

07 Hutongs
Page **65** • The tangle of alleys behind Houhai Lake reveals the city's real, private face.

08 Summer Palace
Page **104** • Once the exclusive retreat of the emperors, this beautiful landscaped park, dotted with imperial buildings, is now open to all.

09 Markets
Page **159** • The city's jumbled cornucopias of bric-a-brac, souvenirs, curios and fake antiques are great for a browse and a haggle.

ACTIVITIES | CONSUME | EVENTS | NATURE | SIGHTS

13

10 **Great Wall at Simatai** Page **113** • A dramatic stretch of crumbly, vertiginous fortifications three hours from Beijing.

11 **Nanluogu Xiang** Page **97**
• This trendy *hutong* of restaurants and boutiques has a Left Bank feel to it.

12 **Baiyun Guan** Page **74** • See China at prayer in this attractive and popular Taoist temple, where devotees play games such as throwing coins at the temple bell.

13 **Night-life** Page **147** • Experience Beijing's cultural explosion by catching one of the new bands in a smoky bar, or just bop with the beautiful people.

14 **Dazhalan** Page **65** • An earthy, hectic shopping street with some grand facades and plenty of opportunities for bargain hunting.

15 **Beijing duck** See *Capital cuisine colour section* • Though heavy on calories and very rich, Beijing's culinary speciality is supremely tasty.

16 **Yonghe Gong** Page **97** • A lively Tibetan temple, flamboyantly decorated and busy with devotees and monks.

17 798 Art District Page 87
• This huge complex of art galleries has become Ground Zero for the city's bohemians and fashionistas.

18
Acrobatics Page **154** • The style may be vaudeville, but the stunts, performed by some of the world's greatest acrobats, are breathtaking.

19 Teahouses Page **151** •
Experience the ancient and relaxing tea ceremony in one of Beijing's elegant new teahouses.

20 Beijing opera Page **151** • Largely incomprehensible to foreigners, and many Chinese, but still a great spectacle.

Basics

Basics

Getting there

Beijing is China's main international transport hub, with plenty of direct flights from European capitals and from American, Australian and Asian cities. Though most travellers arrive by plane, there's also the possibility of arriving by rail from elsewhere in China or, more romantically, from Moscow (on the Trans-Siberian Express; see p.20).

Airfares vary with season, with the highest fares charged from Easter to October and around Christmas, New Year, and just before the Chinese New Year (which falls between late-Jan and mid-Feb). Note also that flying at weekends is slightly more expensive; price ranges quoted below assume midweek travel.

You can often cut costs by going through a **specialist flight agent** – either a consolidator, who buys up blocks of tickets from the airlines and sells them at a discount, or a **discount agent**, who may also offer special student and youth fares plus travel insurance, rail passes, car rentals, tours and the like.

Flights from the UK and Ireland

The only non-stop flights to Beijing **from the UK** are Air China and British Airways flights from London Heathrow (10hr). It's not a problem to fly from other UK airports or **from the Republic of Ireland**, though you'll end up either catching a connecting flight to London or flying via your airline's hub city.

There are plenty of indirect flights to Beijing from London with airlines such as Emirates, Qatar Airways, Lufthansa and Aeroflot, stopping off in the airline's hub city. These are a little cheaper than direct flights, with prices starting from around £380 in low season, rising to £700 in high season. If you're flying from the Republic of Ireland, reckon on €1000 in low season, €1500 in high season.

Flights from the US and Canada

There's no shortage of direct flights to Beijing **from North America**; carriers include Air China, Air Canada and United. It takes around thirteen hours' flying time to reach Beijing **from the West Coast**; add seven hours or more to this if you start **from the East Coast** (including a stopover on the West Coast en route). New routes cross the North pole, shaving a couple of hours off the flight time – currently, it's only Air Canada's Toronto and Continental's Newark flight.

In low season, expect to pay US$600–850/CDN$1000–1250 from the West Coast (Los Angeles, San Francisco, Vancouver), or US$850–1100/CDN$1300–1750 from the East Coast (New York, Montreal, Toronto). To get a good fare during high season it's important to buy your ticket as early as possible, in which case you probably won't pay more than US$200/CDN$320 above low-season tariffs.

Flights from Australia, New Zealand and South Africa

You can fly **direct** to Beijing **from Melbourne and Sydney** with, among others, Singapore Airlines, JAL, Malaysian and China Eastern. Otherwise, you will need to stop over, probably in Hong Kong. Alternatively, once in Hong Kong, you have the option of continuing your journey on the Kowloon–Beijing train (see p.25); consider taking a short hop on the train to Guangzhou and flying on to Beijing from there, as it's much cheaper than flying direct from Hong Kong.

Good deals are the Air China flights from Melbourne or Sydney direct to Beijing (A$1500); and Cathay Pacific to Hong Kong (A$1500 in low season; their fares are steep at other times). Some of the cheapest fares are with Royal Brunei Airlines, though they only serve Brisbane and Darwin. Their return fares to Hong Kong, via a stopover in Brunei, are

Fly less – stay longer! Travel and climate change

Climate change is the single biggest issue facing our planet. It is caused by a build-up in the atmosphere of carbon dioxide and other greenhouse gases, which are emitted by many sources – including planes. Already, flights account for around 3–4 percent of human-induced global warming: that figure may sound small, but it is rising year on year and threatens to counteract the progress made by reducing greenhouse emissions in other areas.

Rough Guides regard travel, overall, as a global benefit, and feel strongly that the advantages to developing economies are important, as are the opportunities for greater contact and awareness among peoples. But we all have a responsibility to limit our personal "carbon footprint". That means giving thought to how often we fly and what we can do to redress the harm that our trips create.

Flying and climate change

Pretty much every form of motorized travel generates CO_2, but planes are particularly bad offenders, releasing large volumes of greenhouse gases at altitudes where their impact is far more harmful. Flying also allows us to travel much further than we would contemplate doing by road or rail, so the emissions attributable to each passenger become truly shocking. For example, one person taking a return flight between Europe and California produces the equivalent impact of 2.5 tonnes of CO_2 – similar to the yearly output of the average UK car.

Less harmful planes may evolve but it will be decades before they replace the current fleet – which could be too late for avoiding climate chaos. In the meantime, there are limited options for concerned travellers: to reduce the amount we travel by air (take fewer trips, stay longer!), to avoid night flights (when plane contrails trap heat from Earth but can't reflect sunlight back to space), and to make the trips we do take "climate neutral" via a carbon offset scheme.

Carbon offset schemes

Offset schemes run by climatecare.org, carbonneutral.com and others allow you to "neutralize" the greenhouse gases that you are responsible for releasing. Their websites have simple calculators that let you work out the impact of any flight. Once that's done, you can pay to fund projects that will reduce future carbon emissions by an equivalent amount (such as the distribution of low-energy light bulbs and cooking stoves in developing countries). Please take the time to visit our website and make your trip climate neutral.

Ⓦ www.roughguides.com/climatechange

---

around A$1100. Qantas or British Airways are the only two operators to fly direct from Perth to Hong Kong (A$1800).

There are no direct flights to Beijing **from New Zealand**. About the best deal is on Air New Zealand or Singapore from Auckland to Hong Kong (NZ$1750). Air New Zealand, Malaysia and other carriers also fly via other Southeast Asian cities to Hong Kong and Beijing.

From Moscow: The Trans-Siberian Express

The classic overland route to Beijing is through Russia on the **Trans-Siberian**

Express, and the journey is a very memorable way to begin or end your stay in China. The fabulous views of stately birch forests, velvety prairies, misty lakes and arid plateaus help time pass, and there are frequent stops during which you can wander the station platform, purchasing food and knick-knacks. The trains are comfortable and clean: second-class compartments contain four berths, while first-class have two, and even boast a private shower. **Private tour companies** offer deals that allow you to stop off for a few days in, for example, Irkutsk or Mongolia.

There are actually two rail lines from Moscow to Beijing: the first, the Trans-Manchurian line, runs almost as far as the sea of Japan before turning south through Dongbei to Beijing, and takes six days. The second Trans-Mongolian line is more popular with tourists as it rumbles past Lake Baikal in Siberia, the grasslands of Mongolia, and the desert of northwest China. It takes around five days.

Meals are included while the train is in China. In Mongolia, the dining car accepts payment in both Chinese and Mongolian currency; while in Russia, US dollars or Russian roubles can be used. It's worth having small denominations of US dollars as you can change these on the train throughout the journey, or use them to buy food from station vendors along the way. Note that trains via Dongbei arrive in Beijing at 5.20am, so remember to change money at the border stop if you're using this route.

Booking tickets independently, you'll need to reserve a couple of weeks ahead to ensure a seat. Sorting out your travel arrangements from abroad is a rather complex business – you'll need transit visas for Russia, and if you use the Trans-Mongolian train you may have to apply for visas for Mongolia as well (US citizens don't need these). For detailed information, check Ⓦwww.seat61/trans-siberian.htm.

You can save complications by using an experienced travel agent who can organize all tickets, visas and stopovers if required, in advance. Monkey Business (Ⓦwww.monkeyshrine.com), based in Hong Kong and Beijing, offers these services, as well as rail packages; for details of companies at home which can sort out Trans-Siberian travel, see the lists of specialist travel agents for your country (see p.23). If you want to book a ticket yourself, reckon on paying the equivalent of at least US$200 for second-class travel from Moscow to Beijing.

If you're planning to take the train home, you could buy your train ticket in Beijing, at the CITS office on the ground floor of the *International Hotel* on Jianguomennei Dajie (daily 8.30am–5pm; ☏010/65120507; see p.135); or you can book the ticket online at Ⓦwww.cits.net/travel/reservation/train. jsp. This is an inexpensive option (tickets for Moscow start at about US$215; visas will cost another US$80 or so), but it involves a certain amount of hassle. Staff there will tell you the hoops to jump through to get the necessary visas.

Airlines, agents and operators

Online booking agents

Many airlines and discount travel websites offer the opportunity to book your tickets online, cutting out the costs of agents and middlemen. Good deals can often be found through discount or auction sites, as well as through the airlines' own websites.

Ⓦ**www.cheapflights.com** (in UK and Ireland),
Ⓦ**www.cheaptickets.com** (in US),
Ⓦ**www.expedia.co.uk** (in UK),
Ⓦ**www.expedia.com** (in US),
Ⓦ**www.expedia.ca** (in Canada),
Ⓦ**www.flyaow.com** (in US),
Ⓦ**www.flychina.com** (in US),
Ⓦ**www.hotwire.com** (in US),
Ⓦ**www.lastminute.com** (in UK),
Ⓦ**www.opodo.co.uk** (in UK),
Ⓦ**www.priceline.com** (in US),
Ⓦ**www.travelocity.co.uk** (in UK),
Ⓦ**www.travelocity.com** (in US),
Ⓦ**www.travelocity.ca** (in Canada),
Ⓦ**www.travelshop.com.au** (in Australia),
Ⓦ**www.zuji.com.au** (in Australia),
Ⓦ**www.zuji.co.nz** (in New Zealand).

Airlines

Aeroflot UK ☏020/7355 2233, US ☏1-888/340-6400, Canada ☏1-416/642-1653, Australia ☏02/9262 2233, Ⓦwww.aeroflot.co.uk, Ⓦwww.aeroflot.com.
Air Canada UK ☏0871/220 1111, Republic of Ireland ☏01/679 3958, US ☏1-888/247-2262, Australia ☏1300/655 767, New Zealand ☏0508/747 767, Ⓦwww.aircanada.com.
Air China UK ☏020/7744 0800, US ☏1-800-9828/802, Canada ☏1-416/581-8833, Australia ☏02/9232 7277, Ⓦwww.airchina.com.cn.
Air France UK ☏0870 142 4343, US ☏1-800/237-2747, Canada ☏1-800/667-2747, Australia ☏1300/390 190, South Africa ☏0861/340 340, Ⓦwww.airfrance.com.
Alitalia UK ☏0870/544 8259, Republic of Ireland ☏01/677 5171, US ☏1-800/223-5730, Canada ☏1-800/361-8336, New Zealand ☏09/308 3357, South Africa ☏11/721 4500, Ⓦwww.alitalia.com.

All Nippon Airways (ANA) UK ☎0870 837 8866,
Republic of Ireland ☎1850/200 058, US and Canada
☎1-800/235-9262, ⓦwww.anaskyweb.com.
American Airlines UK ☎0845 7789 789,
Republic of Ireland ☎01/602 0550, US and Canada
☎1-800/433-7300, Australia ☎1800/673 486,
New Zealand ☎0800/445 442, ⓦwww.aa.com.
Asiana Airlines UK ☎020/7514 0200, US ☎1-
800/227-4262, Australia ☎02/9767 4343, ⓦwww.
flyasiana.com.
Austrian Airlines UK ☎0870/124 2625, Republic
of Ireland ☎1800/509 142, US☎1-800/843-0002,
Canada ☎1888-8174/444, Australia ☎1800/642
438 or 02/9251 6155, ⓦwww.aua.com.
British Airways UK ☎0870 850 9850, Republic
of Ireland ☎1890 626 747, US and Canada
☎1-800/AIRWAYS, Australia ☎1300 767 177, New
Zealand ☎09/966 9777, South Africa ☎011/4418
600, ⓦwww.ba.com.
Cathay Pacific UK ☎020/8834 8888, US
☎1-800/233-2742, Canada ☎1-800-268-6868,
Australia ☎13 17 47, New Zealand ☎09/379
0861, South Africa ☎011/700 8900, ⓦwww.
cathaypacific.com.
China Airlines UK ☎020/7436 9001, US ☎1-
917/368-2003, Australia ☎02/9231 5588, New
Zealand ☎09/308 3364, ⓦwww.china-airlines.com.
China Eastern Airlines UK ☎0870 760 6232, US
☎1-626/1583-1500, Canada ☎1604-6898/998,
Australia ☎02/9290 1148, ⓦwww.chinaeastern.
co.uk.
China Southern Airlines US ☎1-888-388-8988,
Australia ☎02/9231 1988, ⓦww.cs-air.com.
Continental Airlines UK ☎0845 607 6760,
Republic of Ireland ☎1890/925 252, US and
Canada ☎1-800/523-3273, Australia ☎02/92/442
242, New Zealand ☎09/308 3350, ⓦwww.
continental.com.
Finnair UK ☎0870/241 4411, Republic of Ireland
☎01/844 6565, US ☎1-800/950-5000, Australia
☎02/9244 2299, South Africa ☎011/339 4865/9,
ⓦwww.finnair.com.
Garuda Indonesia UK ☎020/7467 8600, US
☎1-212/279-0756, Australia ☎1300/365 330
or 02/9334 9944, New Zealand ☎09/366 1862,
ⓦwww.garuda-indonesia.com.
Gulf Air UK ☎0870 777 1717, Republic of Ireland
☎0818/272 828, Australia ☎1300/366 337, South
Africa ☎011/2688909, ⓦwww.gulfairco.com.
JAL (Japan Air Lines) UK ☎0845 774 7700,
Republic of Ireland ☎01/408 3757, US and
Canada ☎1-800/525-3663, Australia ☎02/9272
1111, New Zealand ☎09/379 9906, South Africa
☎011/214 2560, ⓦwww.jal.com.
KLM (Royal Dutch Airlines)/Northwest See
also Northwest/KLM. UK ☎0870/507 4074,

Republic of Ireland ☎1850/747 400, US and
Canada ☎1-800-225-2525, Australia ☎1300/392
192, New Zealand ☎09/921 6040, South Africa
☎011/961 6727, ⓦwww.klm.com.
Korean Air UK ☎0800 413 000, Republic of
Ireland ☎01/799 7990, US and Canada ☎1-
800/438-5000, Australia ☎02/9262 6000, New
Zealand ☎09/914 2000, ⓦwww.koreanair.com.
Lufthansa UK ☎0870 837 7747, Republic
of Ireland ☎01/844 5544, US ☎1-800-399-
5838, Canada ☎1-800/563-5954, Australia
☎1300/655 727, New Zealand ☎0800 945 220,
South Africa ☎0861/842 538, ⓦwww.lufthansa.
com.
Malaysia Airlines UK ☎0870 607 9090, Republic
of Ireland ☎01/6761 561, US ☎1-800/5529-
264, Australia ☎13 26 27, New Zealand ☎0800
777 747, South Africa ☎011-8809 614, ⓦwww.
malaysia-airlines.com.
Northwest/KLM UK ☎0870 507 4074, US and
Canada ☎1-800-225-2525, Australia ☎1300/392
192; ⓦwww.nwa.com.
PIA (Pakistan International Airlines) UK
☎0800 587 1023, US and Canada ☎1-800/578-
6786, ⓦwww.piac.com.pk.
Qantas Airways UK ☎0845 774 7767, Republic
of Ireland ☎01/407 3278, US and Canada ☎1-
800/227-4500, Australia ☎13 13 13, New Zealand
☎0800 808 767 or 09/357 8900, South Africa
☎011/441 8550, ⓦwww.qantas.com.
Qatar Airways UK ☎0870/770 4215, US
☎1-877/777-2827, Canada ☎1-888/366-5666,
Australia ☎386/054 855, South Africa ☎11/523
2928, ⓦwww.qatarairways.com.
Royal Brunei UK ☎020 7584 6660, Australia
☎1300/721 271, New Zealand ☎09/977 2209;
ⓦwww.bruneiair.com.
Royal Jordanian US ☎1-800/223-0470, Canada
☎1-877/363-0711 or 514-288-1647, UK ☎020
7878 6300, Australia ☎02/9244 2701, New
Zealand ☎03/365 3910; ⓦwww.rja.com.jo.
SAS (Scandinavian Airlines) UK ☎0870 6072
7727, Republic of Ireland ☎01/844 5440, US and
Canada ☎1-800/221-2350, Australia ☎1300/727
707, ⓦwww.flysas.com.
Singapore Airlines UK ☎0844 800 2380,
Republic of Ireland ☎01/671 0722, US ☎1-
800/742-3333, Canada ☎1-800/663-3046,
Australia ☎13 10 11, New Zealand ☎0800/808
909, South Africa ☎011/880 8560 or 11/880 8566,
ⓦwww.singaporeair.com.
Swiss UK ☎0845 601 0956, Republic of Ireland
☎1890 200 515, US ☎1-877/3797-947, Canada
☎1-877-559-7947, Australia ☎1300/ 24 666,
New Zealand ☎09/977 2238, South Africa ☎0860
040 506, ⓦwww.swiss.com.

Thai Airways UK ☎0870/606 0911, US ☎1-212/949-8424, Australia ☎1300/651 960, New Zealand ☎09/377 3886, South Africa ☎011/455 1018, @www.thaiair.com.
United Airlines UK ☎0845 844 4777, US ☎1-800/UNITED-1, Australia ☎13 17 77; @www.united.com.
US Airways US and Canada ☎1-800/428-4322, UK ☎0845 600 3300, Republic of Ireland ☎1890/925 065, @www.usair.com.
Vietnam Airlines UK ☎0870 224 0211, US ☎1-415-677-0888, Canada ☎1-416/599-2888, Australia ☎02/9283 9658, @www.vietnamairlines.com.

Agents and operators

China Highlights China ☎+86/773 2831999, @www.chinahighlights.com. China-based company that offers a set of tours of Shanghai and the surrounding area.
China Odyssey China ☎+86/773 5854000, @www.chinaodysseytours.com. Operates short city tours, or longer trips that take in other destinations in China.
North South Travel ☎ & ⓕ01245 608 291, @www.northsouthtravel.co.uk. Discounted fares worldwide; profits are used to support projects in the developing world, especially the promotion of sustainable tourism.
STA Travel UK ☎0870 1600 599, US & Canada ☎1-800/781-4040, Australia ☎1300/733 035, New Zealand ☎0508/782 872, @www.sta-travel.com. Worldwide specialists in low-cost flights and tours for students and under-26s, though other customers welcome.
Trailfinders UK ☎020 7628 7628, Republic of Ireland ☎01/677 7888 Australia ☎02/9247 7666, @www.trailfinders.com. One of the best-informed and most efficient agents for independent travellers.
Travel China Guide US and Canada ☎ 1-800-892-6988, all other countries ☎+800 6668 8666; @www.travelchinaguide.com. A Chinese company with a wide range of three- and four-day group tours of Beijing and around.

Organized tours

Tour operators generally include Beijing as one of a number of destinations in a tour of China. There are very cheap off-season flight-and-hotel packages to Beijing, which, at prices that often go below £500/US$1000/€700, provide six or seven nights in a four-star hotel effectively for free, considering the cost of the flight alone. Don't forget, though, that quoted prices in brochures usually refer to the low-season minimum, based on two people sharing – the cost for a single traveller in high season will always work out far more expensive.

Specialist tour operators

Abercrombie & Kent ☎1-800/323-7308 or 630/954-2944, @www.abercrombiekent.com. Luxury tours; US$4000 buys you a twelve-day "Highlights of China" trip covering Shanghai, Guilin, Xi'an and Beijing.
Destinations Worldwide Holidays Republic of Ireland ☎01/855 6641, @www.destinations.ie. Two-week tours that include Hong Kong and Beijing.
Hayes and Jarvis UK ☎0870 898 9890, @www.hayesandjarvis.co.uk. Their Beijing flight-and-hotel-only packages are among the most inexpensive.
Intrepid Adventure Travel UK ☎020 73546169, Australia ☎1300 360 667 or 03/9473 2626, New Zealand ☎0800/174 043, @www.intrepidtravel.co.uk, @www.intrepidtravel.com.au. Small-group tours, with the emphasis on cross-cultural contact and low-impact tourism. Covers the staples, including hikes along the Great Wall near Beijing.
The Russia Experience UK ☎020 8566 8846, @www.trans-siberian.co.uk. Besides detailing their Trans-Siberian packages, their website is a veritable mine of information about the railway.
World Expeditions UK ☎020/8870 2600, Australia ☎1300 720 000, US 1-888-464-8735, Canada 1-800-567-22126 @www.worldexpeditions.com. Offers a 21-day Great Wall trek, starting in Beijing and heading well off the beaten track, for £1600, excluding flights.

Arrival

Those who arrive by train are lucky to find themselves already at the heart of the city; all others will find themselves outside the second ring road with a long onward journey. It's best not to tussle with the buses with luggage, so head for the metro or a cab rank. There aren't many shady cabbies in Beijing, but the few there are hang around arrival points – ignore offers from freelance operators and head straight to the officially monitored taxi ranks.

Orientation

Beijing's **ring roads** – freeways arranged in nested rectangles centring on Tian'anmen Square – are rapid-access corridors around the city. The second and third ring roads, Erhuan and Sanhuan Lu, are the two most useful, as they cut down on journey times but extend the distance travelled; they are much favoured by taxi drivers. Within the second ring road lie most of the **historical sights**, while many of the most modern buildings – including the smartest hotels, restaurants, shopping centres and office blocks – are along or close to the third. You'll soon become familiar with the experience of barrelling along a freeway in a bus or taxi, not knowing which direction you're travelling in, let alone where you are, as identical blocks flicker past.

By air

Beijing Capital Airport is 29km northeast of the centre, and, like everything else in the city, is being improved with the Olympics in mind. A third terminal, designed by Norman Foster, will be open from January 2008.

Banks and an **ATM** are on the right as you exit Customs (and there are more ATMs upstairs). There's an accommodation-booking service opposite Customs, but you may get lower prices if you call the hotels yourself and bargain for a discount.

You'll be pestered in the Arrivals Hall itself by charlatan taxi drivers; ignore them. Use the **taxi rank** to the left of the main exit from Arrivals (just outside Gate 9). A trip to the city centre will cost ¥80–¥100, including the ¥10 toll.

A light railway from the airport to Dongzhimen is due to open in July 2008. Until then the most convenient public transport to the centre is the comfortable, if cramped, **airport buses**, which can be found outside Gate 11. Buy tickets (¥16) from the desk directly in front of the exit. They leave regularly on four routes. **Line 1** buses stop at Dongzhimen (for the subway), Dongsishitiao, Yabao Lu and finish at the Airline Office in Xidan. **Line**

Beijing transport terminals

Beijing	北京	*běijīng*
Beijing Capital Airport	北京首都机场	*běijīng shǒudū jīchǎng*
Bus stations		
Deshengmen bus station	德胜门公共汽车站	*déshèngmén gōnggòng qìchēzhàn*
Dongzhimen bus station	东直门公共汽车站	*dōngzhímén gōnggòng qìchēzhàn*
Haihutun bus station	海户屯公共汽车站	*hǎihùtún gōnggòng qìchēzhàn*
Zhaogongkou bus station	赵公口公共汽车站	*zhàogōngkǒu gōnggòng qìchēzhàn*
Train stations		
Beijing Zhan	北京站	*běijīng zhàn*
Xi Zhan	西站	*xī zhàn*
Xizhimen Zhan	西直门站	*xīzhímén zhàn*
Yongdingmen Zhan	永定门站	*yǒngdìngmén zhàn*

Street names

Beijing street names appear bewildering at first, as a road can have several names along its length, but once you know the system, they are easy to figure out. Each name varies by the addition of the word for "inside" or "outside" (**nei** or **wai** respectively), which indicates the street's position in relation to the former city walls, then a direction – **bei**, **nan**, **xi**, **dong** and **zhong** (north, south, west, east and middle respectively). Central streets often also contain the word **men** (gate), which indicates that they once passed through a walled gate along their route. **Jie** and **lu** mean "street" and "road" respectively; the word **da**, which sometimes precedes them, simply means "big". Thus Jianguomenwai Dajie literally refers to the outer section of Jianguomen Big Street. More confusingly, in the northwest section of the third ring road you'll come across both Beisanhuan Xi Lu (for the bit east of the northwest corner) and Xisanhuan Bei Lu (the stretch running south of that corner). Some of these compound street names are just too much of a mouthful and are usually shortened; Gongrentiyuchang Bei Lu, for example, is usually referred to as Gongti Bei Lu.

2 goes to the far north and west of the city, **line 3** to Guomao and Beijing Zhan, and **line 4** to Zhongguancun.

If the airport bus doesn't pass close to your destination, it's a good idea to do the remainder of your journey by taxi rather than tussle with more buses, as the public transport system is confusing at first and the city layout alienating. But be wary of the taxi drivers waiting at the bus stop – hail a cab from the street instead.

By train

Beijing has two main train stations. **Beijing Zhan**, the central station, just south of Jian-guomennei Dajie, is where trains from destinations north and east of Beijing arrive. At the northeastern edge of the concourse is the subway stop, on the network's loop line. The taxi rank is over the road and 50m east of the station; another 50m on is a major bus terminal, from where buses serve most of the city.

Approaching from the south or west of the capital, you'll arrive at the west station, **Xi Zhan**, Asia's largest train terminal and the start of the Beijing–Kowloon line. There are plenty of **buses** from here – bus #122 heads to Beijing Zhan, bus #21 to Fuchengmen subway stop – as well as taxis, from the rank 50m in front of the main entrance.

You're unlikely to use Beijing's new south station (**Yongdingmen Zhan**) just inside the third ring road, unless you have come on the new fast train link from Tianjin.

Leaving Beijing

Booking onward transport is a simple matter. But at the peak seasons – the two-week long holidays and just before Chinese New Year (see p.31) – it's best to organize your onward transport long in advance.

By air

You can buy **airline tickets** from hotels and all travel agencies for a small commission (¥50 or so); the Aviation Office at 15 Xichang'an Jie in Xidan (☎010/66013336 for domestic flights, ☎66016667 international; 24hr); from CAAC offices in the *Beijing Hotel* on Dongchang'an Jie and in the China World Trade Centre (☎010/65053775); or from CITS offices at 103 Fuxingmenwai Dajie (☎010/66039321), and in the *International Hotel* (☎010/65126688), just north of Beijing Zhan. Alternatively, buy your ticket online with ⊛www.elong.com.cn or ⊛www.ctrip.com.cn. Your ticket will be delivered the same day at no extra charge, provided you're within the third ring road. You need a mobile phone number to confirm your purchase.

Airport information Ticket information ☎010/66013336; arrival/departure enquiries ☎010/64599567; shuttle bus information ☎010/64594376; lost luggage ☎010/64599523; ⊛www.bcia.com.cn.
Airline Offices in Beijing The following foreign airlines have offices in Beijing:

Aeroflot, 1st floor, *Jinglun Hotel*, 3 Jianguomenwai Dajie ℡010/65002412; Air Canada, Rm C201, Lufthansa Centre, 50 Lianmaqiao Lu ℡010/64682001; Air China, Xidan Aviation Office, 15 Chang'an Xi Lu ℡800/8101111; Air France, Rm 1606-1611, Building 1, Kuntai International Mansion, 12A Chaowai Dajie ℡400/8808808; Alitalia, Rm 141, *Jianguo Hotel*, 5 Jianguomenwai Dajie ℡010/65918468; All Nippon Airways, Fazhan Dasha, Rm N200, 5 Dongsanhuan Bei Lu ℡010/65909174; Asiana Airlines, 12th floor, Building A, Jiacheng Plaza, 18 Xiaguangli ℡010/64684000; Austrian Airlines, Rm 603, Lufthansa Centre, 50 Liangmaqiao Lu ℡010/64622161; British Airways, Rm 210, SCITECH Tower, 22 Jianguomenwai Dajie ℡010/65124070; Canadian Airlines, Rm C201, 50 Liangmaqiao Lu ℡010/64637901; China Southern Airlines, Building A, AVIC Building, 2 Dongsanhuan Nan Lu, ℡010/9503333; Continental Airlines, 500 Sunflower Tower, 37 Maizidian Jie, ℡010/85726686; Dragonair, Rm 1710, Office Tower 1, Henderson Centre,18 Jianguomennei Dajie, ℡010/65182533; Japan Airlines, 1/F Changfugong Office Building, 26A Jianguomenwai Dajie ℡400/8880808; KLM, 1609-1611 Kuntai International Building, Chaoyangmenwai Dajie, ℡400/8808222; Korean Air, 1602 Hyundai Motor Building, 38 Xiaoyun Lu, ℡400/6588888; Lufthansa, Rm S101, Lufthansa Centre, 50 Liangmaqiao Lu, ℡010/64688838; Northwest Airlines, 501B, West Wing, China World Trade Centre, 1 Jianguomenwai Dajie, ℡400/8140081; Pakistan Airlines, Rm 106A, China World Trade Centre, 1 Jianguomenwai Dajie ℡010/65052256; Qantas, Lufthansa Centre, B7-8, 10th floor, West Tower, LG Twin Tower, B12 Jianguomenwai Dajie, ℡65679006; SAS Scandinavian Airlines, Rm 430, Beijing Sunflower Tower, 37 Maizidian Jie, ℡85276100; Shanghai Airlines, Nanzhuyuan Yiqu, Building 3, Beijing Capital International Airport, ℡010/64569019; Singapore Airlines, Room 801, Tower 2, China World Trade Centre, 1 Jianguomenwai Dajie, ℡010/65052233; Swissair, Room 612, Scitech Tower, 22 Jianguomenwai Dajie, ℡010/65123555; Thai International, Rm 303, W3 Tower, Oriental Plaza, ℡010/85150088; United Airlines, Lufthansa Centre, 50 Liangmaqiao Lu, ℡010/64631111.

The **airport bus** leaves from the Aviation Office at 15 Xi Chang'an Jie (every 15min 5.40am–9pm). A second bus also leaves from the east side of the Beijing Zhan station concourse (every 30min 6am–7pm), but this one is a little confusing to find as there are so many buses in the area. Both trips take an hour and cost ¥16. Inquiries ℡010/64594375.

By train

Train tickets from Beijing are only sold four days in advance, except for the luxury "Z" class trains, which can be bought up to three weeks before (see below).

At Beijing main station, the ticketing office for foreigners (5.30–7.30am, 8am–6.30pm, 7–11pm) is on the northwest corner of the first floor, at the back of the soft seat waiting room. You don't have to buy your tickets here but the queues are much shorter than at the main ticket booking office on the west side of the station; you may be asked to show your passport. At Beijing West station, the foreigners' ticketing office is on the second floor (24hr). You can also book train tickets online at ⊛www.51piao.com/train or call the reservation centre on ℡010/95105105 – and your tickets will be delivered for a ¥10 fee. For train timetables, check ⊛www.chinahighlights.com/china-trains/index.htm.

By boat

International **ferries** to Japan and Korea leave from Tanggu port in Tianjin an hour from Beijing. Boats (run by a Japanese company) are clean and comfortable, (there's ping pong and karaoke) and third class – a *tatami* mat on the floor of a communal dorm – is certainly the cheapest way to do the trip. The trip to Kobe in Japan leaves every Monday and takes two full days. Tickets start at around ¥1600 and can be bought at CITS (see p.46). The twice weekly ferries to Inchon in Korea take 24 hours, and cost around ¥850.

Getting around

BASICS | Getting around

Getting around Beijing can be a challenge, the public transport system is extensive but overstretched and the streets are nearing gridlock – the average speed of a car is less than 10mph. Buses can be a hassle, taxis get stuck in gridlock, so the best way to get around is to hire a bike.

Beijing is divided into **districts** that, unfortunately, aren't marked on standard city maps. Broadly, Dongcheng is the eastern half of the centre, Xicheng the western half. Xuanwu is the southwest, Chongwen the southeast, Haidian the north and west outside the second ring road, and Chaoyang north and east outside the third ring road. It's helpful to know these districts when trying to locate addresses.

By bus

Even though every one of the city's 140 bus and trolleybus services runs about once a minute, you'll find getting on or off at rush hour hard work. **Double-deckers**, operated on five services, are comfortable – you're more likely to get a seat on these – and run along main roads. **Luxury buses**, which run around certain tourist sights, are modern, air-conditioned, and quite pleasant. **Tourist buses** – which look like ordinary buses but have route numbers written in green – make regular trips (mid-April to mid-Oct) between the city centre and certain out-of-town

attractions, including sections of the Great Wall; we've listed useful routes in the text.

The **fare** is a flat ¥1 with double-decker buses charging ¥2. On luxury buses, fares cost between ¥3–10, and on tourist buses ¥10–20. In all cases a conductor will collect fares.

Bus routes are efficiently organized and easy to understand – a handy feature, since stops tend to be a good kilometre apart. The routes are indicated by red or blue lines on all good maps; a dot on the line indicates a stop. Next to the stop on the map you'll see tiny Chinese characters giving the stop's name; you need to know it for the conductor to work out your fare (the Beijing Tourist Map has stops marked in *pinyin*; see p.42). The conductor will alert you when it's time to get off.

Useful bus routes

All buses display their **route numbers** prominently. Routes numbered 1–25 run around the city centre; buses numbered in the 200s run only at night; numbers in the 300s navigate the periphery of the city centre; and numbers in the 800s are the luxury buses.

Long-distance bus stations

There are many terminals for long-distance buses, each terminus serving buses from only a few destinations. Stations are located on the city outskirts, matching the destination's direction.

Dongzhimen, on the northeast corner of the second ring road, is the largest bus station, connected by subway to the rest of the city; it handles services to and from Shenyang and the rest of the northeast. **Deshengmen** (Beijiao), the north station serving Chengde and Datong, is just north of the second ring road (Erhuan Bei Lu); it's on the route of bus #328, which terminates at Andingmen, from where you can catch the subway's loop line. **Zhaogongkou**, on the south side of the third ring road (Nansanhuan Lu), serves southern and eastern destinations including Tianjin; it's on the route of bus #17 from Qianmen. Close by, to the west, **Haihutun**, at the intersection of the third ring road and Yongdingmenwai Dajie, is for buses for Tianjin and cities in southern Hebei; it's connected with the centre by bus #2 to Qianmen.

Bus #1 and double-decker bus #1 From Xi Zhan east along the main thoroughfare, Chang'an Jie.

Double-decker bus #2 From the north end of Qianmen Dajie, north to Dongdan, the Yonghe Gong and the Asian Games Village.

Double-decker #4 From Beijing Zoo to Qianmen via Fuxingmen.

Bus #5 From Deshengmen, on the second ring road in the northwest of the city, south down the west side of the Forbidden City and Tian'anmen to Qianmen Dajie.

Bus #15 From the zoo down Xidan Dajie, past Liulichang, ending at the Tianqiao area just west of Yongdingmennei Dajie, close to Tiantan Park.

Bus #20 From Beijing Zhan to Yongdingmen Zhan, south of Taoranting Park.

Bus #52 From Xi Zhan east to Lianhuachi Qiao, Xidan Dajie, Tian'anmen Square, then east along Chang'an Jie.

Bus #103 From Beijing Zhan, north up the east side of the Forbidden City, west along Fuchengmennei Dajie, then north up Sanlihe Lu to the zoo.

Bus #104 From Beijing Zhan to Hepingli Zhan in the north of the city, via Wangfujing.

Bus #105 From the northwest corner of Tiantan Park to Xidan Dajie, then west to the zoo.

Bus #106 From Yongdingmen Zhan to Tiantan Park and Chongwenmen, then up to Dongzhimennei Dajie.

Bus #300 Circles the third ring road.

Bus #332 From Beijing Zoo to Beijing University and Yihe Yuan (Summer Palace).

Luxury bus #808 From just northwest of Qianmen to the Yiheyuan.

Luxury bus #802 Xi Zhan to Panjiayuan Market in the southeast.

By subway

Clean, efficient and very fast, the **subway**, which operates daily from 5am to 11pm, is a preferable alternative to the bus – though again, be prepared for enforced intimacies during rush hour. Station entrances are marked by a logo of a rectangle inside a "G" shape. All stops are marked in *pinyin*, and announced in English and Chinese over the intercom when the train pulls in.

A loop line runs around the city, making useful stops at Beijing Zhan, Jianguomen (under the flyover, close to the Ancient Observatory and the Friendship Store), Yonghe Gong (50m north of the temple of the same name), Gulou (near the Drum Tower) and Qianmen, at the northern end of Qianmen Dajie. The east–west line runs across the city from the western suburbs,

through Tian'anmen, Wangfujing and the China World Trade Centre, and terminates out beyond the eastern section of the third ring road. There are interchanges between this and the loop line at Fuxingmen and Jianguomen stations.

Line 13 serves the far north of the city: built for the Olympic Village, it's in fact an overground light-rail system, though the stations use the same logo as the subway. You can get onto it from the loop line at Xizhimen or Dongzhimen, though you have to leave the station, walk a short distance and buy new tickets (same price) to do so. The only useful stations for tourists are Dazhongsi – for the Dazhong Si – and Wudaokou – for Beijing Daxue and the summer palaces.

There are so many lines under construction that the present pleasingly minimalist subway map will soon look like a plate of noodles. **Line 5**, which will soon be complete, will run north–south with interchanges at Yonghegong, Dongdan and Chongwenmen; its central stops are shown on our transport map. The potentially handy **Line 4** (north–south) is planned to open in conjunction with the Olympics: running from Yiheyuan (the Summer Palace) to the zoo down to Xidan and then south to Taoranting Park, it will take in plenty of sights. A light-rail line running from Dongzhimen to the airport should also be finished in the near future. Other new lines were still to be finalized at the time of writing. Among these, one will run north–south between Xi Zhan and Yiheyuan, between Haidian and Guomao (for the China World Trade Centre) and between the two main train stations.

Tickets (undated slips of paper) cost ¥3 per journey and can be bought from the ticket offices at the top of the stairs leading down to the platforms. It's worth getting a few tickets at once to save queuing every time you use the system. You need to give your ticket to an attendant before you descend to the platform. Anyone staying more than a couple of weeks should consider buying a stored value swipe card, available from subway stations and valid for bus and subway tickets. The deposit is ¥20, which you receive back when you return it, and you can put as much on it as you like.

Taxis

Taxis cost ¥2 per kilometre, with a minimum charge of ¥10; after 11pm, there's a surcharge of twenty percent. Drivers are good about using their meters; if they don't put them on, insist by saying "dǎ biǎo".

Don't let yourself get hustled into a taxi, as unscrupulous drivers look out for newly arrived foreigners with luggage; walk a short distance and hail one, or find a rank (there's one outside each train station). Having a map open on your lap deters some drivers from taking unnecessary detours. If you feel aggrieved at a driver's behaviour, take his number (displayed on the dashboard) and report it to the taxi complaint office (☏010/68351150). Indeed, just the action of writing his number down can produce a remarkable change in demeanour. If a cab has a red star on the roof, the driver has been voted as exemplary by members of the public.

In consideration for the Olympics, all cab drivers are supposed to be learning English. Most have made no progress, however, explaining (rightly) that they work too hard to study.

Rickshaws

Don't use the ordinary **cycle-rickshaws** you'll see in backstreets. The drivers almost inevitably attempt to overcharge foreigners and use unpleasant tactics such as demanding more money when you get out than originally agreed.

Around the northwestern *hutongs*, drivers in bright waistcoats are employed by tour companies to give tourists rides around the area. You can approach them directly to go on a scenic trip, but be sure to bargain hard.

Bicycle rental

It's worth renting or buying a **bike**, giving yourself much more independence and flexibility – and they're often faster than taxis.

There are bike lanes on all main roads and you'll be in the company of plenty of other cyclists. If you feel nervous at busy junctions, just dismount and walk the bike across – plenty of Chinese do.

Almost all hotels – certainly all the hostels – rent out bikes for around ¥20 a day plus a

¥200–400 deposit. Upmarket hotels charge ¥50 a day for the same bikes. You can also rent from many places in the *hutongs* around Houhai (see map p.95).

You can **buy** cheap city bikes for about ¥250; try Carrefour (see p.146) or the strip of bike shops on the south side of Jiaodaokou, just west of the Ghost Street (Gui Jie; see map pp.90–91) restaurants.

The first thing you'll need is a good **lock**, as theft is very common. Always test the brakes on a rented bike before riding off, and get the tyres pumped up. Should you have a problem, you can turn to one of the bike repair stalls – there are plenty of these on the pavement next to main roads.

The best place to leave a bike is at one of the numerous **bike parks**, where you pay ¥0.3 to the attendant.

Car rental

Given the state of Beijing's traffic, you'd have to be pretty intrepid to want to **drive** yourself around the city, and it's not possible for anyone with an "L" or tourist visa. You'll need a Chinese driver's license, a Beijing Residence Permit and a credit card to cover the deposit. Avis is at 16 Dongzhimennei Dajie (☏84063343; ⊛www.avischina.com).

City tours

Organized tours of the city and its outskirts offer a painless, if expensive, way of seeing the main sights quickly. All big hotels offer them, and CITS has a variety of one- and two-day tour packages, on "Dragon Buses" which you can book from their offices (see p.46), from a BTS office (see p.45) or from the information desk in the Friendship Store. These tours aren't cheap, though the price includes lunch and pays for a tour guide: Beijing By Night – a trip to the opera and a meal at a duck restaurant – costs ¥330; a trip to the Summer Palace, Yonghe Gong and zoo is ¥260. Similar tours are run by two other official agencies, CTS and CYTS.

One good, inexpensive tour that's more imaginative than most is the *hutong* tour (see p.93), which offers the opportunity to see a more private side of the city. The one-day tours offered by the cheaper hotels offer better value than similar jaunts run by classier places, and you don't have to be a resident of theirs to go along. All the youth hostels offer good-value evening trips to the acrobatics shows and the opera a few times a week, and day (and occasionally overnight) trips to Simatai and Jinshanling Great Wall (April–Oct daily; Nov–March weekly; ¥60–80; see p.114). You must book these at least a day in advance.

The media

Xinhua, the Chinese news agency, is a mouthpiece for the state, whose propaganda you can read in the English-language *China Daily*, available from the Friendship Store (see p.160), the Foreign Language Bookstore (see p.162), and the bigger hotels and most newsagents, including the ones on subway platforms. Heavy censorship continues to affect the Chinese-language press, the only thing you can believe in the *China Daily* is the cultural listings section, though more detailed listings can be found in the city's expat-oriented magazines. *Beijing Today* (¥2) is a rather better English-language newspaper, also on sale on subway platforms, but it doesn't carry listings.

Although censorship is stringent, stories sometimes break that the Party would rather people didn't know about; for example, in 2007, the appalling conditions of mineworkers became a national issue, thanks to crusading journalists. It's a brave editor who prints such stuff, however. Imported news publications (sometimes censored) such as *Time*, *Newsweek* and the *Far Eastern Economic Review*, and Hong Kong's *South China Morning Post*, can be bought at the Friendship Store or at the bookstands in four- and five-star hotels.

TV and radio

There is the occasional item of interest on Chinese **television**, though you'd have to be very bored to resort to it for entertainment. Domestic travel and wildlife programmes are common, as are song-and-dance extrava-ganzas, the most enjoyable of which feature dancers in weird fetishistic costumes. Soap operas and historical dramas are popular, and often feature a few foreigners, and *Pop Idol*-esque talent shows are currently all the rage.

CCTV, the state broadcaster, has an English-language channel, **CCTV9**; the news is on at 10pm. CCTV5 is a sports channel and often shows European football games. CCTV2, CCTV4, and local channel BTV1, all have English-language news programmes at 11pm. Satellite TV in English is available in the more expensive hotels.

On the **radio** you're likely to hear the latest ballads by pop-robots from the Hong Kong and Taiwan idol factories, or versions of Western pop songs sung in Chinese. Easy FM (91.5FM) is an expat-geared English-language station carrying music programmes and local information.

Public holidays and festivals

BASICS | Public holidays and fetivals

The rhythm of festivals and religious observances that used to mark the Chinese year was interrupted by the Cultural Revolution, and only now, nearly forty years on, are old traditions beginning to re-emerge. The majority of festivals celebrate the turning of the seasons or propitious dates, such as the Double Ninth festival held on the ninth day of the ninth lunar month, and are times for gift-giving, family reunions and feasting.

Festivals and holidays calendar

Traditional festivals take place according to dates in the Chinese lunar calendar, in which the first day of the month is when the moon is a new crescent, with the middle of the month marked by the full moon; by the Gregorian calendar, these festivals fall on a different date every year.

January/February

New Year's Day (Jan 1).
Spring Festival (starts between late Jan and mid-Feb). The Chinese New Year celebrations extend over the first two weeks of the new lunar year (see box below).

Tiancang (Granary) Festival Chinese peasants celebrate with a feast on the twentieth day of the first lunar month, in the hope of ensuring a good harvest later in the year.

March

Guanyin's Birthday Guanyin, the goddess of mercy and China's most popular Buddhist deity, is celebrated on the nineteenth day of the second lunar month, most colourfully in Taoist temples.

April

Qingming Festival (April 4 & 5). This festival, Tomb Sweeping Day, is the time to visit the graves of ancestors, leave offerings of food, and burn ghost money – fake paper currency – in honour of the departed.

Spring Festival

The **Spring Festival**, usually falling in late January or the first half of February, is marked by two weeks of festivities celebrating the beginning of a new year in the lunar calendar (and thus also called Chinese New Year). In Chinese astrology, each year is associated with a particular animal from a cycle of twelve – 2008 is the Year of the Rat, for example – and the passing into a new astrological phase is a momentous occasion. There's a tangible sense of excitement in the run-up to the festival, when China is perhaps at its most colourful, with shops and houses decorated with good luck messages and stalls and shops selling paper money, drums and costumes. However, the festival is not an ideal time to travel – everything shuts down, and most of the population is on the move, making travel impossible or extremely uncomfortable.

The first day of the festival is marked by a family feast at which *jiaozi* (dumplings) are eaten, sometimes with coins hidden inside. To bring luck, people dress in red clothes (red being regarded as a lucky colour) – a particularly important custom if the animal of their birth year is coming round again – and each family tries to eat a whole fish, since the word for fish (*yu*) sounds like the word for surplus. Firecrackers are let off to scare ghosts away and, on the fifth day, to honour Cai Shen, god of wealth. Another ghost-scaring tradition you may notice is the pasting up of images of door gods at the threshold. If you're in town at this time, make sure you catch a temple fair (see colour insert).

May

Labour Day (May 1). The beginning of a week-long holiday.

Youth Day (May 4). Commemorates the student demonstrators in Tian'anmen Square in 1919, which gave rise to the nationalist "May Fourth" movement. It's marked in Beijing with flower displays in Tian'anmen.

June

Children's Day (June 1). Most school pupils are taken on excursions at this time, so if you're visiting a popular tourist site, be prepared for mobs of kids in yellow baseball caps.

September/October

Moon Festival Also known as the Mid-Autumn Festival, this is marked on the fifteenth day of the eighth lunar month (in 2008, this will be on September 14th). It's a time of family reunion, celebrated with fireworks and lanterns. Moon cakes, containing a rich filling of sweet bean paste, are eaten, and plenty of *maotai* – a strong white spirit distilled from rice – is consumed.

Double Ninth Festival Nine is a number associated with *yang*, or male energy, and on the ninth day of the ninth lunar month qualities such as assertiveness and strength are celebrated. It's believed to be a profitable time for the distillation (and consumption) of spirits.

Confucius Festival (Sept 28). The birthday of Confucius is marked by celebrations at all Confucian temples.

National Day (Oct 1). Everyone has a week off to celebrate the founding of the People's Republic.

Culture and etiquette

When Confucius arrives in a country, he invariably gets to know about its society. Does he seek this information, or is it given him? Confucius gets it through being cordial, good, respectful, temperate and deferential.

Confucius, *The Analects*, 1.10

Privacy is largely an unheard-of luxury in China – indeed, Chinese doesn't have an exact translation of the word. Public toilets are built with low partitions, no one eats alone in restaurants, all leisure activities are performed in noisy groups, and a curiosity – such as a visiting Caucasian, or "big nose" as the Chinese like to say – can find himself or herself the subject of frank stares and attention. The best thing to do in such situations is smile and say nǐhǎo. A desire to be left alone can baffle the Chinese, and is occasionally interpreted as arrogance. Conversely, behaviour seen as antisocial in the West, notably spitting and smoking, is quite normal in China, though government campaigns to cut down on both are having some effect. A particular bugbear with foreigners is queue jumping, so in a bid to teach the populace international standards of manners, the government has deemed first Wednesday of every month is "Queuing Awareness Day".

Skimpy **clothing** is fine (indeed fashionable), but looking scruffy will only induce disrespect: all foreigners are, correctly, assumed to be comparatively rich, so why they would want to dress like peasants is quite beyond the Chinese.

Shaking hands is not a Chinese tradition, though it is now fairly common between men. Businessmen meeting for the first time exchange business cards, with the offered card held in two hands as a gesture of respect – you'll see polite shop assistants doing the same with your change.

In a restaurant, the Chinese don't usually share the bill (*jiao*); instead, diners contest for the honour of paying it, with the most respected usually winning. You should make some effort to stake your claim but, as a visiting guest, you can pretty much guarantee that you won't get to pay a *jiao*.

Tipping is never expected, and though you might sometimes feel it's warranted, resist the temptation – you'll set an unwelcome precedent. A few upmarket places add a service charge, though it's highly unlikely that the serving staff ever see any of it.

If you visit a Chinese house, you'll be expected to present your hosts with a **gift**, which won't be opened in front of you (that would be impolite). Imported whisky and ornamental trinkets are suitable as presents, though avoid giving anything too practical, as it might be construed as charity.

Sex and gender issues

Women travellers in Beijing usually find the incidence of sexual harassment much less of a problem than in other Asian countries. Chinese men are, on the whole, deferential and respectful. Being ignored is a much more likely complaint, as the Chinese will generally assume that any man accompanying a woman will be doing all the talking.

Prostitution, though illegal, has made a big comeback – witness all the new "hairdressers", saunas and massage parlours, almost every one a brothel. Single foreign men are likely to be approached inside hotels; it's common practice for prostitutes to phone around hotel rooms at all hours of the night – so unplug the phone if you don't want to be woken up. Bear in mind that China is hardly Thailand – consequences may be unpleasant if you are caught with a prostitute – and that AIDS is rife and much of the public largely ignorant of sexual health issues.

See p.37 for information on gay and lesbian Beijing.

Travelling with children

Foreigners with kids can be expected to receive lots of attention from curious locals – and the occasional admonition that the little one should be wrapped up warmer.

Local kids don't use **nappies**, just pants with a slit at the back – and when baby wants to go, mummy points him at the gutter. Nappies and baby milk are available from modern supermarkets such as Carrefour (see p.146), though there are few public changing facilities. High-end hotels have baby minding services for around ¥150 an hour. **Breastfeeding** in public is acceptable, though more so outside the train station than in celebrity restaurants.

Sights that youngsters might enjoy are the zoo and aquarium (see p.100), pedal boating on Houhai, (see p.94), the acrobat shows (see p.153) and the Puppet Theatre (see p.153), the waxwork show (see p.55), the Natural History Museum (see p.69) and the Goose and Duck Ranch (see p.111). If you're tired of worrying about them in the traffic, try taking them to pedestrianized Liulichang, the parks, or the 798 Art District.

Travel essentials

Costs

In terms of **costs**, Beijing is a city of extremes. You can, if you wish to live it up, spend as much here as you would visiting any Western capital; on the other hand, it's also quite possible to live extremely cheaply – most locals survive on less than £75/US$150/¥1100 a month.

Generally, your biggest expense is likely to be **accommodation**. Food and transport, on the other hand, are relatively cheap. The minimum you can live on comfortably is about £10/US$16/¥150 a day if you stay in a dormitory, get around by bus and eat in simple restaurants. On a budget of £32/US$50/¥400 a day, you'll be able to stay in a modest hotel, travel in taxis and eat in good restaurants. To stay in an upmarket hotel, you'll need to have a budget of around £80/US$130/RMB1000 a day.

It used to be government policy to **surcharge** foreigners on fares on public transport and for admission to sights. This is no longer the case but the practice lives on, and you might well find price discrimination being exercised by unscrupulous shopkeepers. **Discounts** on admission prices are available to students in China on production of the red Chinese student identity card. A youth hostel card gets a small discount at hostels (and can be bought at the front desk).

Crime and personal safety

With all the careful showcasing of modernity, it's easy to forget that Beijing is the heart of an authoritarian state that has terrorized its subjects for much of its short, inglorious history. Not that this should worry visitors too much; the state is as anxious to keep guests happy as it is to incarcerate democracy activists and the like. Indeed, Chinese who commit crimes against foreigners are treated much more harshly than if their victims had been compatriots.

Crime is a growth industry in China, partly thanks to appalling disparities in income, and the get-rich-quick attitude that has become the prevailing ideology. Official corruption is rampant, and the state sometimes shoots scapegoats in an effort to cut it down (it's called "killing the chicken to frighten the monkeys").

While there is no need for obsessive paranoia – Beijing is still safer than most Western cities – you do need to take care. Tourists are an obvious target for petty thieves. Passports and money should be kept in a concealed money belt; a bum bag offers much less protection and is easy for skilled pickpockets to get into. It's a good idea to keep around £400/US$200 separately from the rest of your cash, together with your travellers'-cheque receipts, insurance-policy

Con artists

Getting scammed is by far the biggest threat to foreign visitors, and there are now so many professional con artists targeting tourists that you can expect to be approached many times a day at places such as Wangfujing and on Tian'anmen Square. A sweet-looking young couple, a pair of girls, or perhaps a kindly old man, will ask to practise their English or offer to show you round. After befriending you – which may take hours – they will suggest some refreshment, and lead you to a teahouse. After a traditional-looking tea ceremony you will be presented with a bill for thousands of *yuan*, your new "friends" will disappear or pretend to be shocked, and some large gentlemen will appear. In another variation, you will be coaxed into buying a painting (really a print) for a ridiculous sum. Never drink with a stranger if you haven't seen a price list.

Emergency numbers

Police ☎110
Fire ☎119
Ambulance ☎120

details, and photocopies of your passport and visa. Be wary on buses, the favoured haunt of pickpockets, and trains, particularly in hard-seat class and on overnight journeys. Take a chain and padlock to secure your luggage in the rack.

Hotel rooms are on the whole secure, dormitories much less so – in the latter case it's often fellow travellers who are the problem. Most hotels should have a safe, but it's not unusual for things to go missing from these.

On the **street**, flashy jewellery and watches will attract the wrong kind of attention, and try to be discreet when taking out your cash. Not looking obviously wealthy also helps if you want to avoid being ripped off by street traders and taxi drivers, as does telling them you are a student – the Chinese have a great respect for education, and more sympathy for foreign students than for tourists.

The police

If you do have anything stolen, you'll need to get the **police**, known as the **Public Security Bureau** or PSB, to write up a loss report in order to claim on your insurance. Their main office is at 2 Andingmen Dong Dajie, 300m east of Yonghe Gong subway stop (Mon–Fri 8am–4.30pm; ☎010/84015292).

The **police** are recognizable by their dark blue uniforms and caps, though there are a lot more around than you might at first think, as plenty are undercover. They have much wider powers than most Western police forces, including establishing the guilt of criminals – trials are often used only for deciding the sentence of the accused, though China is beginning to have the makings of an independent judiciary. Laws are harsh, with execution – a bullet in the back of the head – the penalty for a wide range of serious crimes, from corruption to rape, though if the culprit is deemed to show proper remorse, the result can be a more lenient sentence.

While individual police can be very helpful and go out of their way to help foreigners, the PSB itself has all the problems of any police force in a nation rife with corruption, and it's best to minimize contact with them.

Electricity

The electrical supply is 220V. Plugs come in four types: three-pronged with angled pins, three-pronged with round pins, two flat pins and two narrow round pins. Adaptor plugs are available from hardware and electronic stores; try the Hi-Tech Mall (see p.164).

Entry requirements

Visas

To enter China, all foreign nationals require a **visa**, available worldwide from Chinese embassies and consulates and through specialist tour operators and visa agents. **Single-entry tourist visas** (called "L" visas) must be used within three months of issue, and cost US$30–50, or the local equivalent. They are valid for a month, but the authorities might well grant a request for a two- or three-month visa if asked (which costs the same) though there is no certainty about this.

To apply for a visa you have to submit an application form, one or two passport-size photographs, your passport (which must be valid for at least another six months from your planned date of entry into China, and have at least one blank page for visas) and the fee. If you apply in person, processing should take between three and five working days. Postal applications take three weeks.

You'll be asked your occupation – it's wise not to admit to being a journalist or writer as you might be called in for an interview. At times of political sensitivity you may be asked for a copy of any air tickets and hotel bookings in your name.

A **business visa** (F) costs US$100–150 and is valid for six months and multiple journeys; you'll need an official invitation from a government-recognized Chinese organization to apply for one (except in Hong Kong, where you can simply buy one). Twelve-month work visas (Z) cost US$300 and again require an invitation, plus a health certificate from your doctor. Students intending to study in Beijing for less than six months need an invitation or letter of acceptance from a college there in order to apply for student visas (US$150). If you're intending to go on a longer course, you have to fill in an additional form, available from Chinese embassies, and will also need a health certificate; then you'll be issued with an X visa, valid for a year, and renewable.

Chinese embassies and consulates

Australia 15 Coronation Drive, Yarralumla, Canberra, ACT 2600 ☎02/6273 4780, ⊛http://au.china-embassy.org/eng/. Also consulates at 77 Irving Rd, Toorak, Melbourne (visa and passport enquiries ☎03/9804 3683) and 539 Elizabeth St, Surry Hills, Sydney (☎02/9698 7929).
Canada 515 St Patrick St, Ottawa, Ontario K1N 5H3 ☎613/234 2682, ⊛www.chinaembassycanada.org. Visas can also be obtained from the consulates in Calgary, Toronto and Vancouver.
India 50-D Shantipath, Chanakyapuri, New Delhi, 110021, ☎26781585.
Republic of Ireland 40 Ailesbury Road, Dublin 4 ☎01/2691707.
Laos Thanon Wat Nak Yai, Vientiane ☎315103.
New Zealand 2–6 Glenmore Street, Wellington ☎04/474 9631, ⊛www.chinaembassy.org.nz; plus a consulate in Auckland ☎09/525 1589, ⊛www.chinaconsulate.org.nz.
Russia ul. Druzhby 6, Moscow ☎095/145-1543, ⊛www.chinaembassy.ru.
UK 31 Portland Place, London W1B 1QD ☎020 7631 1430; Denison House, Denison Rd, Victoria Park, Manchester M14 5RX ☎0161/224 7480, ⊛www.chinese-embassy.org.uk.
South Africa 956 Church Street, Arcadia 0083 Pretoria, ☎012/3424194, ⊛www.chinese-embassy.org.au.za.
USA 2300 Connecticut Ave NW, Washington, DC 20008 ☎202/3282517, ⊛www.china-embassy.org. Also consulates in Chicago, Houston, Los Angeles, New York and San Francisco.
Vietnam Tran Phu, Hanoi (round the corner from the main embassy building at 46 Hoang Dieu) ☎04/823 5517, ⊛www.fmprc.gov.cn/eng.

Getting visas in Hong Kong

In Hong Kong, it's easier to obtain visas that are valid for longer than the usual thirty-day period. The standard one-month tourist visa for China can be obtained from any of the numerous travel agencies or direct from the visa office at the Ministry for Foreign Affairs, Floor 5, Low Block, China Resources Building, 26 Harbour Rd (☎0852/2827 1881). For a sixty- or ninety-day multiple-entry visa, issued in two days, visit the China Travel Service (CTS) at 78–83 Connaught Rd or 27–33 Nathan Rd. Note that these visas are valid from the date of issue, not the date of entry. You can get a six-month multiple-entry business visa at Shoestring Travel, 27–33 Nathan Rd, for £38/US$77/HK$600. No invitation letter is required, just a business card. For a next-day, no questions asked, one-year business visa costing £83/US$167/HK$1300 visit Forever Bright Trading Ltd, 707, New Mandarin Plaza, Tower B, 14 Science Museum Road.

British and Irish citizens, nationals of most other European countries, Canadians, Australians and New Zealanders can stay in Hong Kong without a visa for three months; Americans and South Africans for thirty days.

Visa extensions

Once in China, a **first extension** to a tourist visa, valid for a month, is easy to obtain; most Europeans pay ¥160 for this, Americans a little more. To apply for an extension, go to the "Aliens Entry Exit Department" of the PSB at 2 Andingmen Dong Dajie, 300m east of Yonghe Gong subway stop (Mon–Fri 8am–4.30pm; ☎010/84015292). The staff will **keep your passport** for three working days; note that you can't change money, or even book into a new hotel, while they've got it. Subsequent applications for extensions will be refused unless you have a good reason to stay – such as illness. They'll reluctantly give you a couple of extra days if you have a flight out of the country booked; otherwise, you'll be brusquely ordered to leave the country. Don't; simply go to Chengde (see p.121), which has a friendly PSB office where you can get month-long second extensions on the spot.

Don't overstay your visa even for a few hours – the fine is ¥500 per day, and if you're caught at the airport with an out-of-date visa the hassle that will follow may mean you'll miss your flight.

Customs allowances

You're allowed to import into China up to four hundred cigarettes, two litres of alcohol, twenty fluid ounces (590ml) of perfume and up to fifty grams of gold or silver. You can't take in more than ¥6000, and foreign currency in excess of US$5000 or the equivalent must be declared. It's illegal to import printed or filmed matter critical of the country, but confiscation is rare in practice.

Finally, note that **export restrictions** apply on any items over 100 years old that you might buy in China. Taking these items out of the country requires an export form, available from the Friendship Store (see p.160); ask at the information counter for a form, take along the item and your receipt, and approval is given on the spot. You needn't be unduly concerned about the process – the "antiques" you commonly see for sale are all fakes anyway.

Embassies

Most **embassies** are either around Sanlitun, in the northeast, or in the Jianguomenwai compound, north of and parallel to Jianguomenwai Dajie. You can get passport-size photos for visas from an annex just inside the front entrance of the Friendship Store. Visa departments usually open for a few hours every weekday morning (phone for exact times and to see what you'll need to take). During the application process they might take your passport off you for as long as a week; remember that you can't change money or your accommodation without it.

Australia 21 Dongzhimenwai Dajie, Sanlitun ☏010/65322331.
Azerbaijan 7-2-5-1 Tayuan Building ☏010/65324614.
Canada 19 Dongzhimenwai Dajie, Sanlitun ☏010/65323536.
France 3 Dong San Jie, Sanlitun ☏010/65321331.
Germany 5 Dongzhimenwai Dajie, Sanlitun ☏010/65322161.
India 1 Ritan Dong Lu, Sanlitun ☏010/65321856.
Ireland 3 Ritan Dong Lu, Sanlitun ☏010/65322691.
Japan 7 Ritan Lu, Jianguomenwai ☏010/65322361.
Kazakhstan 9 Dong Liu Jie, Sanlitun ☏010/65326183.

Kyrgyzstan 2-4-1 Tayuan Building ☏010/65326458.
Laos 11 Dongsi Jie, Sanlitun ☏010/65321224.
Mongolia 2 Xiushui Bei Jie, Jianguomenwai ☏010/65321203.
Myanmar (Burma) 6 Dongzhimenwai Dajie, Sanlitun ☏010/65321425.
New Zealand 1 Ritan Dong'er Jie, Sanlitun ☏010/65322731.
North Korea Ritan Bei Lu, Jianguomenwai ☏010/65321186.
Pakistan 1 Dongzhimenwai Dajie, Sanlitun ☏010/65322660.
Russian Federation 4 Dongzhimen Bei Zhong Jie ☏010/65322051.
South Korea 3 Sanlitun Sijie, ☏010/65320290.
Thailand 40 Guanghua Lu, Jianguomenwai ☏010/65321903.
UK 11 Guanghua Lu, Jianguomenwai ☏010/65321961 visa and consular section at 21st Floor, Kerry Centre, 1 Guanghua Lu.
Ukraine 11 Dong Lu Jie, Sanlitun ☏010/65324014.
USA 3 Xiushui Bei Jie, Jianguomenwai ☏010/65323831.
Uzbekistan 7 Beixiao Jie, Sanlitun ☏010/65326305.
Vietnam 32 Guanghua Lu, Jianguomenwai ☏010/65321155.

Gay and lesbian Beijing

Beijing, and China as a whole, has become much more tolerant of **homosexuality**, and it's been removed from the list of psychiatric diseases and is no longer illegal. Still, the scene is fairly tame and low key. See p.150 for a list of gay venues.

Health

The most common health hazard in Beijing is the host of **cold and flu infections** that strike down a large percentage of the population, mostly in the winter months. The problem is compounded by the overcrowded conditions, chain-smoking, pollution and the widespread habit of spitting, which rapidly spreads infection. Initial symptoms are fever, sore throat, chills and a feeling of malaise, sometimes followed by a prolonged bout of bronchitis. If you do come down with something like this, drink lots of fluids and get plenty of rest, and seek medical advice if symptoms persist.

Diarrhoea is another common illness to affect travellers, usually in a mild form, while your stomach gets used to unfamiliar food. The sudden onset of diarrhoea with stomach cramps and vomiting indicates food poisoning. In both instances, get plenty of rest, drink lots of water, and in serious cases replace lost salts with oral rehydration solution (ORS); this is especially important with young children. Take a few sachets with you, or make your own by adding half a teaspoon of salt and three of sugar to a litre of cool, previously boiled water. While down with diarrhoea, avoid milk, greasy or spicy foods, coffee and most fruit, in favour of bland foodstuffs such as rice, plain noodles and soup. If symptoms persist, or if you notice blood or mucus in your stools, consult a doctor.

To avoid stomach complaints, eat at places that look busy and clean and stick to fresh, thoroughly cooked food. Beware of food that has been pre-cooked and kept warm for several hours. Shellfish are a potential hepatitis A risk, and best avoided. Fresh fruit you've peeled yourself is safe; other uncooked foods may have been washed in unclean water. You may be advised not to drink **tap water**, and to avoid locally made ice drinks.

AIDS is a growing problem in China, and there's widespread ignorance of sexual health issues; always use a condom. Foreign brands are widely available (see p.39).

Hospitals, clinics and pharmacies

Medical facilities in Beijing are adequate: there are some high-standard international clinics, most big hotels have a resident doctor, and for minor complaints, there are plenty of pharmacies that can suggest remedies. Most doctors will treat you with Western techniques first, but will also know a little Traditional Chinese Medicine (TCM).

If you don't speak Chinese, you'll generally need to have a good phrasebook or be accompanied by a Chinese-speaker. How-

Healing hands

Beijing's massage centres and spas are a great way to unwind from the stresses of city life, and not expensive. Try one of the following:

Aibosen 11 Liufang Bei Lu ℗010/64652044. The staff at this clinic are trained in Chinese medical massages; ¥88/70min.
Bodhi 17 Gongti Bei Lu, close to the Workers' Stadium ℗010/64179595. Ayurvedic and Thai massages are among the many options available at this clinic. Prices begin at ¥138/hr, but it's half price Mon–Thurs before 5pm.
Chi *Shangri-La Hotel*, 29 Zizhuyuan Road ℗010/88826748. Therapies at this luxurious New Age spa claim to use the five Chinese elements – metal, fire, wood, water and earth – to balance your *yin* and *yang*. It might look like a Tibetan temple though there can't be many real Tibetans who could afford to darken its doors; a Chi Balance massage costs ¥1350, a Himalayan Healing Stone Massage ¥1600.
Dragonfly 1st floor, Eastern Inn, Sanlitun Nan Lu ℗010/65936066; 60 Donghuamen Dajie, outside the east gate of the Forbidden City ℗65279368; ℗www.dragonfly.net. cn. This well-reputed Shanghai chain has opened a couple of conveniently located centres in the capital. Their two-hour hangover special (¥320) is always popular.
St Regis Spa Centre St Regis Hotel, 21 Jianguomenwai Dajie ℗010/64606688. Traditional Chinese massage, aromatherapy and facials are among the treatments on offer at this very upscale hotel. Prices start at ¥250 for a head and shoulders massage.
Taipan 6 Ritan Lu ℗010/65035701; ℗www.taipan.com.cn. A popular chain, no frills, but clean and cheap.
The Heping Centre 11 Xiushui Jie, Jianguomen ℗010/64367370. A foot massage parlour that's handy for stressed out shoppers from the Silk Market.
Zen Spa House 1, 8A Xiaowuji Lu, ℗010/87312530; ℗www.zenspa.com.cn. This spa, located in a courtyard house full of antique furniture, offers Thai and Chinese massages as well as all sorts of scrub and detox treatments. A full two-and-a-half-hour treatment costs ¥1700, but there are cheaper options.

Rough Guides insurance

Rough Guides has teamed up with **Columbus Direct** to offer you travel insurance that can be tailored to suit your needs. Products include a low-cost backpacker option for long stays; a short break option for city getaways; a typical holiday package option; and others. There are also annual multi-trip policies for those who travel regularly. Different sports and activities (trekking, skiing, etc) can be usually be covered if required.

See our website (ⓦwww.roughguides.com/website/shop) for eligibility and purchasing options. Alternatively, UK residents should call ☏0870 033 9988; Australians should call ☏1300/669 999 and New Zealanders should call ☏0800/55 9911. All other nationalities should call ☏+44 870 890 2843.

ever, the following **hospitals** have foreigners' clinics where some English is spoken: Peking Union Medical College Hospital at 1 Shuaifuyuan, Wangfujing (Mon–Fri 8am–4.30pm; ☏010/65295284); Friendship Hospital, 95 Yongan Lu, west of Tiantan Park (Mon–Fri 8am–4pm; Sat & Sun 8am–noon; ☏010/63014411); and Sino Japanese Friendship Hospital, in the northeast of the city just beyond Beisanhuan Dong Lu (daily 8–11.30am & 1–4.30pm; ☏010/64221122). At each of the above you will have to pay a consultation fee of around ¥200.

For services run by and for foreigners, try the International Medical and Dental Centre at S111 in the Lufthansa Centre, 50 Liangmaqiao Lu (☏010/64651384); the Hong Kong International Clinic on the 3rd floor of the Swissôtel Hong Kong Macau Centre, Dongsi Shitiao Qiao (daily 9am–9pm; ☏010/65012288, ext 2346); or the United Family Hospital, the only completely foreign-operated clinic, at 2 Jingtai Lu (☏010/64333960). Expect to pay at least ¥500 for a consultation.

For **emergencies**, the AEA International Clinic has English-speaking staff and offers a comprehensive (and expensive) service at 14 Liangmahe Lu, not far from the Lufthansa Centre (clinic ☏010/64629112, emergency calls ☏010/64629100).

Pharmacies are marked by a green cross. There are large ones at 136 Wangfujing and 42 Dongdan Bei Dajie (daily 9am–8pm) or you could try the well-known Tongrentang Pharmacy on Dazhalan for traditional remedies (see p.65). For imported non-prescription medicines, try Watsons (daily 9am–9pm) at the Holiday Inn Lido, Shoudujichang Lu,

in the northeast of the city, or at the Full Link Plaza on Chaoyangmenwai Dajie (daily 10am–9pm).

Insurance

You'd do well to take out an **insurance** policy before travelling, to cover against theft, loss and illness or injury. Before paying for a new policy, however, it's worth checking whether you are already covered: some all-risks home insurance policies may cover your possessions when overseas, and many private medical schemes include cover when abroad.

There's little opportunity for dangerous sports in Beijing (unless crossing the road counts) so a standard policy should be sufficient.

Internet

Smoky **Internet cafés** full of kids playing Couterstrike and MMUDs are legion, and looked on with some disquiet – Beijing's vice mayor has called them the new opium dens, and Internet addiction clinics have opened to deal with young adults whose online use has become excessive. At these "vice dens", you'll be asked to show your passport before being allowed near a computer. They're on every back street, but are particularly prevalent close to colleges. There's never an English sign; look out for the character for "net", *wang* – two crosses inside an "n" (see p.192)

There's a handy **Internet café** on the 3rd floor of The Station, the shopping centre on the east side of Qianmen; aggravatingly though, there's one section for locals at ¥7/hr, and one for foreigners that charges ¥20/hr. Another large café is on Diananmen Dajie,

The new Great Wall of China

Tireless as ever in controlling what its citizens learn and know about, the Chinese government has built a sophisticated **firewall** – nicknamed the new Great Wall of China – that blocks access to undesirable websites. The way this is administered shifts regularly according to the mood of the powers that be – restrictions were loosened, for example, while Beijing was campaigning to be awarded the 2008 summer Olympics (the government was anxious to be seen not to be oppressing its subjects). In general, you can be pretty sure you won't be able to access the BBC, CNN, the White House, or anything about Tibetan freedom, though newspaper websites tend to be left unhindered. You can access banned sites by using a proxy server, but it will slow the connection; try dowloading tor (🌐www.tor.eff.org) which works well with Firefox, or anonymouse (🌐www.anonymouse.org).

opposite the south entrance to Nanluogu Xiang (24hr; ¥3/hr). All hotels have business centres where you can get online, but this can be ridiculously expensive, especially in the classier places. Better value are the hostels (see the "Accommodation" chapter for details), where getting online costs around ¥5/hr. Free Wi-Fi is widespread, and it's safe to assume that cafés will have it – they even have it at McDonalds.

Laundry

You might have a tough time finding a self-service **laundry**; it's said that Chinese housewives wouldn't trust a stranger with the family's clothes. Hotels all offer a laundry service.

Left luggage

The main **left-luggage** office at Beijing Zhan is on the east side of the station (daily 5am–midnight; ¥10/day). There's also a left-luggage office in the foreigners' waiting room, signposted at the back of the station, with lockers for ¥20 (5am–midnight). The left-luggage office at Xi Zhan is downstairs on the left as you enter (¥15 a day; 5am–midnight).

Libraries

The **Beijing National Library**, at 39 Baishiqiao Lu (Mon–Fri 8am–5pm; ☎010/68415566), just north of Zizhuyuan Park, is one of the largest in the world, with more than ten million volumes, including ancient manuscripts and a Qing-dynasty encyclopedia; the very oldest of its texts are Shang-dynasty inscriptions on bone. To take books out, you need to be resident

in the city, though you can just turn up and get a day pass that lets you browse (apply in the office on the south side; ¥5). The Capital Library at 88 Dongsanhuan Nan Lu (☎010/67358114) is smaller, but will let foreign visitors borrow books, though you have to pay a deposit of ¥250. There are some foreign magazines and newspapers. The library of the British Embassy, on the fourth floor of the Landmark Building, 8 Dongsanhuan Bei Lu (Mon–Fri 9am–5pm; 🌐www.britishcouncil.org.cn), has a wide selection of books and magazines and is open to all.

Living in Beijing

Foreigners are allowed to reside anywhere in the city, though most live in **expat housing**, often in Chaoyang in the east of the city. Rent in these districts is expensive, usually at least £1000/US$2000/¥16,000 a month, which gets you a rough imitation of a Western apartment. Living in ordinary neighbourhoods is much cheaper: a furnished two-bedroom apartment can cost around £250/US$500/¥4000 a month.

The easiest way to find an apartment is through a **real estate agent**, who will usually take a month's rent as a fee. There are plenty of agents, and many advertise in the expat magazines – Wo Ai Wo Jia (44 Chengfu Lu ☎010/62557602, 🌐www.5i5j.com) is one of the better ones. Homestays can be cheap, but you won't get much privacy; check 🌐www.chinahomestay.org. For anywhere, as soon as you move in, you and the landlord should register with the local PSB office. See p.45 for further publications.

Anyone intending to live in Beijing should get hold of the fat **Insider's Guide to Beijing** published by Middle Kingdom Press, which includes information on finding housing and doing business. It's available in the Friendship Store.

Working in Beijing

There are plenty of jobs available for foreigners in mainland China, with a whole section of expat society surviving as actors, cocktail barmen, models and so on. Many foreign workers are employed as **English-language teachers** – most universities and many private colleges now have a few foreign teachers.

There are schemes to place foreign teachers in Chinese educational institutions – contact your nearest Chinese embassy (see p.36 for addresses) for details, or check the list of organizations given below. **Teaching** at a university, you'll earn about ¥2000 a month, more than your Chinese counterparts do, though your workload of between ten and twenty hours a week is correspondingly a lot heavier. The pay isn't enough to allow you to put much aside, but is bolstered by on-campus accommodation. Contracts are generally for one year. Most teachers find their students keen, hard-working, curious and obedient, and report that it was the contact with them that made the experience worthwhile. That said, avoid talking about religion or politics in the classroom, as this could get you into trouble.

You'll earn more – up to ¥150 per hour – in a **private school**, though be aware of the risk of being ripped off (you might be given more classes to teach than you'd signed up for, for example).

Studying in Beijing

There are plenty of opportunities to **study** in Beijing but note that most courses are in Chinese (for details of courses in the Chinese language itself, see below). Beijing Daxue (usually referred to as Beida; see p.103; ®www.pku.edu.cn) and Tsinghua Daxue (®www.tsinghua.edu.cn), both in Haidian in the northwest of the city, are the most famous universities in China.

Studying Chinese

You can do short courses (from two weeks to two months) in Mandarin Chinese at Beijing Foreign Studies University, 2 Xi Erhuan Lu (℡010/68468167; ®www.bfsu.edu.cn); at Berlitz at 6 Ritan Lu (℡65930478; ®www.berlitz.com) at the Bridge School in Jianguomenwai Dajie (℡010/64940243), which offers evening classes; or at the Cultural Mission at 7 Beixiao Jie in Sanlitun (℡010/65323005), where most students are diplomats. For courses in Chinese lasting six months to a year, apply to the Beijing International School at Anzhenxili, Chaoyang (℡010/64433151; ®www.isb.bj.edu.cn); Beida in Haidian (see p.103); or Beijing Normal University.

Useful resources

Chinatefl ®www.chinatefl.com. Gives a good overview of English-teaching opportunities in the Chinese public sector.
Council on International Educational Exchange ®www.ciee.org. Exchange programmes for US students of Mandarin or Chinese studies, with placements in Beijing.
Teach Abroad ®www.teachabroad.com. A website where you can post your CV.
Zhaopin ®www.zhaopin.com. A huge jobs site, in Chinese and English.

Mail

Main **post offices** are open seven days a week between 9am and 5pm; smaller offices may close for lunch or at weekends. The International Post Office is on Chaoyangmen Dajie, just north of the intersection with Jianguomen Dajie (Mon–Sat 8am–7pm; ℡010/5128114). At the latter office it's also possible to rent a PO Box, use their packing service for parcels, and buy a wide variety of collectable stamps, but staff are not very helpful. This is where poste restante letters end up, dumped in a box; you'll have to rifle through them all to find your mail – bring your passport as identification. Have letters addressed to you c/o Poste Restante, GPO, Beijing. Letters are only kept for a month and are then sent back. You can also leave a message for someone in the poste restante box, but you'll have to buy a stamp at the post office. There are other post offices in the basement of the World Trade Centre; on Xi Chang'an Jie, just east of the Concert Hall; on Wangfujing Dajie; and at the north end of Xidan Dajie (all Mon–Sat 9am–5pm).

More convenient are the offices in the *New Otani Hotel* (daily 8am–6pm; ☎010/65211309) and at L115, China World Trade Centre (daily 8am–8pm).

The Chinese postal service is, on the whole, as fast and reliable as in western countries. Overseas postage rates are becoming expensive; a postcard costs ¥4.2, while a standard letter is ¥6 or more, depending on the weight. As well as at post offices, you can post letters in green **post-boxes**, or at tourist hotels, which usually have a postbox at the front desk. Envelopes can be frustratingly scarce; try the stationery sections of department stores.

An Express Mail Service (**EMS**) operates to most countries and to most destinations within China and is available from all post offices. Besides cutting delivery times, the service ensures the letter or parcel is sent by registered delivery – though note that the courier service of DHL (24hr office at 2 Jiuxian Qiao in the Chaoyang district, ☎010/64662211) is rather faster, and costs about the same.

To send **parcels**, turn up at a post office with the goods you want to send and the staff will sell you a box to pack them in for ¥15 or so. Once packed, but before the parcel is sealed, it must be checked at the customs window in the post office. A one-kilogram parcel should cost upwards of ¥70 to send surface mail, ¥120 by airmail to Europe; the largest box available holds 30kg and costs about ¥750 to send. If you are sending valuable goods bought in China, put the receipt or a photocopy of it in with the parcel, as it may be opened for customs inspection farther down the line.

Maps

A large fold-out **map** of the city is vital. In general, the free tourist maps – available in large hotels and printed inside tourist magazines – don't show enough detail. A wide variety of city maps are available at all transport hubs and from street vendors, hotels and bookshops. The best map is widely available *Beijing Tourist Map* (¥8), which is labelled in English and Chinese and has bus routes, sights and hotels marked.

Worth seeking out before you go is the *Berndtson and Berndtson* map, which is laminated, and the *Periplus Beijing* map, which has all the street names, including those of many *hutongs* (alleyways), in English. Whatever map you get, you can gauge if it's really up to date by whether it includes the newer subway lines.

Money

Chinese **currency** is formally called the **yuan** (¥), more colloquially known as renminbi (RMB) or kuai; a yuan breaks down into units of ten **jiao** (also called mao). One jiao is equivalent to ten **fen**, though these are effectively worthless – you'll only ever be given them in official currency transactions, or see the tiny notes folded up and used to build model dragons or boats. Paper money was invented in China and is still the main form of exchange, available in ¥100, ¥50, ¥20, ¥10, ¥5, and ¥1 notes, with a similar selection of jiao. At the time of writing the exchange rate was approximately ¥15 to £1, ¥8 to $1 and ¥10 to €1.

China is suffering from a rash of **counterfeiting**. Check your change carefully, as the locals do – hold 100s and 50s up to the light and rub them; fakes have no watermarks and the paper feels rougher.

Banks and ATMs

Banks are usually open Monday to Friday (9am–5pm), though some branches open on weekends too. All banks are closed on New Year's Day, National Day, and for the first three days of the Chinese New Year, with reduced hours for the following eleven days.

The Commercial Bank (Mon–Fri 9am–noon & 1–4pm) in the CITIC Building, 19 Jianguomenwai Dajie, next to the Friendship Store, offers the most comprehensive exchange service: here, you can change money and travellers' cheques, or use most credit cards to obtain cash advances or buy American dollars (if you present exchange certificates).

All branches of the Bank of China will give cash advances on Visa cards, incurring a three percent commission. Their main branch is at 108 Fuxingmennei Dajie (Mon–Fri 9am–

noon & 1.30–5pm), off Chaoyangmen Dajie, just north of the International Post Office. You'll find other branches in the SCITECH Plaza (Mon–Fri 9am–noon & 1–6.30pm), the China World Trade Centre (Mon–Fri 9am–5pm, Sat 9am–noon), the Sun Dong'an Plaza (Mon–Fri 9.30am–noon & 1.30–5pm) and the Lufthansa Centre (Mon–Fri 9am–noon & 1–4pm), among others.

Cirrus and Plus cards can be used to make cash withdrawals from **ATMs** operated by the Bank of China, the Industrial and Commercial Bank of China, China Construction Bank and Agricultural Bank of China. For a list of ATMs, see ⓦwww.moveandstay. com/beijing/guide_banks.asp.

Travellers' cheques and foreign currency

Travellers' cheques are a good way to carry your funds around, as they can be replaced if lost or stolen – for which contingency, it's worth keeping a list of the serial numbers separate from the cheques. They also attract a slightly better rate of exchange than cash. Available through banks and travel agents, they can be cashed only at branches of the Bank of China and at tourist hotels.

It's still worth taking along a small quantity of **foreign currency** – such as US, Canadian or Australian dollars, British pounds or euros – as cash is more widely exchangeable than travellers' cheques. Don't try to change money on the **black market** as you'll almost certainly get ripped off.

Credit cards and wiring money

Major **credit cards**, such as Visa, American Express and MasterCard, are accepted at big tourist hotels and restaurants, and by some tourist-oriented shops. It's straightforward to obtain cash advances on a Visa card at Bank of China branches (however, the commission is a steep three percent). Visa-card holders can also get cash advances using ATM machines bearing the "Plus" logo. It's possible to **wire money** to Beijing through Western Union (ⓦwww.westernunion.com); funds can be collected from one of their agents in the city, in post offices and the Agricultural Bank of China.

Opening hours and public holidays

Offices and **government agencies** are open from Monday to Friday, usually from 8am to noon, then from 1pm to 5pm; some open on Saturday and Sunday mornings, too. **Shops** are generally open from 9am to 7pm Monday to Saturday, with shorter hours on Sunday. **Museums** are either open all week or are shut on one day, usually Monday.

Public **holidays** (see p.31) have little effect on business, with only government departments and certain banks closing. However, on New Year's Day, during the first three days of the Chinese New Year, and on National Day, most businesses, shops and sights will be shut, though some restaurants stay open.

The best time to sightsee is during the week, as all attractions are swamped with local tourists at weekends. Some attractions have separate low- and high-season opening times and prices; in high season (end March to early November), places open usually half an hour earlier, and close half an hour later, while prices rise by ¥5 or ¥10.

Phones

Local calls are free from landlines, and long-distance China-wide calls are fairly cheap. Note that everywhere in China has an area code that must be used when phoning from outside that locality; area codes are given for Chinese phone numbers throughout the book. International calls cost at least ¥8 a minute (cheaper if you use an IC card and even cheaper with an IP Internet phone card – see below).

The most prevalent **public phones** are attached to small stores; simply pick up, dial and pay the amount on the meter afterwards. Most of these however, will not handle international calls. The cheapest way to make long-distance calls is with card phones (¥0.2 for 3min), and these can also be used for international calls. They take **IC Cards** (I-C ka˜ in Mandarin), which are sold at every little store and in hotels, in units of ¥20, ¥50 and ¥100. There's a fifty percent discount after 6pm and at weekends. You will be cut off when the credit left on the card drops below the amount needed for the next minute. You'll find a card phone in every hotel lobby, and there are many booths on the street.

Useful dialling codes

To call mainland China from abroad, dial your international access code (℗00 in the UK and the Republic of Ireland, ℗011 in the US and Canada, ℗0011 in Australia, ℗00 in New Zealand and South Africa), then 86 (China's country code), then the number (minus the initial zero).

Phoning from China to abroad

To call abroad from China dial ℗00 from mainland China, then the country code (see below), then the area code (if any, omitting the initial zero), then the number.

UK international access code + 44 + city code.
Republic of Ireland international access code + 353 + city code.
US and Canada international access code + 1 + city code.
Australia international access code + 61 + city code.
New Zealand international access code + 64 + city code.
South Africa international access code + 27 + city code.

Another option is the **IP (Internet Phone) card**, which can be used from any phone, and comes in ¥50 and ¥100 denominations (though the card is always discounted). You dial the number on the card, then instructions in Chinese and English ask you to dial a PIN printed under a silver strip on the card, which activates the account; finally you call the number you want. Rates are as low as ¥2.4 per minute to the USA and Canada, ¥3.2 to Europe. The cards are widely available, but check that you are buying a card that can be used for international calls, as some are China only (ask for a *guoji* card).

Note that calling from **tourist hotels,** whether from your room or from their business centres, will attract a surcharge and may well be extortionate.

Mobile phones

Your home **cellular phone** may already be compatible with the Chinese network (visitors from North America should ensure their phones are GSM/Triband), though note that you will pay a premium to use it abroad, and that callers within China have to make an international call to reach you. For more information, check the manual that came with your phone, or with the manufacturer and/or your telephone service provider. Call your phone company to find out whether or not they do calling cards that can be charged to your home bill. Alternatively, once in Beijing you can buy a GSM SIM card from any China Mobile shop or street kiosk, which allows you to use your phone as though it's a local mobile, with a new number, as long your phone is unlocked. The SIM card costs around ¥100, with some variation according to how lucky the digits are – favoured sixes and eights bump up the price, unlucky fours make it cheaper. Additionally, you'll need to buy prepaid cards to pay for the calls. Making and receiving domestic calls this way costs ¥0.6 per minute, international calls considerably more.

You can also **rent** mobile phones – look for the ads in expat magazines or ask at your hotel (around ¥30 a day). The cheapest phones **to buy** are around ¥400 (make sure the staff change the operating language into English for you).

Time

Beijing, like the rest of China, is eight hours ahead of GMT, thirteen hours ahead of US Eastern Standard Time, sixteen hours ahead of US Pacific Time and two hours behind Australian Eastern Standard Time. It does not have daylight saving time.

Tourist information

In Beijing, **BTS (Beijing Travel Service)** is a tourist agency focusing on the capital whose main role is to sell tours. However, they will also book train and plane tickets for a small commission and hand out free maps. They have offices at the locations below (daily 9am–6pm). For more information on their tours, check ⓦwww.english.bjta.gov.cn.

There's also a tourism hotline for enquiries or complaints (☎010/065130828).

Of the many other agencies, the government-run CITS (China International Tourist Service; 28 Jianguomenwai Dajie ☎010/65157671) and CYTS (China Youth Travel Service, 3C Dongjiaominxiang ☎010/65243388) are the largest. Again, they run tours and sell tickets but don't expect too much from them.

Chinese tourist offices abroad

For additional locations, see ⊛www.cnto. org/offices.htm.

UK 4 Glentworth St, London NW1 5PG ☎020 7373 0888.
Australia 19th floor, 44 Market St, Sydney, NSW 2000 ☎02/9299 4057.
Canada 480 University Ave, Suite 806, Toronto, Ontario M5G 1V2 ☎0416/5996636.
USA Suite 6413, 350 Fifth Ave, Empire State Building, New York, NY 10018 ☎212/760-8218; Suite 201, 333 W Broadway, Glendale, CA 91024 ☎818/545-7505.

BTS offices in Beijing

Beijing Zhan Jie Just south of the COFCO Plaza, Jianguomen.
Haidian District South Lobby, Modern Plaza, Dong Dai shopping Centre, 40 Zhongguancun Nan Dajie ☎010/62622895.
Dongcheng District 10 Dengshikou Xi Jie, opposite Lao She's Residence ☎010/65123043.
Xicheng District 1st floor, Xidan Science and Technology Plaza, 131 Xidan Bei Dajie ☎010/66160108.
Chaoyang District 27 Gongrentiyuchang Bei Lu.

Useful publications

The English-language **Beijing This Month** has listings and light features aimed at tourists; you can pick it for free in the lobbies of the upmarket hotels, from any tourist office or the counter inside the front door at the Friendship Store on Jianguomenwai Dajie, along with leaflets containing basic tourist information.

Much more useful, though, are the free magazines aimed at the **expat** community, which contain up-to-date entertainment and restaurant listings and are available at expat

bars and restaurants. Look for *City Weekend* (⊛www.cityweekend.com) and *That's Beijing* (⊛www.thatsbeijing.com). Both have listings sections that include club nights, art happenings and gigs, with addresses written in *pinyin* and Chinese.

Online resources

There's plenty of **online information** about China in general and Beijing specifically, though as a general rule, avoid websites run by official agencies such as CITS; they're dry as dust. Here's a selection of sites to start you off:

The Beijing Page ⊛www.beijingpage.com. A comprehensive and well-organized page of links, with sections on tourism, entertainment, reference and industry.
Beijing Opera Page ⊛www.geocities. com/Vienna/Opera/8692/index0.html. More than most people would want to know about Beijing opera, including story rundowns and a frank essay about why hardly anyone bothers watching it any more.
Beijing Guo'an ⊛www.soccerage.com/ en/02/01278.html. All about Guo'an, Beijing's football team, including fixture lists.
CCTV 9 ⊛www.cctv-9.com. Featuring a live video stream plus other programmes available to watch on demand, this is the website of the Chinese state television's English-language channel.
China Business World ⊛www.cbw.com. A corporate directory site with a useful travel section, detailing tours and allowing you to book flights and hotels.
China Vista ⊛www.chinavista.com. China-based website with snippets about Chinese culture, history, attractions and food.
Friends of the Great Wall ⊛www. friendsofgreatwall.org/English. Covers efforts to maintain and clean up the Great Wall, with useful links.
Niubi ⊛www.niubi.com. This website, named after a very rude phrase in Chinese, is dedicated to Beijing's more underground rock bands.
Sinomania ⊛www.sinomania.com. A California-based site with links to current Chinese news stories and a good popular music section, with MP3 downloads available.
Yesasia ⊛www.yesasia.com. Online shopping for Chinese movies, CDs, books, collectables, etc.
Zhongwen.com ⊛www.zhongwen.com Especially interesting if you're a student of Chinese, this site includes background on the Chinese script, several classic texts (with links to some English translations) and even a bunch of suggested renderings into Chinese of common first names.

Travellers with disabilities

Beijing makes few provisions for **disabled** people. Undergoing an economic boom, the city resembles a building site, with uneven, obstacle-strewn paving, intense crowds and vehicle traffic, and few access ramps. Public transport is generally inaccessible to wheelchair users, though a few of the upmarket hotels are equipped to assist disabled visitors; in particular, Beijing's several *Holiday Inns* (*Holiday Inn Downtown* at 98 Beilishi Lu ☎010/68132299) and *Hiltons* (there's one at 1 Dongfang Lu ☎010/58655000) have rooms designed for wheelchair users.

The disabled in Chinese are usually kept hidden away; attitudes are not, on the whole, very enlightened, and disabled visitors should be prepared for a great deal of frank staring. Given the situation, it may be worth considering an **organized tour** – the contacts given below will be able to help you arrange this or aid you in researching your own trip. Make sure you take spares of any specialist clothing or equipment, extra supplies of drugs (carried with you if you fly), and a prescription including the generic name – in English and Chinese characters – in case of emergency. If there's an association representing people with your disability, contact them early on in the planning process.

Contacts for travellers with disabilities

UK and Republic of Ireland

Irish Wheelchair Association Blackheath Drive, Clontarf, Dublin 3 ☎01/818 6400, 🌐www.iwa. ie. A source of useful information on travelling abroad with a wheelchair.

Tripscope Alexandra House, Albany Rd, Brentford, Middlesex TW8 0NE ☎0845/7585 641, ✆020/8580 7021, 🌐www.tripscope.org.uk. Advice on transport for those with a mobility problem.

US and Canada

Access-Able 🌐www.access-able.com. Online resource for travellers with disabilities, with limited coverage of Beijing.

Directions Unlimited 123 Green Lane, Bedford Hills, NY 10507 ☎1-800/533-5343 or 914/241-1700. Travel agency specializing in bookings for people with disabilities.

Disability Travel 🌐www.disabilitytravel.com. Arranges all aspects of travel for the mobility-impaired, including tours to Beijing.

Society for the Advancement of Travelers with Handicaps (SATH) 347 5th Ave, New York, NY 10016 ☎212/447-7284, 🌐www.sath.org. Non-profit educational organization that has actively represented travellers with disabilities since 1976.

Australia and New Zealand

ACROD (Australian Council for Rehabilitation of the Disabled) PO Box 60, Curtin ACT 2605; Suite 103, 1st floor, 1–5 Commercial Rd, Kings Grove, NSW 2208; ☎02/6282 4333, TTY ☎02/6282 4333, 🌐www.acrod.org.au. Provides lists of travel agencies and tour operators for people with disabilities.

Disabled Persons Assembly 4/173–175 Victoria St, Wellington, New Zealand ☎04/801 9100 (also TTY), 🌐www.dpa.org.nz. Resource centre with lists of travel agencies and tour operators for people with disabilities.

Travel agents

There are plenty of travel agents in Beijing. The biggest is the state-run CITS. They offer tours of the city and surroundings, and advance ticket booking within China for trains, planes and ferries, with a commission of around ¥20 added to ticket prices. You'll find CITS next to the Gloria Plaza Hotel at 28 Jianguomenwai Dajie (daily 8.30–11.30am & 1.30–4.30pm; ☎010/65050231); next to the Parkson Building at 103 Fuxingmen Dajie (daily 9am–5pm; ☎010/66011122); in the *Beijing Hotel*, 33 Dongchang'an Jie (☎010/65120507); and at the *New Century Hotel* (☎010/68491426), opposite the zoo. Good, privately run alternatives to CITS include China Swan International Tours on the 4th floor of the Longhui Building, 1 Nanguang Nanli, Dongsanhuan Lu (☎010/67316393; 🌐www.china-swan. com) and BTG International at 206 Beijing Tourism Building, (☎010/96906798; 🌐www. btgtravel.cn); both are well geared up for corporate groups. For adventure travel within China, contact Wildchina, Room 801, Oriental Place, 9 Dongfang Dong Lu, Dongsanhuan Bei Lu (☎010/64656602, 🌐www.wildchina. com). Beijing's most unusual tour agency is Koryo Tours (Room 43, *Red House Hotel*, 10 Taiping Zhuang; ☎010/64167544; 🌐www. koryogroup.com), who arrange visits (heavily controlled, of course) to the paranoid hermit kingdom of North Korea. Expect to pay at least two thousand dollars for the privilege.

The City

The City

1

Tian'anmen Square
and the
Forbidden City

The first stop for any visitor to Beijing is **Tian'anmen Square**, which at over 400,000 square metres, is the greatest public space on earth. Right in the city centre, the square is symbolically the heart of China, and the events it has witnessed have shaped the history of the People's Republic from its inception. Laid out in 1949, it is a modern creation in a city that traditionally had no places where crowds could gather. As one of the square's architects put it: "Beijing was a reflection of a feudal society . . . We had to transform it, we had to make Beijing into the capital of socialist China." So they created a vast concrete plain dotted with worthy statuary and bounded by stern, monumental buildings: the **Great Hall of the People** to the west and the **Museums of History** and the **Revolution** to the east. To the north you'll see Tian'anmen, a gateway of great significance to both imperial and communist China.

The Chairman Mao's Memorial Hall	毛主席纪念堂	*máozhǔxí jìniàntáng*
The Forbidden City	故宫	*gùgōng*
The Great Hall of the People	人民大会堂	*rénmín dàhuìtáng*
Museum of Chinese History	中国历史博物馆	*zhōngguó lìshǐ bówùguǎn*
Museum of the Revolution	中国革命博物馆	*zhōngguó gémìng bówùguǎn*
Museum of Urban Planning	规划博物馆	*guī huà bó wù guǎn*
National Opera House	中国国家大剧院	*zhōngguó guójiā dàjùyuàn*
Tian'anmen	天安门	*tiān'ān mén*
Tian'anmen Square	天安门广场	*tiān'ānmén guǎngchǎng*
Working Peoples' Cultural Palace	劳动人民文化宫	*láodòngrénmín wénhuàgōng*
Zhengyangmen	正阳门	*zhèngyáng mén*
Zhong Shan park	中山公园	*zhōngshān gōngyuán*

Beyond it, and in its luxury and ornament a complete contrast to the square's austerity, is the Gugong, or Imperial Palace, better known in the West by its unofficial title, the **Forbidden City** – a reference to its exclusivity. Indeed, for the five centuries of functioning, through the reigns of 24 emperors of the Ming and Qing dynasties, civilian Chinese were forbidden from even approaching the walls. With its maze of eight hundred buildings and nine thousand chambers, it was the core of the capital, the empire, and (so the Chinese believed) the universe. From within, the emperors – the **Sons of Heaven** – issued commands with absolute authority to their millions of subjects. It remains an extraordinary place today, unsurpassed in China for monumental scale, harmonious design and elegant grandeur.

Tian'anmen Square

For many Chinese tourists, **Tian'anmen Square** is a place of pilgrimage. Crowds flock to see the corpse of Chairman Mao in his **mausoleum** and to see the most

▲ Guards at Tian'anmen Square

potent symbols of power in contemporary China: the Great Hall of the People and Tian'anmen Gate. Some quietly bow their heads before the **Monument to the People's Heroes**, a thirty-metre-high obelisk commemorating the victims of the revolutionary struggle. Its foundations were laid on October 1, 1949, the day that the establishment of the People's Republic was announced. Bas-reliefs around it illustrate key scenes from China's revolutionary history; one of these, on the east side, shows the Chinese burning British opium (see p.172) in the nineteenth century. The calligraphy on the front is a copy of Mao Zedong's handwriting and reads "Eternal glory to the Heroes of the People". The platform on which the obelisk stands is guarded, and a prominent sign declares that commemorative gestures, such as the laying of wreaths, are banned. In 1976, riots broke out when wreaths honouring the death of the popular politician Zhou Enlai were removed; the demonstrations of 1989 began here with the laying of wreaths to a recently deceased liberal politician.

For a great view over the square head to the south gate, **Zhengyangmen** (daily 9am–4.30pm; ¥5). Similar to Tian'anmen (North Gate), this squat, forty-metre-high structure with an arched gateway through the middle once marked the boundary between

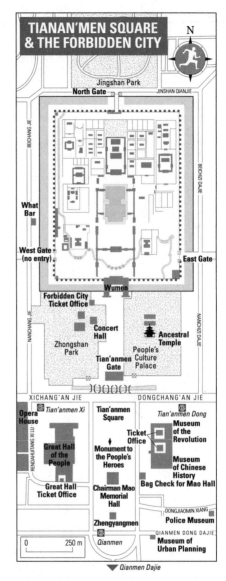

Tricksters

Around Tian'anmen be wary of young couples and cute little girls who say they want to practise their English or claim to be art students. Their aim is to coax you into accompanying them to a "teahouse" or "art gallery", where you'll end up being persuaded, cajoled or even forced into paying hundreds of dollars for a few cups of tea or a worthless print. See p.34 for more.

Dissent in Tian'anmen Square

Though it was designed as a space for mass declarations of loyalty, Tian'anmen Square has as often been a venue for expressions of popular **dissent**. The first mass protests here occurred on May 4, 1919, when students gathered in the area to demonstrate against the disastrous terms of the Treaty of Versailles, under which the victorious Allies granted several former German concessions in China to the Japanese. The protests, and the movement they spawned, marked the beginning of the painful struggle for Chinese modernization. In 1925, the inhabitants of Beijing again occupied the square, to protest over the massacre in Shanghai of Chinese demonstrators by British troops. The following year, protesters angered at the weak government's capitulation to the Japanese marched on government offices and were fired on by soldiers.

The first time the square became the focus of outcry in the communist era was in 1976, when thousands assembled here, without government approval, to voice their dissatisfaction with their leaders; in 1978 and 1979, large numbers came to discuss new ideas of democracy and artistic freedom, triggered by writings posted along "Democracy Wall" on the edge of the Forbidden City. People gathered again in 1986 and 1987, remonstrating the Party's refusal to allow limited municipal elections to be held. But it was in **1989** that Tian'anmen Square became the venue for the largest expression of popular dissent in China in the twentieth century; from April to June of that year, nearly a million protesters demonstrated against the slow reform, lack of civil liberties and widespread corruption. The government, infuriated at being humiliated by their own people, declared martial law on May 20, and on June 4 the military moved into the square. The ensuing **killing** was indiscriminate; tanks ran over tents and machine guns strafed the avenues. No one knows exactly how many demonstrators died in the massacre – probably thousands; hundreds were arrested afterwards and some remain in jail (though others have since joined the administration).

These days the square is occasionally the venue for small protests by foreigners or members of the cultish, religious sect Falun Gong – hence the many closed-circuit TV cameras and large numbers of Public Security men, not all in uniform; look out, for example, for the plainclothes bruisers who stand either side of Tian'anmen's Mao painting.

the imperial city and the commoners outside. Avoid the tacky souvenir stores on the first two floors and head to the top; you'll get a good idea of how much more impressive the square looked before Mao's mausoleum was stuck in the middle of it.

At dawn, the flag at the northern end of the square is raised in a military ceremony. It's lowered again at dusk, which is when most people come to watch, though foreigners complain that the regimentation of the crowds is oppressive. After dark, the square is at its most appealing and, with its sternness softened by mellow lighting, it becomes the haunt of strolling families and lovers.

As a transport hub, the square is easy to get to: Qianmen subway stop is just south of the square, with Tian'anmen Xi and Tian'anmen Dong stops nearby to the west and east respectively; you can also get here on buses #1, #4, #10, #22, #52 or #57.

The Museum of Urban Planning

Beijing's newest attraction, just off Qianmen Dong Dajie, is the six-storey, marble-faced **Museum of Urban Planning** (Tues–Sun 9am–5pm; ¥30). Along with a host of rather banal displays and presentations on Beijing's bright urban future, a fascinating model shows the city as it used to look in imperial times when every significant building was part of an awesome, grand design. The star attraction, though, is an enormous model of the city that takes up the entire top floor: it illustrates what the place will look like once it's finished being ripped up and redesigned by 2020. Visitors can wander around the amazingly detailed mock-up: the z-shaped CCTV Tower (see p.176) looks like it's going to be an impressive building.

The Chairman Mao Memorial Hall

Mao's **mausoleum** (daily 8.30–11.30am, plus April–Oct 2–4pm Mon, Wed & Fri; free), constructed in 1977 by an estimated million volunteers, is an ugly building that looks like a drab municipal facility. It contravenes the principles of *feng shui* (see box on p.57) – presumably deliberately – by interrupting the line from the palace to Qianmen and by facing north. Mao himself wanted to be cremated, and the erection of the mausoleum was apparently no more than a power assertion by his would-be successor, Hua Guofeng. In 1980 Deng Xiaoping, then leader, said it should never have been built, although he wouldn't go so far as to pull it down.

After depositing your bag and camera at the Bag Check over the road to the east

Chairman Mao

A revolution is not a dinner party.

Mao Zedong

Mao Zedong, the son of a well-off Hunnanese farmer, believed social reform lay in the hands of the peasants. Having helped found the Chinese Communist Party, on the Soviet model, in Shanghai in 1921, he quickly organized a peasant workers militia – the Red Army – to take on the Nationalist government. A cunning guerrilla leader, Mao was said to have learnt his tactics from studying the first tyrant Emperor Qin Shihuang, Sun Tzu's *Art of War*, and from playing the East Asian game of Go. In 1934 Mao's army was encircled; the epic retreat that followed, the **Long March** – eighty thousand men walking ten thousand kilometres over a year – solidified Mao's reputation and spread the message of the rebels through the countryside. They joined another rebel force at Yan'an, in northern China, and set up the first soviets, implementing land reform and educating the peasantry.

In 1949, now at the head of a huge army, Mao finally vanquished the Nationalists and became the "Great Helmsman" of the new Chinese nation – and here the trouble started. The chain-smoking poet rebel indulged what appeared to be a personal need for permanent revolution in catastrophes such as the **Great Leap Forward** of the Fifties and the **Cultural Revolution** of the Sixties (see p.174). His policies caused enormous suffering; some estimate Mao was responsible for the deaths of over 38 million people – mostly from famine as a result of incompetent agricultural policies. Towards the end of his life Mao became increasingly paranoid and out of touch, surrounded by sycophants and nubile dancers – a situation vividly described by his physician, Zhisui Li, in his book *The Private Life of Chairman Mao*.

Today the official Chinese position on Mao is that he was "seventy percent right". Although public images of him have largely been expunged, the personality cult he fostered lives on, particularly in taxis where his image is hung like a lucky charm from the rear-view mirror, and he's often included among the deities in peasant shrines. Today his **Little Red Book**, source of political slogans such as "power grows from the barrel of a gun", is no longer required reading but English translations are widely available in Beijing – though from souvenir vendors rather than bookshops. His poetry is highly regarded; check it out at Ⓦ www.mzdthought.com.

(¥10), join the orderly queue of Chinese – almost exclusively working class out-of-towners – on the northern side. The queue advances surprisingly quickly, and takes just a couple of minutes to file through the chambers in silence. Mao's pickled **corpse**, draped with a red flag within a crystal coffin, looks unreal, which it may well be; a wax copy was made in case the preservation went wrong. Mechanically raised from a freezer every morning, it is said to have been embalmed with the aid of Vietnamese technicians who had previously worked on the body of Ho Chi Minh. Apparently, 22 litres of formaldehyde went into preserving his body; rumour has it that not only did the corpse swell grotesquely when too much fluid was used, but that Mao's left ear fell off during the embalming process, and had to be stitched back on.

Much of the interest of a visit here lies in witnessing the sense of awe of the Chinese confronted with their former leader, the architect of modern China who was accorded an almost god-like status for much of his life. The atmosphere is one of reverence, though once through the marble halls, you're herded past a splendidly wide-ranging array of tacky Mao souvenirs. The flashing Mao lighter that plays the national anthem is a perennial favourite (¥10).

The Great Hall of the People

Taking up almost half the west side of the square is the monolithic **Great Hall of the People** (daily 8.30am–3pm when not in session; ¥20; buy tickets and leave bags at the office on the southern side), one of ten Stalinist wedding-cake-style buildings constructed in 1959 to celebrate "ten years of liberation" (others include Beijing Zhan and the Military Museum – see p.25 and p.77 respectively). This is the venue of the National People's Congress (the Chinese legislature), and the building is closed to the public when the Congress is in session – you'll know by the hundreds of black Audis with darkened windows parked outside. It's not really a sight as such, but you can take a turn around the building; what you see on the roped-off route through is a selection of the 29 cavernous, dim reception rooms,

▲ The Great Hall of the People

decorated in the same pompous but shabby style seen in the lobbies of cheap Chinese hotels – badly fitted red carpet, lifeless murals and armchairs lined up against the walls and draped with fiddly antimacassars.

Each room is named after a part of China; one is called "Taiwan Province". The route ends at the massive five-thousand-seater banqueting hall where you can buy a bland canteen lunch (¥10).

When Mrs Thatcher came here in 1982 she tripped on the steps – this was regarded in Hong Kong as a terrible omen for the negotiations she was having over the territory's future. In 1989, the visiting Mikhail Gorbachev had to be smuggled in through a side entrance to avoid the crowds of protesters outside (see p.52). If you're not a national leader on a meet-and-greet, you'll be better rewarded elsewhere; the Russian-built Exhibition Hall (see p.100) is a more pleasing example of monumental communist architecture.

The museums

On the east side of the square is a giant digital clock designed to count down the seconds till the start of the Olympic Games. It was used before, to count down till the handovers of Hong Kong and then Macau. Behind it are two museums (both daily 8.30am–5pm; last entry 4.15pm; exhibitions ¥10–20), housed in the same building but with separate ticket offices. At the time of writing both were closed for a huge spruce up; they will be open in time for the Olympics.

The **Museum of the Revolution** covers China in the nineteenth and twentieth centuries. It's full of propaganda, and seems almost always to be shut for refits (during the Cultural Revolution it was shut for twelve years) as its curators are constantly having to reinvent the displays according to the latest Party line. The exhibits from the twentieth century – mostly photos of politicians – are dull (and the coverage terminates at 1949, post-liberation history being just too contentious), but those from the nineteenth century, including such oddments as a contract signed by a peasant selling his wife, and "Weapons used by the British against the Tibetan People", are fascinating. There are copious English captions, full of terms like "foreign aggression" and "colonial oppressors".

One exhibition hall holds the **historical waxworks show** (¥10), which displays 35 figures, including heroes of the people: devoted Party member Lei Feng rubs shoulders with Norman Bethune (the only foreigner, a Canadian surgeon who worked with the Red Army), the historian Sima Qian, Confucius and, of course, Mao, whose figure here looks more realistic than the one in the tomb. Sadly there are no English captions, but the figure of the little girl staring up in homage at the red flag at the entrance drives home the point well enough – this is art to inspire patriotism, the latest incarnation of Socialist Realism.

The south side of the building is the **Museum of Chinese History**. It is intended more for the education of the Chinese masses than foreign tourists – it will be interesting to see whether, when it reopens, the exhibits are still divided according to a Marxist reading of history, into "primitive", "slave", "feudal" and "semi-colonial".

Tian'anmen

Tian'anmen (daily 8am–5pm; ¥15), the Gate of Heavenly Peace, is the main entrance to the Forbidden City (buy tickets from the Forbidden City ticket office, further north on the right: see map on p.58). An image familiar across the world, Tian'anmen occupies an exalted place in Chinese iconography, appearing on policemen's caps, banknotes, coins, stamps and most pieces of official paper.

The emperor speaks to his people

In the Ming and Qing dynasties, Tian'anmen was where the **ceremony** called "the golden phoenix issues an edict" took place. The minister of rites would receive an imperial edict inside the palace, and take it to Tian'anmen on a silver "cloud tray", he and his charge under a yellow umbrella. Here, the edict was read aloud to the officials of the court who knelt below, lined up according to rank. Next, the edict was placed in the mouth of a gilded wooden phoenix, which was lowered by rope to another cloud tray below. The tray was then put in a carved, wooden dragon and taken to the Ministry of Rites to be copied out and sent around the country.

Mao too liked to address his subjects from here; on October 1, 1949, he delivered the **liberation speech** to jubilant crowds below, declaring that "the Chinese people have now stood up"; in the 1960s, he spoke from this spot to massed ranks of Red Guards and declared that it was time for a "cultural revolution" (see p.174).

As such it's a prime object of pilgrimage, with many visitors milling around and taking pictures of the large **portrait of Mao** (the only one still on public display), which hangs over the central passageway. Once reserved for the sole use of the emperor, but now standing wide open, the entrance is flanked by the twin slogans "Long Live the People's Republic of China" and "Long Live the Great Union between the Peoples of the World".

The entry ticket allows you to climb up onto the **viewing platform** above the gate. Security is tight: all visitors have to leave their bags, be frisked and go through a metal detector before they can ascend. Inside, the fact that most people cluster around the souvenir stall – which only sells official certificates to anyone who wants their visit here documented – reflects the fact that there's not much to look at.

The parks

The two parks either side of Tian'anmen, **Zhongshan** to the west and the grounds of the **People's Culture Palace** to the east, are great places to escape the square's rigorous formality (both open daily 6am–9pm; ¥3).

Zhongshan park boasts the ruins of the Altar of Land and Grain, a site of biennial sacrifice during the Qing and Ming dynasties, with harvest-time events closely related to those of the Temple of Heaven (see p.68). There's a concert hall here too (see p.154). The People's Culture Palace – symbolically named in deference to the fact that only after the communist takeover in 1949 were ordinary Chinese allowed within this central sector of their city – has a number of modern exhibition halls, often worth checking out for their temporary art shows, and a scattering of original fifteenth-century structures, most of them Ming or Qing ancestral temples.

The Forbidden City

Lying at the heart of the city, the Imperial Palace, Gugong, or, most evocatively, the **Forbidden City**, is Beijing's finest monument. To do it justice, you should plan to spend a whole day here, though you could wander the complex for a week and keep discovering new aspects. The central halls, with their wealth of imperial pomp, may be the most magnificent buildings, but for many visitors it's the side rooms, with their displays of the more intimate accoutrements of court life, that bring home the realities of life for the inhabitants in this, the most gilded of cages.

Although the earliest structures (none of which survive today) on the site of the Forbidden City began with Kublai Khan during the Mongol dynasty, the **plan** of the palace buildings is essentially Ming. Most date back to the fifteenth century and the ambitions of the **Emperor Yongle**, the monarch responsible for switching the capital from Nanjing back to Beijing in 1403 (see p.171). His programme to construct a complex worthy enough to house the Son of Heaven was concentrated between 1407 and 1420, involving up to ten thousand artisans and perhaps a million labourers.

All the halls of the Forbidden City were laid out according to geomantic theories – the balance between *yin* and *yang*, or negative and positive energy. The buildings, signposted in English, face south in order to benefit from the invigorating advantages of *yang* energy, and as a protection against harmful *yin* elements from the north, both real and imagined – cold winds, evil spirits and steppe barbarians. Ramparts of compacted earth and a fifty-metre-wide moat isolated the complex from the commoners outside, with the only access being through four monumental gateways in the four cardinal directions. The layout is the same as that of any grand Chinese house of the period; pavilions are arranged around courtyards, with reception rooms and official buildings at the front (south), set out with rigorous symmetry, and a labyrinthine set of private chambers to the north.

Visiting the Forbidden City

You can get to the Forbidden City on **bus** #5 from Qianmen; #54 from Beijing Zhan; or #1, which passes the complex on its journey along Chang'an Jie; all three buses drop you at the north end of Tian'anmen Square. The nearest **subways** are Tian'anmen Xi and Tian'anmen Dong, each about 300m away. Once through Tian'anmen, you find yourself on a long walkway, with the moated palace complex and massive main gate, Wumen, directly ahead; this is where you buy your ticket. If you're in a taxi, you can be dropped right outside the ticket office. The complex is **open** daily from 8.30am to 4.30pm (last admission 4pm April–Sept, 3.30pm Oct–March) and **tickets** cost ¥40.

Note that as well as the main gate, you can enter the complex through the smaller north and east gates (there are ticket offices just inside both gates). You can get to the north gate on bus #101, #103, or #109, which pass right by, and to the east gate on bus #819.

Visitors have freedom to wander most of the one-square-kilometre site, though not of all the buildings. If you want detailed explanations of everything you see, you can tag along with one of the numerous tour groups, buy one of the

Feng shui

Feng shui, literally "wind and water", is a form of geomancy, which assesses how objects must be positioned so as not to disturb the spiritual attributes of the surrounding landscape. This reflects Taoist cosmology, which states that the inner harmonies of the landscape must be preserved to secure all other harmonies. Buildings should be favourably oriented according to the compass – tombs, for example, should face south – and protected from unlucky directions by other buildings or hills.

Even the minutiae of interior **decor** are covered by *feng shui*. Some of its handy rules for the modern home include: don't have a mirror at the foot of the bed; don't have sharp edges pointing into the room; cover the television when it's not in use; and don't leave the lavatory seat up.

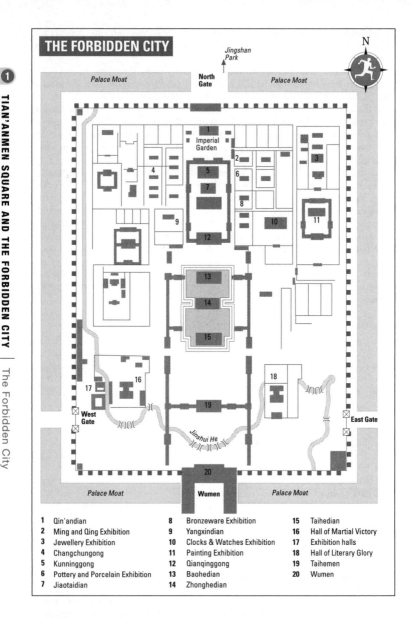

1 Qin'andian	**8** Bronzeware Exhibition	**15** Taihedian
2 Ming and Qing Exhibition	**9** Yangxindian	**16** Hall of Martial Victory
3 Jewellery Exhibition	**10** Clocks & Watches Exhibition	**17** Exhibition halls
4 Changchungong	**11** Painting Exhibition	**18** Hall of Literary Glory
5 Kunninggong	**12** Qianqinggong	**19** Taihemen
6 Pottery and Porcelain Exhibition	**13** Baohedian	**20** Wumen
7 Jiaotaidian	**14** Zhonghedian	

many specialist books on sale at Wumen, or take the **audio tour** (¥40), available at the main gate. On the audio tour, you're provided with a cassette player and headphones, and talked through the complex. If you take this option, it's worth retracing your steps afterwards for an untutored view, and heading off to the side halls that aren't included on the tour. There are plenty of fancy toilets inside the complex.

From Wumen to Taihemen

A huge building, whose central archway was reserved for the emperor's sole use, **Wumen** (Meridian Gate) is the largest and grandest of the Forbidden City gates. From a vantage point at the top, each new lunar year the Sons of Heaven would announce to their court the details of the forthcoming calendar, including the dates of festivals and rites, and, in times of war, inspect the army. It was customary for victorious generals returning from battle to present their prisoners here for the emperor to decide their fate. He would be flanked, as on all such imperial occasions, by a guard of elephants, the gift of Burmese subjects. In the Ming dynasty, this was also where disgraced officials were flogged or executed.

In the wings on either side of the Wumen are two drums and two bells; the drums were beaten whenever the emperor went to the Temple of the Imperial Ancestors, the bells rung when he visited the temples of Heaven (see p.68) and Earth (see p.98).

Passing through Wumen, you find yourself in a vast paved court, cut east–west by the **Jinshui He**, or Golden Water Stream, with its five marble bridges, one for each Confucian virtue (see p.98). They're decorated with carved torches, a symbol of masculinity. Beyond is another ceremonial gate, **Taihemen**, the Gate of Supreme Harmony, its entrance guarded by a magisterial row of lions, and further on a larger courtyard where the principal imperial audiences were held. Within this space the entire court – up to a hundred thousand people – could be accommodated. They made their way in through the lesser side gates – military men from the west, civilian officials from the east – and waited in total silence as the emperor ascended his throne. Then, with only the Imperial Guard remaining standing, they prostrated themselves nine times.

The galleries running round the courtyard housed the imperial storerooms. The buildings either side are the Hall of Martial Victory to the west and Hall of Literary Glory to the east; the latter, under the Ming emperors, housed the 11,099 volumes of the encyclopedia Yongle commissioned.

The ceremonial halls

The three main **ceremonial halls** stand directly north of Taihemen, dominating the court. The main halls, made of wood, are traditionally built all on the same level, on a raised stone platform. Their elegant roofs, curved like the wings of a bird, are supported entirely by pillars and beams; the weight is cleverly distributed

Imperial symbolism

Almost every colour and image in the palace is richly **symbolic**. Yellow was the imperial colour; only in the palace were yellow roof tiles allowed. Purple was just as important, though used more sparingly; it symbolized joy and represented the pole star, centre of the universe according to Chinese cosmology (the implication of its use – usually on wall panels – was that the emperor resided in the earthly equivalent of the celestial zenith). The sign for the emperor was the dragon and for the empress, the phoenix; you'll see these two creatures represented on almost every building and stairway. The crane and turtle, depicted in paintings, carved into furniture or represented as freestanding sculptures, represent longevity of reign. The numbers nine and five crop up all over the complex, manifested in how often design elements are repeated; nine is lucky and associated with *yang*, or male energy, while five, the middle single-digit number, is associated with harmony and balance. Nine and five together – power and balance – symbolize "the heavenly son" – the emperor.

Dining, imperial style

The emperor ate twice a day, at 6.30am and around noon. Often meals consisted of hundreds of dishes, with the emperor eating no more than a mouthful of each – to eat more would be to express a preference, and that information might reach a potential poisoner. According to tradition, no one else was allowed to eat at his table, and when banquets were held he sat at a platform well above his guests. Such occasions were extremely formal and not to everyone's liking; a Jesuit priest invited to such a feast in 1727 complained, "A European dies of hunger here; the way in which he is forced to sit on the ground on a mat with crossed legs is most awkward; neither the wine nor the dishes are to his taste . . . Every time the emperor says a word which lets it be known he wishes to please, one must kneel down and hit one's head on the ground. This has to be done every time someone serves him something to drink."

by ceiling consoles, while the walls beneath are just lightweight partitions. Doors, steps and access ramps are always odd in number, with the middle passageway reserved for the emperor's palanquin.

Raised on a three-tiered marble terrace is the first and most spectacular of the halls, the **Taihedian**, Hall of Supreme Harmony. The vast hall, nearly 38m high, was the tallest in China during the Ming and Qing dynasty – no civilian building was permitted to be taller. Taihedian was used for the most important state occasions: the emperor's coronation, birthday or marriage; ceremonies marking the new lunar year and winter solstice; proclamations of the results of the imperial examinations; and the nomination of generals at the outset of a military campaign. During the Republic, it was proposed that parliament should sit here, though the idea wasn't put into practice.

Decorated entirely in red and gold, Taihedian is the most sumptuous building in the complex. In the central coffer, a sunken panel in the ceiling, two gold-plated dragons play with a huge pearl. The gilded rosewood chair beneath, the dragon throne, was the exact centre of the Chinese universe. A marble pavement ramp, intricately carved with dragons and flanked by bronze incense burners, marks the path along which the emperor's sedan chair was carried whenever he wanted to be taken somewhere. The grain measure and sundial just outside are symbols of imperial justice.

Moving on, you enter the **Zhonghedian**, Hall of Middle Harmony, another throne room, where the emperor performed ceremonies of greeting to foreign dignitaries and addressed the imperial offspring (the progeny of his several wives and numerous concubines). It owes its name to a quote from the *I-Ching* (see p.76), a Chinese tome dating back to 200 BC: "avoiding extremes and self control brings harmony" – the idea being that the middle course would be a harmonious one. The emperor also examined the seed for each year's crop in the hall, and it was used, too, as a dressing room for major events held in the Taihedian.

The third of the great halls, the **Baohedian**, or Preserving Harmony Hall, was the venue for state banquets and imperial examinations; graduates from the latter were appointed to positions of power in what was the world's first recognizably bureaucratic civil service. Huge ceremonies took place here to celebrate Chinese New Year; in 1903, this involved the sacrifice of ten thousand sheep. The hall's galleries, originally treasure houses, display various finds from the site, though the most spectacular, a vast marble block carved with dragons and clouds, stands at the rear of the hall. A Ming creation, reworked in the eighteenth century, it's among the finest carvings in the palace and certainly the largest – the 250-tonne chunk of marble was slid here from well outside the city by flooding the roads in winter to form sheets of ice.

The imperial living quarters

To the north, repeating the hierarchy of the ceremonial halls, are the three principal palaces of the **imperial living quarters**. Again, it's the first of these, the **Qianqinggong**, or Palace of Heavenly Purity, that's the most extravagant. Originally the imperial bedroom, its terrace is surmounted by incense burners in the form of cranes and tortoises. It was here in 1785 that Qianlong presided over the famous "banquet of old men" that brought together three thousand men of over sixty years of age from all corners of the empire. Used for the lying in state of the emperor, the hall also played a role in the tradition that finally solved the problem of **succession** (hitherto fraught with intrigue and uncertainty, as the principle of primogeniture was not used). The practice was begun by Qing Emperor Yongzheng: keeping an identical document on his person, Yongzheng and his successors deposited the name of his chosen successor in a sealed box hidden in the hall. When the emperor died, it was sufficient to compare the two documents to proclaim the new Son of Heaven.

Eunuchs and concubines

For much of the imperial period, the Forbidden City was home to members of the royal household. Around half of these were **eunuchs**, introduced into the imperial court as a means of ensuring the authenticity of the emperor's offspring and, as the eunuchs would never have any family, an extreme solution to the problem of nepotism. As virtually the only men allowed into the palace, they came into close contact with the emperor and often rose to positions of considerable power. Their numbers varied greatly from one dynasty to the next – the Ming court is supposed to have employed twenty thousand, but this is probably an overestimate; the relatively frugal Qing Emperor Kangxi reduced the number to nine thousand.

Most of the eunuchs (or "bob-tailed dogs" as they were nicknamed) came from poor families, and volunteered for their emasculation as a way of acquiring wealth and influence. The operation cost six silver pieces and was performed in a hut just outside the palace walls. Hot pepper-water was used to numb the parts, then after the blade had flashed the wound was sealed with a solder plug. The plug was removed three days later – if urine gushed out, the operation was a success. If it didn't, the man would die soon, in agony. Confucianism held that disfiguration of the body impaired the soul, so in the hope that he would still be buried "whole", the eunuch carried his severed genitalia in a bag hung on his belt. One problem eunuchs were often plagued with was bed-wetting; hence the old Chinese expression, "as stinky as a eunuch".

Eunuchry was finally banned in 1924, and the remaining 1500 eunuchs were expelled from the palace. An observer described them "carrying their belongings in sacks and crying piteously in high pitched voices".

Scarcely less numerous than the eunuchs were the **concubines**, whose role varied from consorts to whores. At night, the emperor chose a girl from his harem by picking out a tablet bearing her name from a pile on a silver tray – though the court astrologer had to OK the decision. She would be delivered to the emperor's bedchamber naked but for a yellow cloth wrapped around her, and carried on the back of one of the eunuchs, since she could barely walk with her bound feet. Eunuchs would be on hand for the event, standing behind a screen and shouting out cautions for the emperor not to get too carried away and risking harming the Imperial body. Favoured wives and concubines were the only women in dynastic China with power and influence; see the box on Cixi (p.106) for a telling example of just how successful a concubine could be.

Beyond is the **Jiaotaidian**, Hall of Union, the empress's throne-room, where the 25 imperial document seals were kept. The ceiling here is possibly the finest in the complex, a gilt confection with a dragon surrounded by phoenixes at the centre; also here is a fine, and very hefty, water clock. The two characters *wu wei* at the back of the hall mean "no action" – a reference to the Taoist political ideal of not disturbing the course of nature or society.

Lastly, the **Kunninggong**, or Palace of Earthly Tranquillity, was where the emperor and empress traditionally spent their wedding night. By law the emperor

Exhibitions in the Forbidden City

The Palace is increasingly being devoted to museum space – fifty thousand square metres today and, in a few years, four hundred thousand. It's becoming arguably the best museum in China, and after appreciating the palace itself it's worth visiting a second time just to take in the exhibits. There's a strip of exhibition halls on the western side of the complex and a few more in the northeast: all exhibitions are free unless specified otherwise. Check out what's on at ⓦ www.dpm.com.cn; new exhibitions are opening all the time. There's a map showing the location of the exhibitions on the back of your entrance ticket.

Insignia of the Qing Court Lots of fans and canopies.

Qing Dynasty Weapons Most of the exhibits here reflect the Qing armies' mounted archers, with plenty of bows and saddles. There are also some early firearms.

Qing Dynasty Musical Instruments As well as displaying lots of instruments, you can listen to extracts of Imperial music.

Qing Treasures Exquisite lacquerware, and carvings of jade, wood, bamboo and ivory.

History of the Qing Council A rather dry show of bureaucratic accoutrements.

Imperial Birthday Celebrations The emperor's birthday was an occasion for spectacle; check out the sumptuous gifts that he received here.

Qing Dynasty Imperial Weddings Dowry gifts and extravagant costumes.

Gifts Presented to the Museum Qing dynasty finery and oddments.

The Life of Qing Concubines Costumes and accessories for the court ladies.

Empress Dowager Cixi Formal costumes and fine objects.

Life of the Last Emperor Puyi Mostly photos and the emperor's personal possesssions.

Pottery and porcelain Seven hundred pieces of pottery and porcelain from the Stone Age to the Qing dynasty.

Bronzeware Five hundred pieces of bronzeware from the Shang dynasty to the Warring States period (sixteenth century BC to 200 BC).

Painting Thousands of magnificent paintings from the Jin to the Qing dynasties, with displays changing monthly.

Jewellery (¥10) In Yangxindian and Leshoutang, north of the painting exhibition. The first hall houses mostly gold, silver and jade tableware and tea and wine utensils. There are also gold chimes, seals, books and a pagoda that was used to store any hair that fell out, on brushing, from the imperial head of Emperor Qianlong's mother. The second hall holds the costumes and utensils the emperor and empress used. Particularly impressive is a huge jade carving illustrating a Taoist immortal taming the waves. It weighs over five tonnes and reputedly took ten years to carve.

Clocks and watches (¥10). In Fengxiandian, the eastern palace quarters. This hall, always a favourite, displays the result of one Qing emperor's passion for liberally ornamented Baroque timepieces, most of which are English and French, though the rhino-sized water clock by the entrance is Chinese. There's even one with a mechanical scribe who can write eight characters. Some clocks are wound to demonstrate their workings at 11am and 2pm.

had to spend the first three nights of his marriage, and the first day of the Chinese New Year, with his new wife. On the left as you enter is a large sacrificial room, its vats ready to receive offerings (1300 pigs a year during the Ming dynasty). The wedding chamber is a small room off to one side, painted entirely in red and covered with decorative emblems symbolizing fertility and joy. It was last pressed into operation in 1922 for the wedding of 12-year-old Puyi, the last emperor, who, finding it "like a melted red wax candle", decided that he preferred the Mind Nurture Palace and went back there.

One of a group of palaces to the west, the Mind Nurture Palace, or **Yangxindian**, was where emperors spent most of their time. Several of these palaces retain their furniture from the Manchu times, most of it eighteenth-century; in one, the **Changchungong** (Palace of Eternal Spring), is a series of paintings illustrating the Ming novel, *The Story of the Stone*.

The northern museums

To the east of the **Kunninggong** is a group of palaces, once residences of the emperor's wives and now adapted as **museum galleries** (see box, opposite). The atmosphere here is much more intimate than in the state buildings, and you can peer into well-appointed chambers full of elegant furniture and ornaments, including English clocks decorated with images of English gentlefolk, looking very out of place among the jade trees and ornate fly whisks.

The Imperial Garden

From the Inner Court, the Kunningmen (Gate of Terrestrial Tranquility) opens north onto the **Imperial Garden**, by this stage something of a respite from the elegant buildings. There are a couple of **cafés** here (and toilets) amid a pleasing network of ponds, walkways and pavilions, designed to be reminiscent of southern Chinese landscapes. In the middle of the garden, the **Qin'andian**, or Hall of Imperial Tranquillity, was where the emperor came to worship a Taoist water deity, Xuan Wu, who was responsible for keeping the palace safe from fire. You can exit here into Jingshan Park, which provides an overview of the complex – see p.91.

2

South of the centre

Most visitors head south to sample the glorious Temple of Heaven, but there's plenty to distract you on your way: just south of Tian'anmen Square, the **Qianmen district** offers a tempting antidote to the square's formality and grandeur – and a dramatic change of scale. The lanes and *hutongs* here comprise a **traditional shopping quarter**, full of small, specialist stores which, to a large extent, remain grouped according to their particular trades – though how much of its earthy flavour will survive the present enormous reconstruction is debatable. Still, it's a part of the city that lends itself to browsing and wandering, as well as being a good place to eat, with one of the best selections of snacks available in the capital.

Down Qianmen Dajie, once the Imperial Way, now a clogged road, lies ravishing **Tiantan**, the **Temple of Heaven**. An example of imperial architecture at its best, it's perfectly set in one of Beijing's prettiest parks. Another site of Imperial ritual nearby, the Temple of Agriculture, has become an engrossing **Museum of Ancient Architecture**. Also in the area is the rather less glamorous **Museum of Natural History**, which contains a gruesome surprise. West of here, **Niu Jie** – at the heart of the city's Muslim quarter – and the **Museum of Ancient Architecture** are both worth a diversion. A very different sort of large-scale project is on show back near Qianmen in the **Underground City**, a shabby relic of communist paranoia.

Qianmen and around

The northern entrance to this quarter is marked by the imposing, fifteenth-century, double-arched **Qianmen**, the gate just south of Tian'anmen Square. Before

Dazhalan Jie	大珊栏街	*dàzhàlán jiē*
Fayuan Si	法源寺	*fǎyuán sì*
Liulichang Jie	琉璃厂街	*gǔdàijiànzhù bówùguǎn*
Museum of Ancient Architecture	古代建筑博物馆	*gǔdài jiànzhù bówùguǎn*
Natural History Museum	自然博物馆	*zìrán bówùguǎn*
Niu Jie	牛街	*niú jiē*
Qianmen	前门	*qiánmén*
Temple of Heaven	天坛	*tiāntán*
Tiantan Park	天坛公园	*tiāntán gōngyuán*
Underground City	地下城	*dìxià chéng*

Temple life

In a chaotic urban landscape, Beijing's Taoist and Buddhist temples are some of the city's most valuable repositories of heritage: as well as being often the only recognizably Chinese buildings around, they are rich with artefacts and long-preserved traditions. Outside, you'll see a glorious array of tat for sale – from flashing Buddhas to credit card-sized images of Gods, to be kept in your wallet for luck. Inside, smoke billows from burners – as well as incense, you'll see worshippers burning fake money, ingots or even paper cars to enrich ancestors in heaven. The atmosphere is lively but nonetheless devout; devotees kowtow before fantastic images and robed monks genuflect.

Detail on Yonghe Gong

Buddhist pillars

Design

In Beijing, as in China as a whole, temples are not as old as they look; most were trashed during the Cultural Revolution and have been rebuilt from scratch. But the layout and design elements are genuinely ancient, and based on principles set down thousands of years ago.

Like private houses, all Chinese temples face **south** (as barbarians and evil spirits come from the north), and are surrounded by walls. Gates are sealed by heavy doors and guarded by statues – Buddhists use the four Heavenly Kings, Taoists a dragon and a lion. Further protection is afforded by a spirit wall in the first courtyard – easy enough for the living to walk around but a block to evil, which can supposedly only travel in straight lines.

The halls are supported by lacquered **pillars** – Buddhists colour them bright red, Taoists use black. Some of the most elegant details of the temple are in the **roof**, where interlocking beams create a characteristic curved roofline and cantilevered brackets allow the jauntily curving eaves to extend well beyond the main pillars.

A Monk's life

Buddhist monks wear orange robes and keep their heads shaved, while Taoist monks wear blue and keep their long hair tied up. Both sets of monks are celibate and vegetarian, and avoid garlic or onion as it is said to enflame the passions. A monk's life is taken up with study, prayer and observance and celebration of significant dates.

Coin-throwing

Temple fairs

Every Beijing temple holds a **fair** at Chinese New Year, integrating worship, entertainment and commerce. At these boisterous carnivals, the air is thick with incense, and locals queue to kneel to altars and play games that bring good fortune – such as trying to hit the temple bell by lobbing coins at it. Priests are on hand to perform rituals and write prayers. Beijing's biggest fairs are at the Tibetan Yonghe Gong (see p.97) and the Taoist Baiyun Guan (see p.74): pick one or the other to visit, as it's regarded as inauspicious to get to both during the same festival. To help you decide, Taoist festivals concentrate on **renewal**, Tibetan Lamaist ones on **enlightenment**.

The lion dance

Symbols

Lion carving at Yonghe Gong

The main hall of a Buddhist temple is dominated by **three large statues** – the Buddhas of the past, the present and the future – while the walls are lined by rather outlandish looking *arhats*, or saints. Around the back of the Buddhist trinity is a statue of **Guanyin**, the multi-armed Goddess of Mercy.

The Taoist **holy trinity** is made up of the three immortals, who each ride different animals (a crane, tiger and deer) and represent the three levels of the Taoist afterlife. You're also likely to see Guanyin represented in Taoist temples – her help in childbirth makes her universally accepted.

Animal carvings are more popular with the animist Taoists: look out for bats and cranes – symbols, respectively, of good luck and longevity. Other figures in Taoist temples include the red-faced God of War, Guan Yu, and the general Zhuge Liang – characters in the ancient story, the *Three Kingdoms* (see "Contexts", p.173), and based on real life figures.

the city's walls were demolished, this controlled the entrance to the inner city from the outer, suburban sector. In imperial days, shops and places of entertainment were banned from the interior city and became concentrated around Qianmen. The quarter's biggest street, **Qianmen Dajie**, runs immediately south from the gate. The area south and off to either side was until recently the city's liveliest *hutong* district, but has been comprehensively bulldozed though a few of the more famous streets are being preserved.

Dazhalan Jie

One of the few Qianmen lanes to escape the wrecking ball, the cramped street of **Dazhalan Jie** leads west off Qianmen Dajie; the entrance is marked by a white arch, opposite the *Qianmen Quanjude Roast Duck* restaurant, on the east side of the road. Where theatres were once concentrated, it's now a hectic, pedestrianized shopping district, its genteel old buildings mostly occupied by tea merchants and clothing stores. It's a good place to pick up tea, silk clothes and souvenirs.

You'll find the Ruifuxiang, a venerable **fabric shop**, just beyond the entrance on the right – look for the storks on its facade, above the arched entrance. This is the place to get silk and satin fabrics, and *qipaos* (see p.163); whether or not you're buying, take a look at the exhibition, on the top floor, of old photos of the street. On the other side of the road at no. 24, the Tongrengtang is a famous **traditional Chinese pharmacy**, whose reputation has spread as far as Korea and Japan. The place even has its own foreign-exchange counter and a booth where a resident pharmacist offers on-the-spot diagnoses. Head upstairs for the weird stuff – aphrodisiacs, deer antlers and ginseng "children" (the more the root looks like a person, the more efficacious it's said to be). Finally, check in at no. 34 for handmade shoes and slippers (see p.163)

At the end of the pedestrianized area, the street narrows and you enter a district of **hutongs**. A stroll here offers a glimpse of the bustle and decay that remains typical of Chinese metropolitan life but is vanishing from Beijing; you'll come across cobblers and knife sharpeners and dubious masseurs, stone lions flanking sagging courtyard doors, and furtive fruit vendors with an eye out for the police. The prevalence of public toilets hints at one reason why the locals don't care much that the *hutongs* are being ripped up – the buildings have terrible plumbing. If you keep going straight, you'll pass backpacker mecca the *Yuandong Hotel* and eventually rejoin the traffic at Nanxinhua Jie. Head off either side and you're likely to get lost – not an unpleasant experience if you're not in a hurry; Liulichang (see below) is a good destination to ask for.

Liulichang Jie

Turn north at the western end of Dazhalan, then head west along a *hutong*, then north and west again, to reach **Liulichang Jie** – split into "dong" (east) and "xi" (west) on the map – parallel to Dazhalan Jie. If you're approaching from Hepingmen subway stop, you can get here by heading south down Nanxinhua Jie, which cuts Liulichang Jie at right angles – look for the marble bridge over the road. Liulichang – whose name literally means "glaze factory street", after the erstwhile factories here making glazed tiles for the roofs of the Forbidden City – has been rebuilt as a heritage street, using Ming-style architecture; today it's full of curio stores (remember to bargain hard, and that every antique is fake). Though there is nothing to distinguish it outwardly from the shops, no. 14 is a small and rather charming museum of folk carving (daily 9am–6pm;

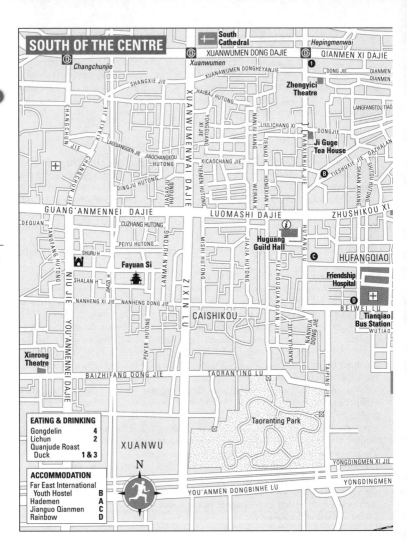

South Cathedral

XUANWUMEN DONG DAJIE

Hepingmenwai

QIANMEN XI DAJIE

Changchunjie

Xuanwumen

DONG JIE

QIANMEN
QIANMEN

XUANWUMEN DONGHEYANJIE

SHANGXIE JIE

HAIBAI HUTONG

LANGFANGTOU TIAO

Zhengyici Theatre

X
U
A
N
W
U
M
E
N
W
A
I

D
A
J
I
E

YONGGUANG XI JIE

NANLU XIANG

LIULICHANG XI

KIAXIE JIE

CHANGCHUN JIE

DONGJIE

Ji Guge Tea House

LAOQIANGGEN JIE

JIAOCHANGKOU HUTONG

TIENAO H.

TIEMEN HUTONG

XINHUA JIE

TIESHUXIE JIE

SHAN XIXIANG

SHITOU HUTONG

DAZHALAN

XICAOCHANG JIE

WEIRAN H.

HONGXIAN H.

DINGJU HUTONG

JIADONG HUTONG

JIADONG HUTONG

GUANG'ANMENNEI DAJIE

LUOMASHI DAJIE

ZHUSHIKOU XI

DEQUAN

CUZHANG HUTONG

HUANG LU

TANGGANG HUTONG

PEIYU HUTONG

MISHI HUTONG

JIAJIA HUTONG

Huguang Guild Hall

i

HUFANGQIAO

SHURU H.

Fayuan Si

LANMAN HUTONG

ZIXIN LU

FUZHOUGUANGAN LU

Friendship Hospital

NIU JIE

SHALAN H.

NANHENG XI JIE

NANHENG DONG JIE

BEIWEI LU

YOU'ANMENNEI DAJIE

CAISHIKOU

NANHUA XIJIE

NANHUA DONG JIE

Tianqiao Bus Station

WUTIAO

PENYA HUTONG

TAIPING JIE

Xinrong Theatre

BAIZHIFANG DONG JIE

TAORANTING LU

EATING & DRINKING

Gongdelin	4
Lichun	2
Quanjude Roast Duck	1 & 3

XUANWU

N

Taoranting Park

ACCOMMODATION

Far East International Youth Hostel	B
Hademen	A
Jianguo Qianmen	C
Rainbow	D

YONGDINGMEN XI JIE

YOU'ANMEN DONGBINHE LU

YONGDINGMEN

free), full of screen doors, woodblocks and the like, with some very skilfully crafted pieces. The **Ji Guge teahouse** at no. 136 offers a welcome respite for shoppers.

Underground City

In response to the perceived nuclear threat from the Soviet Union, Chairman Mao charged "volunteers" to construct a warren of bunkers under the city in the 1960s. The tunnel network had entrances all over the city, a control centre in the western hills, and supply arteries big enough for trucks to drive down. Fortunately it was never put to use; it was too close to the surface to offer protection against any but the smallest conventional bombs.

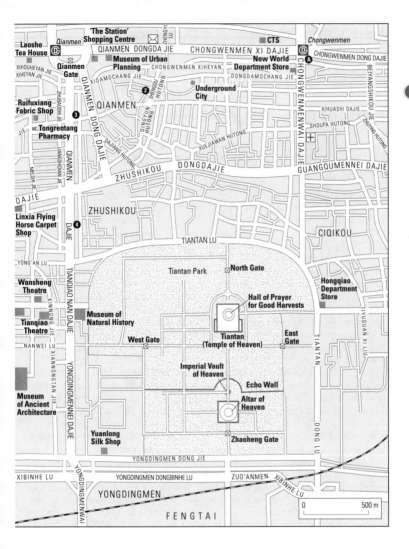

Today the tunnels are falling into disrepair and most of the entrances are sealed, but it's worth visiting to get a sense of the old days of communist paranoia. You can get in using an **entrance** sunk deep in the *hutongs* southeast of Qianmen (daily 8.30am–5pm; ¥20): maps of the *hutongs* aren't reliable, but one foolproof approach is to head east from Qianmen along the north side of Qianmen Dong Dajie. When you reach Zhengyi Lu, which leads north off the road, cross to the south side of Qianmen Dong Dajie and head down the narrow *hutong* here, then take the first left past a sign in English for the *Liyun Duck* restaurant. Head left at the end of this *hutong*, and the entrance is 300m down here on the right. From the entrance, stairs lead down to a claustrophobic, dimly lit, arched tunnel that echoes with your footsteps. The walls are covered with camouflage netting and posters of soldiers, there's an arbitrary showroom selling quilts for no good reason, and rusty metal doors, labelled with landmarks, lead off to the rest of the network. If it's your sort of thing, make sure you check in on the Red Capital Residence (see p.135), whose bar is located in an old bomb shelter.

Tiantan and around

Set in its own large, tranquil park about 2km south of Tian'anmen, **Tiantan**, the Temple of Heaven, is widely regarded as the pinnacle of Ming design. For five centuries it was at the very heart of imperial ceremony and symbolism, and for many modern visitors its architectural unity and beauty remain more appealing – and on a much more accessible scale – than the Forbidden City.

Construction of the sumptuous temple was begun during the reign of Emperor Yongle and completed in 1420. It was conceived as the prime meeting point of earth and heaven, and symbols of the two are integral to its design. Heaven was considered round, earth square; thus the round temples and altars stand on square bases, while the park has the shape of a semicircle beside a square.

The intermediary between earth and heaven was of course the **Son of Heaven**, the emperor, and the temple was the site of the most important ceremony of the imperial court calendar, when the emperor prayed for the year's harvests at the **winter solstice**. Purified by three days of fasting, he made his way to the park on the day before the solstice, accompanied by his court in all its magnificence. On arrival at Tiantan, the emperor would meditate in the Imperial Vault, ritually conversing with the gods on the details of government, before spending the night in the Hall of Prayer for Good Harvests. The following day he sacrificed animals before the Altar of Heaven. It was forbidden for commoners to catch a glimpse of the great annual procession to the temple, and they were obliged to bolt their windows and remain, in silence, indoors. Indeed, the Tiantan complex remained sacrosanct until it was thrown open to the people on the first Chinese National Day of the Republic, in October 1912. The last person to perform the rites was General Yuan Shikai, the first president of the republic, on December 23, 1914. He planned to declare himself emperor but died a broken man, his plans thwarted by opponents, in 1916.

Tiantan Park (daily 8.30am–7pm; ¥10 low season, ¥15 high season) is possibly the best in the city, and worth a visit in its own right; it's easy to find peaceful seclusion away from the temple buildings. Old men gather here with their pet birds and crickets, while from dawn onwards, *tai ji* practitioners can be seen lost in concentration among the groves of 500-year-old *thuja* trees. A variety of **buses** pass by: #106 from Dongzhimen (for the north gate); bus #17 or #54 from Qianmen (west gate); bus #41 from Qianmen (east gate); and bus #120 from Beijing Zhan or #803 from Qianmen (south gate).

The temple buildings

Although you're more likely to enter the park from the north or the west, to appreciate the temple buildings (daily 9am–5pm; combined ticket ¥30 low season, ¥35 high season, or individual building tickets ¥20), it's best initially to skirt round onto the ceremonial route up from the **Zhaoheng Gate**, the park's south entrance. This main pathway leads straight to the circular **Altar of Heaven**, consisting of three marble tiers representing (from the top down) heaven, earth and man. The tiers are comprised of blocks in various multiples of nine, cosmologically the most powerful number, symbolising both heaven and emperor. The centre of the altar's bare, roofless top tier, where the Throne of Heaven was placed during ceremonies, was considered to be the middle of the Middle Kingdom – the very centre of the earth. Various acoustic properties are claimed for the altar; from this point, it is said, all sounds are channelled straight upwards to heaven. To the east of the nearby fountain, which was reconstructed after fire damage in 1740, are the ruins of a group of buildings used for the preparation of sacrifices.

Directly ahead, the **Imperial Vault of Heaven** is an octagonal tower made entirely of wood, with a dramatic roof of dark blue glazed tiles, supported by eight pillars. This is where the emperor would change his robes and meditate. The shrine and stone platforms inside held stone tablets representing the emperor and his ancestors, and the two chambers either side held tablets representing the elements. The tower is encircled by the **Echo Wall**, said to be a perfect whispering gallery, although the unceasing cacophony of tourists trying it out makes it impossible to tell.

The principal temple building – the **Hall of Prayer for Good Harvests**, at the north end of the park – amply justifies all this build-up. Made entirely of wood, without the aid of a single nail, the circular structure rises from another tiered marble terrace and has three blue-tiled roofs. Four compass-point pillars, representing the seasons, support the vault, enclosed in turn by twelve outer pillars (one for each month of the year and the hour of the day). The dazzling colours of the interior, surrounding the central dragon motif on the coffered ceiling, give the hall an ultramodern look; it was in fact rebuilt, faithful to the Ming design, after the original was destroyed by lightning in 1889. The official explanation for this appalling omen was that it was divine punishment meted out on a sacrilegious caterpillar, which was on the point of crawling to the golden ball on the hall's apex when the lightning struck. Thirty-two court dignitaries were executed for allowing this to happen.

The museums

Two museums are worth combining with a visit to Tiantan. Just north of Tiantan Park's western gate, the **Museum of Natural History** (daily 8.30am–4.30pm; ¥15)

Tai ji

In every park, in the early morning, you'll see folk going through the mesmerising, slow moves of **tai ji quan**. It may not look it, but *tai ji* is actually a martial art, developed by Taoist monks. It's all about augmenting the body's natural energy (*qi*), which supposedly circulates around the body along particular channels – the same idea lies behind acupuncture and traditional Chinese medicine. *Qigong* – breath skills – are used to build up an awareness of *qi* and the ability to move it around, eventually replacing excess muscular movements and rendering all actions fluid and powerful.

Forms – pre-arranged movement sets – are used to develop speed and power. Acute sensitivity is cultivated, allowing the martial artist to anticipate attacks and strike first; counter-attacks are made with the body in a state of minimal tension, creating *tai ji's* characteristic **soft appearance**. Students are taught not to directly resist but to redirect the attackers' energy, applying a principle from the Taoist Tao de Qing, "the soft and the pliable will defeat the hard and the strong".

The original Chen form is closely related to kung fu, but the form that you'll most often see is a slowed down and simplified version, stripped of explicit martial content and used to promote health. *Tai ji* was codified in 1949 to make it easier to teach, and so bring it to the masses: to see the best *tai ji*, visit Tiantan Park (see oppposite), and Beijing's gymnasiums (see p.67).

▲ Exhibit at the Museum of Ancient Architecture

includes a terrific room full of dinosaur skeletons. One display that you won't find in a similar Western museum is held in a separate building on the right before the main entrance. Pickled legs, arms, brains and foetuses are arranged around the stars of the show, two whole adult corpses: a woman wearing socks, gloves and a hood; and a man with all his skin removed, leaving just the fingernails and lips. Few foreigners emerge from here unshaken, shown up by the Chinese kids who take it all in their stride.

A short walk to the southwest is the former **Xiannong Temple**, reconverted from a school into a rather fine little **Museum of Ancient Architecture** (daily 9am–5pm; ¥15). Look for the red arch south off Beiwei Lu; the ticket office is just beyond here and the museum itself is further down the road on the right. The temple, twin of the nearby Temple of Heaven, was dedicated to the god of earth, and every year the emperor ritually ploughed a furrow to ensure a good harvest. The buildings and the flat altar are refined, though not spectacular. The **Hall of Worship** holds oddments such as the gold-plated plough used by the emperor, as well as a display explaining the building's history. More diverting is the main **Hall of Jupiter**, with its beautifully ornate ceiling and an enlightening collection of architectural exhibits, showing how China's traditional buildings were put together. There are wooden models, many with cutaways, of famous and distinctive buildings, including Yingxian's pagoda (west of Beijing in Shanxi province), and a stilt house of Yunnan province's Dong people. Also on hand are samples of **dougongs**, interlocking, stacked brackets, as complex as puzzle boxes. The giant floor model (1:1000 scale) of how Beijing looked in 1949 – before the communists demolished most of it – is informative, revealing how all the surviving imperial remnants are fragments of an awesome grand design, with a precise north–south imperial axis and sites of symbolic significance at each of the cardinal points. For those who prefer spectacle, there's a great sinuous wooden dragon on show, once part of a temple ceiling.

Niu Jie and the Fayuan Si

Some 3km southwest of Qianmen, **Niu Jie** (Ox Street) is a conjested thoroughfare in the city's **Muslim quarter**, in a rather shabby section of the city. It's a one-kilometre walk south along Changchun Jie from Changchun Jie subway stop, or you could get here on bus #6 from the north gate of Tiantan Park. Head under the arch at the north end of Niu Jie and you enter a chaotic street lined with offal stalls, steamy little restaurants and hawkers selling fried dough rings, rice cakes and *shaobing*, Chinese-style muffins with a meat filling. The white caps and the beards sported by the men distinguish these people of the Muslim **Hui minority** – of which there are nearly two hundred thousand in the capital – from the Han Chinese.

The street's focus is the bright green **mosque** at its southern end (daily 8am–5pm; ¥10), an attractive and colourful marriage of Chinese and Islamic design, with abstract and flowery decorations and text in Chinese and Arabic over the doorways. You won't get to see the handwritten copy of the Koran, dating back to the Yuan dynasty, without special permission, or be allowed into the main prayer hall if you're not a Muslim, but you can inspect the courtyard, where a copper cauldron, used to cook food for the devotees, sits near the graves of two Persian imams who came here to preach in the thirteenth century. Also in the courtyard is the "tower for viewing the moon", which allows imams to ascertain the beginning and end of Ramadan, the Muslim period of fasting and prayer.

Head south from the mosque, take the second *hutong* on the left, and after a few hundred metres you'll come to the **Fayuan Si**. This is one of Beijing's oldest temples, though the present structures are in fact Qing and thus relatively recent. It's appealingly ramshackle, with the well-worn prayer mats and shabby fittings of a working temple. Monks sit outside on broken armchairs counting prayer beads or bend over books in halls that stink of butter – burnt in lamps – and incense. There are two great Ming bronze lions in the first courtyard, resembling armoured were-puppies, and more fine bronzes of the four Heavenly Guardians and a chubby Maitreya in the hall beyond. The halls behind are home to a miscellany of Buddhist sculpture, the finest of which is a five-metre-long wooden reclining Buddha in the back hall.

West of the centre

Heading west from Tian'anmen Square along **Chang'an Jie**, the giant freeway that runs dead straight east–west across the city, you pass a string of grandiose buildings, the headquarters of official and corporate power. Architectural styles are jumbled together here, with international style, Postmodern whimsy and brute Stalinism side by side. Though most of the sites and amenities are elsewhere, and the area has not modernized as fast as the rest of the city, western Beijing has enough of interest tucked away to entertain the curious for a few days. Along Chang'an Jie itself, there's a hectic shopping district, **Xidan**, where you can rub shoulders with locals, and visit two impressive museums: **Capital Museum** and the **Military Museum**. Just off Chang'an Jie is the pleasant **Baiyun Guan**, a Taoist temple that seems worlds away from its surroundings.

Zhongnanhai to Xidan

As you head west from Tian'anmen Square along Xichang'an Jie, the first major building you pass is, on the left, the new **National Grand Opera House**. Designed by French architect Paul Andreu and nicknamed, for obvious reasons, the "Egg" the glass and titanium dome houses a concert hall, two theatres and a 2500-seat opera house. Visitors enter through a tunnel under the lake outside. Critics already call it a white elephant but it makes an undeniably striking contrast to the surrounding, somewhat po-faced, monumentalism.

Communist Party Headquarters is on the north side of the road. Named **Zhongnanhai**, the walled complex isn't hard to spot, as armed sentries stand outside the gates, ensuring that only invited guests get inside. Once home to the Empress Dowager Cixi (see p.106), since 1949 it's been the base of the Communist Party's Central Committee and the Central People's Government; Mao Zedong and Zhou Enlai both worked here. In 1989, pro-democracy protesters camped

Baiyun Guan	白云观	báiyún guān
Capital Museum	首都博物馆	shǒudū bówùguǎn
Cultural Palace of National Minorities	民族文化宫	mínzú wénhuà gōng
Military Museum	军事博物馆	jūnshì bówùguǎn
TV Tower	电视塔	diànshì tǎ
Xidan	西单	xīdān
Yuyuantan Park	玉渊潭公园	yùyuāntán gōngyuán
Zhongnanhai	中南海	zhōngnánhǎi

outside hoping to petition their leaders, just as commoners with grievances waited outside the Forbidden City in imperial times. In 1999, a similar, large protest was held by **Falun Gong**, a quasi-religious sect followed mostly by the aged in search of health and longevity. Ten thousand devotees sat down cross-legged on the pavement for the afternoon. Religious groups and secret societies have always flourished in China – the Boxers (see p.106) are a particularly prominent example – and governments have tended to treat them warily, as potential sources of organized dissent. Falun Gong have been ruthlessly suppressed ever since.

After the next junction, the boxy **Beijing Telecom Office** rears above you – like the buildings around Tian'anmen Square, it's another of the "ten years of **liberation**" construction projects (see p.54). Just to the west, the **Aviation Office**, the place to buy tickets for internal flights (see p.26) and catch the airport bus, stands on the site of Democracy Wall, which received its name in 1978, when, as part of the so-called "Beijing Spring", posters questioning Mao and his political legacy, and calling for political freedoms, were pasted up here. The movement was suppressed the following year.

The next major junction is **Xidan**, site of some of the capital's most ambitious modern buildings, the most ambitious of which is I.M. Pei's Bank of China at the northwest corner. Inside, the giant atrium leads the eye up to his signature glass pyramids in the ceiling. The shopping district of **Xidan Bei Dajie**, the street running north of here, is worth exploring, at least along its initial few blocks (though not at a weekend when it's heaving with people). This is where trendy Beijingers shop, and the area encloses a dense concentration of **department stores and stalls**, selling everything the burgeoning middle class requires. The sixth and seventh floors of the Xidan Shopping Centre (the ugly brown glass building) are the places to go to check out pop fashions; the taste – at least at the time of writing – was for a Japanese-influenced sartorial excess. When you've had enough of feeling trapped in a pop video, head upstairs to the giant **food court** and **games arcade**. A more upmarket (but just as claustrophobic) shopping experience is on offer at the Xidan CVIK Store, a couple of hundred metres further north of here on the west side of the street. It mostly sells clothes and household goods.

▲ Bank of China building, Xidan

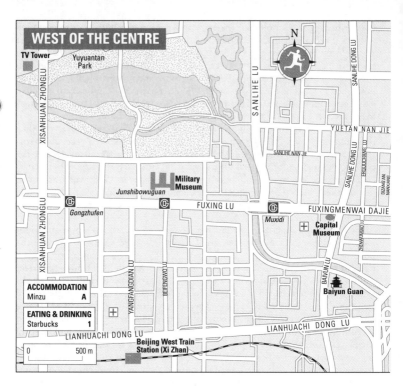

Xichang'an Jie continues west into Fuxingmennei Dajie. On the north side of the street, 400m west of Xidan intersection, the **Cultural Palace of National Minorities** is used for trade fairs, which is a shame, as it is quite striking architecturally, with some grand Socialist-Realist wall reliefs of minority peoples and Tibetan and Islamic elements incorporated into the decoration. Plans are afoot to convert it back to its original function, as a centre for minority culture. Across the road nearby, the pleasant **Sanwei Bookstore** has its own tea house where evening performances of jazz and Chinese folk music are staged (see p.151).

The Parkson Building, at the next large intersection, is an upmarket **mall**. Skip the overpriced clothes and head for the sixth floor, which holds an **arts and crafts exhibition** – most showpieces are in jade but there are ceramics and ivory too – by contemporary masters. Look out for the four renowned jade works, each over a metre high: a dragon relief, a mountain, a vase with chains on the handles and a two-eared cup. Begun in 1985, each piece took forty or so craftsmen four years to make.

Baiyun Guan

A kilometre south of Fuxingmenwai Dajie, **Baiyun Guan** (White Cloud Temple; daily 8am–5.30pm; ¥10) is well worth hunting out; it's signposted in English from Baiyun Lu whose northern end is not far from Muxidi subway stop, and can also

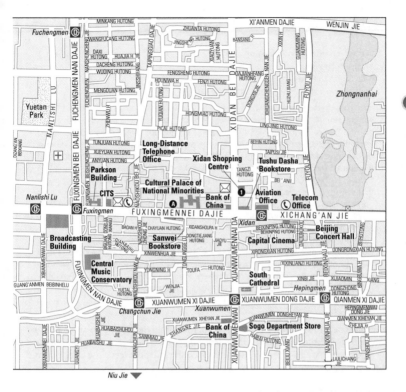

Niu Jie ▼

be reached on bus #212 from Qianmen or #40 from Nansanhuan Zhong Lu. Once the most influential Taoist centre in the country, the temple was renovated after a long spell as a barracks during communist times, and now houses China's national Taoist association, as well as being home to thirty monks. A popular place for pilgrims, with a busy, thriving feel, it's at its most colourful during the Chinese New Year temple fair (see colour insert).

Though laid out in a similar way to a Buddhist temple, Baiyun Guan has a few distinctive features, such as the three gateways at the entrance, symbolizing the three states of Taoism – desire, substance and emptiness. Each hall is dedicated to a different deity, whose respective domains of influence are explained in English outside; it's from the hall to the gods of wealth that the thickest plumes of incense emerge. The eastern and western halls hold a great collection of Taoist relics, including some horrific paintings of hell showing people being sawn in half. An attached bookshop has plenty of tapes of devotional music and lucky charms, though only one text in English, the *I-Ching* (see p.76). In the western courtyard, a shrine houses twelve deities, each linked with a different animal in the Chinese version of the zodiac; here, visitors light incense and kowtow to the deity that corresponds to their birth year. Also in the courtyard is a shrine to **Wen Cheng**, the deity of scholars, with a three-metre bronze statue of him outside. Rubbing his belly is supposed to bring success in academic examinations.

Worship in China can be a lively affair, and there are a number of on-site amusements. Three **monkeys** depicted in relief sculptures around the temple are believed to bring you good luck if you can find, and stroke, them all. One is on

Humans model themselves on earth
earth on heaven
heaven on the way
and the way on that which is naturally so

Lao Zi, *Daodejing*

Taoism is a religion deriving from the *Daodejing* or "Way of Power", an obscure, mystical text (see p.179) comprising the teachings of the semi-mythical Lao Zi, who lived around 500 BC. The Tao (spelt *dao* in *pinyin*), which literally means "Way", is defined as being indefinable; accordingly the book begins: "The Tao that can be told/is not the eternal Tao/The name that can be named/is not the eternal name."

But it is the force that creates and moves the natural world, and Taoists believe that the art of living lies in understanding it and conforming to it. Taoism emphasizes contemplation, meditation, a non-committance to dogma, and going with the flow. Its central principle is that of *wu wei*, literally non-action, perhaps better understood as "no action which goes against nature".

In part Taoism developed in reaction to the rigour and formality of state-sponsored Confucianism (see p.98). Taoism's holy men tend to be artisans and workmen rather than upright advisers, and in focusing on the relationship of the individual with the natural universe, Taoism represents a retreat from the political and social. The communists, accordingly, regard Taoism as fatalistic and passive.

the gate, easy to spot as it's been rubbed black, while the other two are in the first courtyard. Another playful diversion is trying to ding the bell under the courtyard bridge by throwing a coin at it. In the back courtyard, devotees close their eyes and try to walk from a wall to an incense burner.

Capital Museum

Back on Fuxingmenwai Dajie, on the south side of the street and not far from Muxidi subway stop, the new **Capital Museum** (Tues–Sun 9am–5pm; ¥30; Ⓦwww.capitalmuseum.org.cn/en) is easy to miss, despite its size – from the outside it rather resembles the bank headquarters that precede it. Inside, the architecture is much more interesting; a bronze cylinder shoots down through the roof as if from heaven.

Though a lot of money has obviously been spent, the museum doesn't quite reach its full potential: considering the size of the building the exhibition spaces are measly, there's a lot of walking to get from one to another and the exhibits have few English captions. The layout is simple: Beijing exhibition halls are in the **cube**, cultural relics in the **cylinder**. If you're short on time or energy skip the cube and head for the rarer pieces instead.

The cylinder's ground floor gallery holds Ming and Qing paintings, mostly landscapes. They're well presented but the collection is not as comprehensive as the display in the Forbidden City (see p.62). The calligraphy upstairs can be safely missed unless you have a special interest, but the bronzes on level three are pretty interesting: a sinister third-century BC owl-headed dagger, for example, or the strangely modern-looking three-legged cooking vessels decorated with geometrical patterns – which are more than three thousand years old. The display of jade on the fourth floor is definitely worth lingering over; the particular qualities that combine to create the best jade is an esoteric subject (it's all about colour, lustre and clarity) but anyone can appreciate the workmanship that has gone into the buckles, boxes and knick knacks here; the white quail-shaped vessels are particularly lovely.

The cube of exhibition halls on the building's west side can be travelled round rather faster. The bottom level hosts a confusing and disappointing show on the history of Beijing: exhibits are jumbled together – a modern lathe is displayed next to a stele, for example – without enough English captions to make any sense of the showcase at all. The next level up contains models of historical buildings, which can be skipped in favour of the show-stealing Buddhist figurines on the top floor. As well as depictions of serene long-eared gentlemen, there are some very esoteric lamaist figures from Tibet; the Goddess Marici, for example, comes with her own pig-drawn chariot and other fierce deities have lion heads or many arms.

Yuyuantan Park and around

Yuyuantan Park offers respite from the traffic: it's low on trees and grass, but there's a large, pleasant lake; you can take out a pedal boat for ¥10/hr. In the southwest corner stands the dome-shaped China Millennium Monument, a sterile public work and "Centre for Patriotic Education". The Communist Party's version of Chinese history is inscribed on bronze plates that form a walkway leading up to a flat altar.

Now that all the communists have been to marketing school, it's almost refreshing to be confronted with the old-fashioned Soviet-style brutalism of this stern building in front of the park – the **Military Museum** (daily 8am–4.30pm; ¥15; Military Museum subway stop) – subtle as a jackboot. The entrance hall is full of big and bad art, photo-collages of Mao inspecting his army and soldiers performing an amphibious landing (a hint at Taiwan's fate perhaps) and the like. The last Chinese public image of Marx hung here until 1999. The hall beyond has a wealth of Russian and Chinese weaponry on show, including tanks and rockets, with – in case martial feelings have been stirred – an air-rifle shooting gallery at the back. In the rear courtyard a group of miscellaneous old aircraft includes the shells of two American spy planes (with Nationalist Chinese markings) shot down in the 1950s. Upstairs, you'll find plaster casts of statues of military and political leaders.

Head back to the lobby, turn west and climb the unsignposted, dim staircase to the much more engaging **upper halls**. The exhibition on the third floor commemorates the Korean War, whose chief interest for foreign visitors lies in the fact that it's one of those places that isn't meant for them – captions are only in Chinese and there is much crowing over what is presented as the defeat of American power. There are also more paintings of lantern-jawed soldiers charging machine-gun posts and the like. The fourth floor holds a large exhibition on historical warfare, this time with English captions. Arranged in chronological order, it presents Chinese history as a series of bloody conflicts between rival warlords – which is, actually, not far from the truth. The suits of armour worn by Qing soldiers and Japanese pirates are intimidating even when empty. Also on display are mock-ups of ingenious Chinese siege weapons, Ming dynasty gunpowder-driven devices for firing eighty arrows at a time, and the world's earliest handgun, from the fifteenth century. Opposite this hall lies another treat for the connoisseur of kitsch – the "Friendship Hall", containing gifts given to representatives of the Chinese military abroad. Competition for the most tasteless item is fierce, but the gold sub-machine gun from Lebanon and the silver model tractor from Romania certainly deserve a mention.

The TV tower

Northwest of the Military Museum, a three-kilometre walk away through Yuyu-antan Park, lies Beijing's **TV tower** (daily 8am–5pm; ¥50). A giant, needle-like structure on the third ring road, the tower stands on the foundation of the Altar of the Moon, a Ming-dynasty sacrificial site. You ride up to the top in a lift and are given a Coke and some cake once you get there. Though these don't justify the steep price of admission, the outdoor viewing platform 400m above ground does offer stunning views of the city on a clear day. Telescopes are dotted around for closer examination – unfortunately the view into Zhongnanhai is blocked by some judiciously placed buildings.

East of the centre

EAST OF THE CENTRE | The foreign legations and the Police Museum

If you head east from Tian'anmen, the first thing you encounter, setting the tone for the rest of this cosmopolitan sector of the city, is the incongruously European architecture of the **legations quarter**, once home to foreign diplomats. Just to the north, the eastern section of **Chang'an Jie** is glamorous and commercial, with lashings of shopping – the best in China outside Shanghai and Hong Kong – plus flashy hotels and plenty of restaurants and amenities. It's Beijing's most fashionable area; for anyone who's been in China for a while it's the place to come to stock up on luxuries, and for newcomers it offers the chance to experience the new realities of life for privileged locals. The most obvious landmark here is the **Beijing Hotel**, on the corner where **Wangfujing Dajie**, Beijing's most famous shopping street, leads north off Dongchang'an Jie.

Beyond the intersection with Dongdan Bei Dajie and Chongwenmennei Dajie, about 1500m east of Tian'anmen Square, Dongchang'an Jie becomes **Jianguomen Dajie**. The strip around here is a ritzy area with an international flavour and a casual, affluent atmosphere thanks to its large contingent of foreigners, many of them staff from the Jianguomen embassy compound. Eating and staying here will soon sap many tourists' budgets (first-time visitors can be heard expressing disappointment that China is as expensive as New York), but the wide variety of shopping on offer – cheap clothes markets, the best Friendship Store in China and plazas that wouldn't look out of place in Hong Kong – will suit all pockets. Jianguomen Dajie is about as far away from traditional China as you can get, but the **Ancient Observatory** halfway along, and the unusual **Dongyue Temple** to the north, offer respite from rampant modernity.

The foreign legations and the Police Museum

Head east down Dongjiaomin Xiang, the first alley opposite the Mao Memorial Hall, and, still within sight of the Soviet-inspired symbols of Chinese power, you'll come to an odd stretch of street that shows very different influences. This was the **legation quarter**, created at the insistence of foreign officials in 1861, and run as an autonomous district with its own postal system, taxes and defences; initially, Chinese were not permitted entry without a pass. By the 1920s over twenty countries had legations here, most built in the style of their home countries, with imported fittings but using local materials, and today you'll see plenty of Neoclas-

79

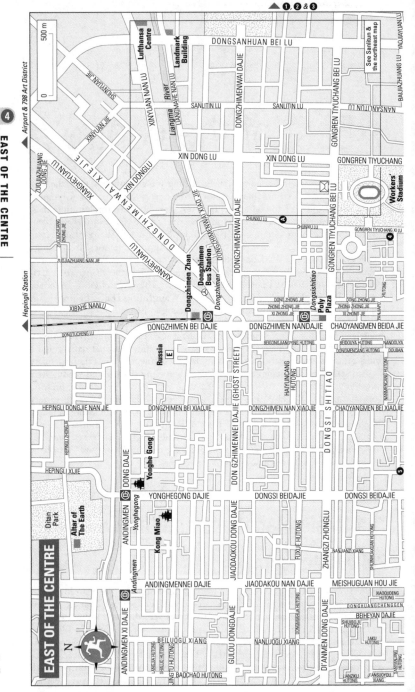

EAST OF THE CENTRE

N

500 m
0

Airport & 798 Art District

Hepingli Station

ZUOJIAZHUANG DONG JIE

SHUNYUAN JIE

XIN JIE KOU

XINYUAN NAN LU

Lufthansa
Centre

Landmark
Building

River
Liangma / LIANGMAHE NAN LU

DONGSANHUAN BEI LU

DONGZHIMENWAI DAJIE

See Sanlitun &
the northeast map

BAIJIAZHUANG LU   YAOJIAYUAN LU

SANLITIN LU

SANLITIN LU

GONGREN TIYUCHANG BEI LU

NANSANLITUN LU

XIANGHEYUAN LU

XIN DONG LU

XIN DONG LU

GONGREN TIYUCHANG

ZUOJIAZHUANG ZHONG JIE

ZUOJIAZHUANG NAN JIE

DONGZHIMEN WAI XIE JIE

DONGZHIMENWAI XIAO JIE

CHUNXIU LU

CHUNXIU LU

GONGREN TIYUCHANG BEI LU

Workers'
Stadium

GONGREN TIYUCHANG XI LU

DONGZHIMENWAI DAJIE

XIBAHE NANLU

Dongzhimen Zhan

Dongzhimen
Bus Station

Dongzhimen

Dongsishitiao

DONG ZHONG JIE

ZHONG ZHONG JIE

XI ZHONG JIE

Poly
Plaza

DONG ZHONG JIE

ZHONG ZHONG JIE

XI ZHONG JIE

PAILAROU

HUTONG

DONGTUCHENG LU

DONGZHIMEN BEI DAJIE

DONGZHIMEN NANDAJIE

CHAOYANGMEN BEIDA JIE

Russia
E

BEIGONGJIANGYING HUTONG

BEIDOUYA HUTONG   NANDOUYA

DONGMENCANG HUTONG   DOUBAN

HEPINGLI DONGJIE NAN JIE

DONGZHIMEN BEI XIAOJIE

DONGZHIMEN NAN XIAOJIE

HAIYUNCANG HUTONG

CHAOYANGMEN BEI XIAOJIE

NANMENCANG HUTONG

HEPINGLI ZHONG JIE

DON GZHIMENNEI DAJIE (GHOST STREET)

DONGSI SHITIAO

SHIJIAJIAOJIAN HUTONG

HEPINGLI XIJIE

Ditan
Park

Altar of
The Earth

ANDINGMEN

Yonghegong

DONG DAJIE

Yonghe Gong

YONGHEGONG DAJIE

DONGSI BEIDAJIE

DONGSI BEIDAJIE

Kong Miao

JIAODAOKOU DONG DAJIE

FUXUE HUTONG

ZHANGZI ZHONGLU

NANLUANZI XIANG

ANDINGMEN XI DAJIE

Andingmen

ANDINGMENNEI DAJIE

JIAODAKOU NAN DAJIE

MEISHUGUAN HOU JIE

XIAOQUDENG
HUTONG

DONGHUANGCHENGGEN

BEIHEYAN DAJIE

LANGJIA HUTONG

SIFALU HUTONG

JINGTU HUTONG

BEILUOGU XIANG

BAOCHAO HUTONG

GULOU DONGDAJIE

NANLUOGU XIANG

DONGJIAMIN HUTONG

DI'ANMEN DONG DAJIE

SHUIBOJU
HUTONG

LAKU
HUTONG

SANYANJING

HUTONG

LIANZIKU
HUTONG

FANSUOYOU
XIANG

①, ② & ③

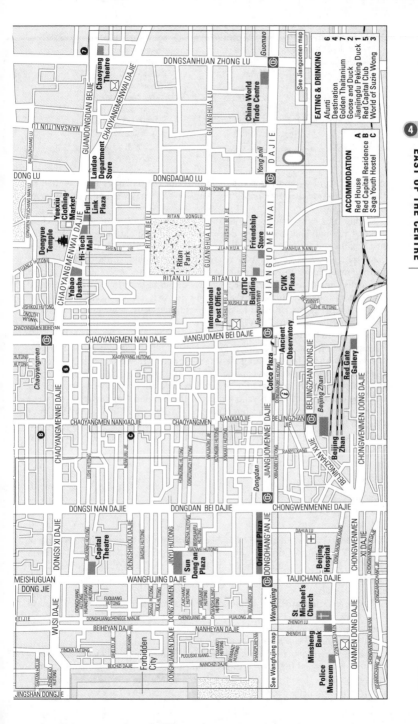

DONGSANHUAN ZHONG LU

Guomao

See Jianguomen map

EATING & DRINKING

Afunti	6
Destination	4
Golden Thaitanium	7
Goose and Duck	2
Jianjingdu Peking Duck	1
Red Capital Club	5
World of Suzie Wong	3

ACCOMMODATION

Red House	A
Red Capital Residence	B
Saga Youth Hostel	C

Chaoyang
Theatre

NANSANLITUN LU

GUANDONGDIAN BEIJIE

CHAOYANGMENWAI DAJIE

GUANGHUA LU

**China World
Trade Centre**

DONG LU

GONGREN TIYUCHANG NAN LU

BAIJIACHUANG LU

**Landao
Department
Store**

DONGDAQIAO LU

Yong'anli

DAJIE

CHAOYANGMENWAI DAJIE

XIUSHUI DONG JIE

**Yuexiu
Clothing
Market**

**Full
Link
Plaza**

**Hi-Tech
Mall**

**Dongyue
Temple**

RITAN BEILU

RITAN DONGLU

GUANGHUA LU

XIUSHUI BEI JIE

XIUSHUI NAN JIE

JIANGUOMENWAI

**Friendship
Store**

YUANLU HUTONG

SHENLU JIE

**Ritan
Park**

JIANHUA LU

JIANHUA NANLU

JISHIKOU HUTONG

YANGJIA HUTONG

CHAOYANGMEN BEIHEYAN

**Yabao
Dasha**

CHAOYANGMENWAI DAJIE

RITAN LU

RITAN LU

RITAN LU

YABAO LU

XIUSHUI BEIJIE

**International
Post Office**

**CITIC
Building**

JIANGUOMENWAI

DAJIE

Jianguomen

**CVIK
Plaza**

HUTONG

HUTONG

Chaoyangmen

CHAOYANGMENNEI DAJIE

6

CHAOYANGMEN NAN DAJIE

JIANGUOMEN BEI DAJIE

Cofco Plaza

**Ancient
Observatory**

DONGBIAOBEI HUTONG

XIAOPAIYANG HUTONG

ℹ

BEIJINGZHAN DONGJIE

Beijing Zhan

**Red Gate
Gallery**

8

CHAOYANGMEN NANXIAOJIE

CHAOYANGMEN

NANXIAOJIE

LISHI HUTONG

NEW JIE LU

WUDAOBU JIE

XIZONGBU HUTONG

XINKAILU HUTONG

BEIJINGZHAN
JIE

XIANYU LU

XUEHE HUTONG

BEIJINGZHAN XIJIE

CHONGWENMEN DONG DAJIE

C

CHAOYANGMENNEI DAJIE

CHAOYANGMEN

XIAOPAIYANG HUTONG

**Beijing
Zhan**

Dongdan

HONGXING HUTONG

DONGTANGZI HUTONG

XIANYU XIANG

XIAOBAOFANG HUTONG

DONGSI NAN DAJIE

DONGDAN BEI DAJIE

CHONGWENMENNEI DAJIE

DONGSI XI DAJIE

DENGSHIKOU DAJIE

BAOFANG HUTONG

BAISHU HUTONG

**Capital
Theatre**

JINYU HUTONG

**Sun
Dong'an
Plaza**

JIAODAOKOU DAJIE

MEISHUGUAN HOU JIE

XIAOWEI HUTONG

Oriental Plaza

DONGCHANG'AN JIE

DAHUA LU

**Beijing
Hospital**

JIAODAOKOU XIANG

CHONGWENMEN

XI DAJIE

CHONGWENMENNEI XI LU

MEISHUGUAN
DONG JIE

WANGFUJING DAJIE

TAIJICHANG DAJIE

CHONGWENMEN DONG DAJIE

CHONGWENMEN PANG LU

WUSI DAJIE

DONGCHANG
HUTONG

HUANGCHENGGEN
HUTONG

FUQIANG
HUTONG

DONG ANMEN

CAOFANG
HUTONG

JIABIANLI
HUTONG

DATIANSHUILING
HUTONG

XIGANGZI JIE

WANGFUJING
JIE

Wangfujing

**St
Michael's
Church**

SI JIE

DONGHUANGCHENGGE NANJIE

CHENGGUANG JIE

HUALONG JIE

XIAOGANGZI JIE

ZHENGYI LU

ZHENGYI LU

**Minsheng
Bank**

✉

BEIHEYAN DAJIE

NANHEYAN DAJIE

YINCHA HUTONG

QINGLONG JIE

BEIJING
SI JIE

NANHEYAN DAJIE

JINYU
HUTONG

CHANGGONG JIE

DONGJIAOMIN XIANG

**Forbidden
City**

DONGHUAMEN DAJIE

PUDUSIXI XIANG

BEIXIANG

CHANGCHUYAN

ZHENGYI LU

QIANMEN DONG DAJIE

DONGJIAOMIN XIANG

See Wangfujing map

SHATAN HOUJIE

ZHONGLAO HUTONG

BEICHIZI DAJIE

NANCHIZI DAJIE

DONGJIAOMIN XIANG

XI DAJIE

QIANMEN XI DAJIE

DONGJIAOMIN PANG LU

JINGSHAN DONGJIE

**Police
Museum**

798 Art District	朝阳区大山子798艺术区	*cháoyángqū dàshānzi qījiǔbā yìshùqū*
The Ancient Observatory	古观象台	*gǔguānxiàngtái*
Chaoyangmen	朝阳门	*cháoyáng mén*
Dongyue Temple	东岳庙	*dōngyuè miào*
Jianguomen	建国门	*jiànguó mén*
Police Museum	警察博物馆	*jǐngchá bówùguǎn*
Ritan Park	日坛公园	*rìtán gōngyuán*
St Michael's Church	东交民巷天主堂	*do1ngjiāomínxiàng tiānzhǔtáng*
Sanlitun Lu	三里屯路	*sānlǐtún lù*
Wangfujing	王府井	*wángfǔ jǐng*

sical facades and wrought-iron balconies. Most of the buildings are now used by the police and are therefore politically sensitive – the area was left blank on maps until the 1980s.

Heading east past what used to be the French and Russian concession – where most of the buildings have been destroyed (though the old French hospital, the first building on the left, still stands), you come to the **Police Museum** (Tues–Sun 9am–4pm; ¥5). Anything vaguely related to crime or public order is exhibited on its four sand floors, including murder weapons, forensics tools, uniforms and an ingenious Qing dynasty fire engine, as well as details of notorious crimes captioned in excited prose – the "forces of the law" always catch the "despicable ruffians", of course. There's plenty of English labelling, and, unusually, some of it is critical of the Cultural Revolution. For ¥15 you can finish off your visit with a blast on the firing range on the fourth floor – though all you get to shoot, alas, is a laser gun.

Keep heading east, over Zhengyi Lu, and you'll find the best-preserved concession architecture. The **Minsheng Bank**, just after the crossroads on the north side, is a Gothic Revival building constructed by the Japanese in the 1930s. Much of the opulent interior, including the chandeliers, tiled floor and balustrades, is original. You can't miss the steep yellow roofs of the **Belgian Concession** – now the *Zhengyi Hotel* – a little further on. Opposite it, the Gothic Revival **St Michael's Church** is worth a poke about if you find it open. Yielding to local taste, the pillars are painted red as in Chinese temples, and the statues of the saints are labelled in Chinese characters.

Wangfujing

Wangfujing Dajie is where the capital gets down to the business of **shopping** in earnest. The haunt of quality stores for over a century, it was called Morrison Street before the communist takeover. The western side of the street has plenty of department stores, small clothes shops and photo studios; the eastern side holds two giant malls.

The new **Oriental Plaza**, at the south end of the street, is the biggest mall in Asia, stretching east for nearly a kilometre. As well as interminable clothes stores (fancy on ground level, affordable below) at the eastern end there are a couple of good restaurants (*South Beauty* and *Crystal Jade*).

Back on Wangfujing, for "shock the folks back home" food – silk worms and sparrows on skewers and the like – visit **Xiaochi Jie**, an alley leading west at the south end of the street. It's lined with small stalls run by Muslim Uigurs from northwest China, who compete fiercely, haranguing passers-by. As well as exotica, plenty of

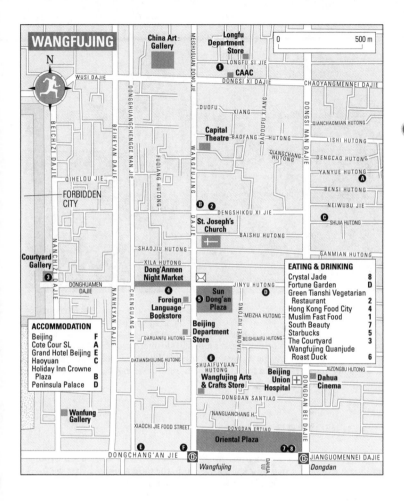

N

WUSI DAJIE

China Art Gallery

Longfu Department Store

MEISHUGUAN DONG JIE

LONGFU SI JIE

CAAC

DONGSI XI DAJIE

CHAOYANGMENNEI DAJIE

0   500 m

DONGHUANGCHENGGE NAN JIE

BEICHIZI DAJIE

BEIHEYAN DAJIE

DUOFU

XIANG

DUOFU XIANG

Capital Theatre

BAOFANG HUTONG

FUDIANG HUTONG

WANGFUJING DAJIE

QIANGCHANG HUTONG

DONGSI NAN DAJIE

QIANCHAOMIAN HUTONG

LISHI HUTONG

DENGCAO HUTONG

YANYUE HUTONG

QIHELOU JIE

FORBIDDEN CITY

BENSI HUTONG

DENGSHIKOU XI JIE

NEIWUBU JIE

St. Joseph's Church

BAISHU HUTONG

SHIJIA HUTONG

NANCHIZI DAJIE

SHAOJIU HUTONG

XILA HUTONG

GANMIAN HUTONG

Courtyard Gallery

DONGHUAMEN DAJIE

Dong'Anmen Night Market

JINYU HUTONG

EATING & DRINKING

Crystal Jade   8
Fortune Garden   D
Green Tianshi Vegetarian
  Restaurant   2
Hong Kong Food City   4
Muslim Fast Food   1
South Beauty   7
Starbucks   5
The Courtyard   3
Wangfujing Quanjude
  Roast Duck   6

CHENGUANG JIE

NANHEYAN DAJIE

Foreign Language Bookstore

Sun Dong'an Plaza

DARUANFU HUTONG

Beijing Department Store

MEIZHA HUTONG

XIAOWEI HUTONG

BEISHUAIFU HUTONG

DATIANSHUIJING HUTONG

SHUAIFUYUAN HUTONG

XIZONGBU HUTONG

ACCOMMODATION

Beijing   F
Cote Cour SL   A
Grand Hotel Beijing E
Haoyuan   C
Holiday Inn Crowne
  Plaza   B
Peninsula Palace   D

Wanfung Gallery

Wangfujing Arts & Crafts Store

Beijing Union Hospital

DONGDAN BEI DAJIE

Dahua Cinema

DONGDAN SANTIAO

NANGUANCHANG H.

XIAOCHI JIE FOOD STREET

DONGDAN ERTIAO

Oriental Plaza

DONGCHANG'AN JIE

Wangfujing

JIANGUOMENNEI DAJIE

DAHUA LU

Dongdan

EAST OF THE CENTRE | Wangfujing

stalls do tasty bowls of noodles for a few yuan and coconuts for ¥10 (you stick in a straw). Back on the main street, the store most frequented by visitors is the Foreign Language Bookstore at no. 235 (see p.162); opposite, the **Sun Dong'an Plaza**, another glitzy mall, is convenient for a snack – the place is home to a food court and several fast-food chain restaurants – and also has a cinema and a games arcade. The tacky dioramas of old city life in the basement are best avoided. Continue heading north up Wangfujing for a kilometre and you'll come to the **China Art Gallery**, a huge exhibition hall showcasing state-approved works (see p.157).

A number of *hutongs* lead east from Wangfujing Dajie into a quiet area well away from the bustle of the main street. If you're here in the evening, don't miss the **Donghuamen Yeshi night market**, at the intersection of Wangfujing Dajie and Jinyu Hutong, where all sorts of food, from regional delicacies, scorpions and starfish to simple street snacks, are sold at the rows of red stalls: nothing costs more than ¥15. At the end of Shuaifuyuan Hutong, the graceful medical college building is a former palace where the ten brothers of a Ming-dynasty emperor were once

▲ Wangfujing Dajie

persuaded to live, so that he could keep a wary eye on them. Today, it's been so rebuilt that only the ornate flying eaves hint at its former function. Continuing east for about 300m through the *hutongs*, you'll reach Dongdan Bei Dajie, parallel to Wangfujing, a shopping area full of boutiques, mostly selling Western imports.

Jianguomen

As you head east towards **Jianguomen**, another cluster of lustrous buildings hoves into view around the Beijing Zhan subway stop, the most striking being the *International Hotel* on the north side of the street, which resembles a toy robot in all but scale. Opposite, just north of Beijing Zhan, the Henderson Centre is yet another glossy mall. On the north side of Chang'an Jie, the **Chang'an Theatre** has nightly performances of Beijing opera (see p.151).

The Ancient Observatory

Beside the concrete knot that is the intersection between Jianguomennei Dajie and the second ring road, the **Ancient Observatory** (Wed–Sun 9–11.30am, 1–4.30pm; ¥15), an unexpected survivor marooned amid the high-rises, comes as a delightful surprise. The first observatory on the site was founded in the thirteenth century on the orders of Kublai Khan; the astronomers were commissioned to reform the inaccurate calendar then in use. Subsequently the observatory was staffed by Muslim scientists, as medieval Islamic science enjoyed pre-eminence, but, strangely, in the early seventeenth century it was placed in the hands of Jesuit missionaries (see box on opposite). Led by one Matteo Ricci, they proceeded to astonish the emperor and his subjects by making a series of precise astronomical forecasts. The Jesuits re-equipped the observatory and remained in charge until the 1830s.

The Jesuits in China

Jesuit missionaries began to arrive in China in the seventeenth century. Though they weren't allowed to preach freely at first, they were tolerated for their scientific and astronomical skills, and were invited to stay at court: precise astronomical calculations were invaluable to the emperor who, as master of the calendar, was charged with determining the cycle of the seasons in order to ensure good harvests, and observing the movement of celestial bodies to harmonize the divine and human order. Some Jesuits rose to high positions in the imperial court, and in 1692 they finally won the right to preach in China. The missionaries made little headway in spreading Catholicism, however, as a Vatican edict forced them to condemn all Chinese rites and rituals, such as sacrifices to ancestors, as anti-Christian.

Matteo Ricci (1552–1610) was the most illustrious of the early Jesuit missionaries to China. A keen Chinese scholar, he translated the Confucian analects into Portuguese and created the first system for romanizing Chinese characters. He began studying the Chinese language in 1582, when he arrived in Macau. In 1603 he moved to Beijing and won the respect of the local literati with his extensive knowledge of cartography, astronomy, mathematics and the physical sciences.

Today the squat, unadorned building is empty, and visitors aren't allowed inside. The best features of the complex are, however, accessible: its garden, a placid retreat; and the eight Ming-dynasty **astronomical instruments** sitting on the roof – stunningly sculptural armillary spheres, theodolites and the like, all beautifully ornamented with entwined dragons, lions and clouds. The small museum attached, displaying pottery decorated with star maps, as well as navigational equipment dating from the Yuan dynasty onwards, is well worth a wander round.

Jianguomenwai Dajie

Beyond the observatory and the second ring road, the **International Club** is the first sign that you're approaching the capital's diplomatic sector. Turn left at the International Club up Ritan Lu and you'll come to the **Jianguomenwai diplomatic compound**, the first of two embassy complexes (the other is at Sanlitun, well northeast of here). It's an odd place, a giant toy-town with neat buildings in ordered courtyards and frozen sentries on plinths.

Ritan Park is just one block north from the International Club, a five-minute walk from Jianguomen Dajie. The park was one of the imperial city's original four, one for each cardinal direction; Tiantan (to the south; see p.68), Ditan (north) and Yuetan (west) were the others. Each park was the location for a yearly sacrificial ritual performed by the emperor but today, Ritan Park is popular with embassy staff and courting couples, who make use of its numerous secluded nooks. The *Stone Boat Café* makes an excellent pit stop (see p.148). It's a very attractive park, with paths winding between groves of cherry trees, rockeries and ponds.

North of the park you enter the city's Russian zone, where all the shop signs are in the Cyrillic alphabet: to the north, Shenlu Jie is full of fur shops aimed squarely at the Russian moll. The street ends in the giant **Aliens Street Market** (9.30am–6pm), a chaotic mall of gaudy trinkets, fakes and questionable fashion, thronging with Russian tourists and traders.

Back on Jianguomenwai Dajie, beyond the CITIC building, you reach the Friendship Store (see p.160), which hosts, at the back, the expat favourite *Steak and Eggs* (see p.143). On the south side of the street, the CVIK Plaza (daily 9am–9pm) is a more modern shopping centre with five floors of clothes and accessories.

The main reason to continue beyond here is to head for the **Silk Market**, a giant

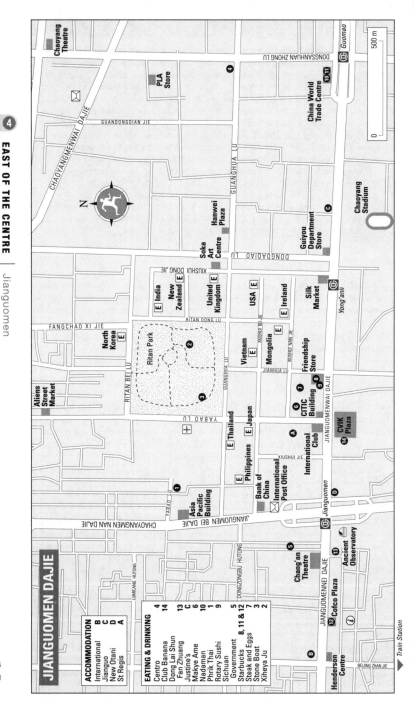

JIANGUOMEN DAJIE

ACCOMMODATION

International	B
Jianguo	C
New Otani	D
St Regis	A

EATING & DRINKING

Centro	4
Club Banana	14
Dong Lai Shun	13
Fan Zhuang	C
Justine's	6
Makye Ame	10
Nadaman	1
Phrik Thai	9
Rotary Sushi	
Sichuan	5
Government	
Starbucks	8, 11 & 12
Steak and Eggs	3
Stone Boat	2
Xiheya Ju	

Chaoyang Theatre

PLA Store

China World Trade Centre

Guomao

Chaoyang Stadium

Guiyou Department Store

Hanwei Plaza

Soka Art Centre

India

New Zealand

United Kingdom

USA

Ireland

Silk Market

Vietnam

Mongolia

Friendship Store

North Korea

Ritan Park

Thailand

Japan

CITIC Building

Philippines

International Club

CVIK Plaza

Aliens Street Market

Bank of China

International Post Office

Jianguomen

Asia Pacific Building

Chang'an Theatre

Ancient Observatory

Cofco Plaza

Henderson Centre

Train Station

six-storey mall of fake goods (see p.163), just north of Yong'an Li subway stop. From here, it's a dull couple of kilometres to the **World Trade Centre** just before the intersection with the third ring road. Dedicated consumers who make it here are rewarded with Beijing's most exclusive mall, boasting four gleaming storeys of pricey goods, as well as a basement ice skating rink.

Chaoyangmenwai Dajie and Sanlitun

North of Jianguomenwai Dajie, the **Dongyue Temple** (Tues–Sun 8am–5pm; ¥10), a short walk from Ritan Park or Chaoyangmen subway stop, is an intriguing place, in pointed contrast to all the shrines to materialism outside. Dating back to the Ming dynasty, it's been restored, though it doesn't seem to attract too many devotees – perhaps it's a little too large. Pass under the Zhandaimen archway – originally constructed in 1322 – and you enter a courtyard holding around thirty annexes, each of which deals with a different aspect of Taoist life, the whole making up a sort of surreal spiritual bureaucracy. There's the "Department of Suppressing Schemes", "Department of Wandering Ghosts", even a "Department for Fifteen Kinds of Violent Death". In each, a statue of Taoist deity Lao Zi holds court over brightly painted figures, many with monstrous animal heads, too many limbs and the like. The temple shop sells red tablets for worshippers to sign and leave outside the annexes as petitions to the spiritual officials. Departments dealing with longevity and wealth are unsurprisingly popular, but so, tellingly, is the "Department for Official Morality".

Not far north of here is the **Poly Plaza**, at Dongsishitiao subway stop. It's mostly offices, but at the back lies a small **museum** (Mon–Sat 9.30am–4.30pm; ¥50) that, though pricey, has one of the most select collections of antiquities in the capital. In the hall of ancient bronzes you'll find four of the twelve bronze animals that were looted from the Old Summer Palace (see p.104); all were bought in the west by patriotic businessmen, and their return was much heralded. The second hall displays ancient Buddha statues.

East of here is the **Sanlitun** bar district (see map on p.88). By night it's raucous and gaudy, but during the day beguilingly civilized, with many small cafes and restaurants that are good for people-watching. As well as drinking, there are plenty of opportunities to eat and shop here.

798 Art District

Though it's way out on the way to the airport, the **798 Art District**, a collection of **art galleries**, **boutiques** and **cafés** is the hotspot for the arty crowd; take bus #915, #918 or #934 from Dongzhimen Station. Originally it was an electronics factory, built by East Germans; when that closed down in the 1990s, artists moved in and converted the airy, light, and above all, cheap spaces into studios. As the Chinese art market blossomed, galleries followed, then shops and cafes – a gentrification that would take fifty years in the West happened here in about five. Fortunately, plans to bus in tour groups to observe the bohemians in their natural environment have been thus far shelved, as have the landlord's attempts to redevelop. The future of the place looks rosy, as it's been designated a Centre of Creative Culture.

There are exhibition openings every week, and every art form is well represented – though with such a lot of it about, it varies in quality. The **most established gal-**

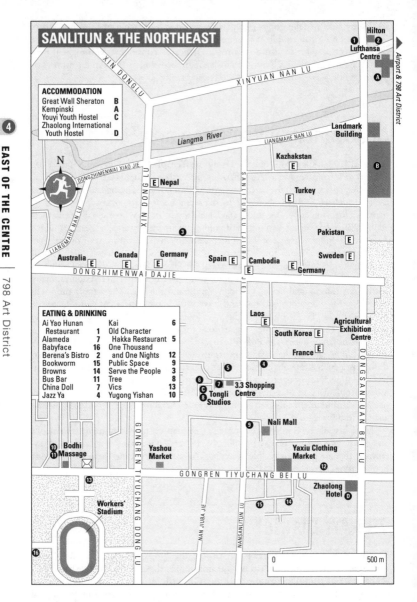

SANLITUN & THE NORTHEAST

ACCOMMODATION
Great Wall Sheraton   **B**
Kempinski   **A**
Youyi Youth Hostel   **C**
Zhaolong International
Youth Hostel   **D**

EATING & DRINKING
Ai Yao Hunan   Kai   6
  Restaurant   1   Old Character
Alameda   7   Hakka Restaurant   5
Babyface   16   One Thousand
Berena's Bistro   2   and One Nights   12
Bookworm   15   Public Space   9
Browns   14   Serve the People   3
Bus Bar   11   Tree   8
China Doll   7   Vics   13
Jazz Ya   4   Yugong Yishan   10

Hilton
Lufthansa Centre
Airport & 798 Art District
Landmark Building
Kazhakstan
Nepal
Turkey
Pakistan
Germany   Spain   Cambodia   Sweden
Australia   Canada   Germany   Germany
Laos
Agricultural Exhibition Centre
South Korea
France
3.3 Shopping Centre
Tongli Studios
Nali Mall
Yaxiu Clothing Market
Bodhi Massage
Yashou Market
Zhaolong Hotel
Workers' Stadium

0   500 m

leries are Beijing Commune, Marcella Gallery, the huge Beijing Tokyo Art Projects and White Space (see p.157). There's a good English language art bookstore, Timezone 8, and plenty of places for food; for crêpes, try *Vincents* and for a cappuccino, the *At Café*.

If it's just too commercial for you, head for the **Songzhuang Artists Village**, 5km north, which is where the hardcore avant gardists escaped to when 798 became overly mainstream for them.

North of the centre

The area north of the Forbidden City has a good collection of sights you could happily spend days exploring. Just outside the Forbidden City are **Jingshan and Beihai parks**, two of the finest in China; north of here, the area around the Shicha Lakes is filling up with bars, restaurants and cafés along the lakesides. Around the lakes you'll find the last big **hutong** district, once the home of princes, dukes and monks. The alleys are a labyrinth, with something of interest around every corner; some regard them as the final outpost of a genuinely Chinese Beijing. Buried deep within them is **Prince Gong's Palace**, with the **Bell and Drum towers**, once used to mark dawn and dusk, standing on the eastern edge of the district.

A kilometre east of here you'll find the appealing street, **Nanluogu Xiang**, where the artsy set hang out, the best place in the city for people watching over

Baita Si	白塔寺	*báitǎ sì*
Beihai Park	北海公园	*běihǎi gōngyuán*
Beijing Aquarium	北京海洋馆	*běijīng hǎiyángguǎn*
Bell Tower	钟楼	*zhōng lóu*
Confucius Temple	孔庙	*kǒng miào*
Ditan Park	地坛公园	*dìtán gōngyuán*
Drum Tower	鼓楼	*gǔ lóu*
Exhibition Centre	展览馆	*zhǎnlǎn guǎn*
Guangji Si	广济寺	*guǎngjì sì*
Guo Morou's Residence	郭沫若故居	*guo1mòruò gùjū*
Houhai	后海	*hòu hǎi*
Jingshan Park	景山公园	*jǐngshān gōngyuán*
Lu Xun Museum	鲁迅博物馆	*lǔxùn bówùguǎn*
Mei Lanfang Museum	梅兰芳纪念	*méilánfāng jìniànguǎn*
Nanluogu Xiang	南锣鼓巷	*nánluógǔ xiàng*
National Swimming Centre	国家游泳中心	*guójiā yóuyǒng zho1ngxīn*
Olympic Park	北京奥林匹克公园	*běijīng áolínpǐkè go1ngyuán*
Olympic Stadium	奥林匹克体育馆	*àolínpǐkè tǐyùguǎn*
Prince Gong's Palace	恭王府	*gōngwáng fǔ*
Qianhai	前海	*qián hǎi*
Song Qingling's Residence	宋庆龄故居	*sòngqìnglíng gùjū*
Wanshou Si	万寿寺	*wànshòu sì*
Wuta Si	五塔寺	*wǔtǎ sì*
Xu Beihong Museum	徐悲鸿纪念馆	*xúbēihóng jìniànguǎn*
Yonghe Gong	雍和宫	*yōnghé gōng*
Zizhuyuan Park	紫竹院公园	*zǐzhúyuàn gōngyuán*
Zoo	北京动物园	*běijīng dòngwùyuán*

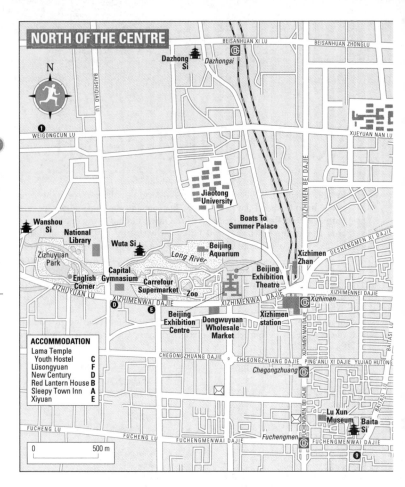

NORTH OF THE CENTRE

BEISANHUAN XI LU   BEISANHUAN ZHONGLU

Dazhong Si   Dazhongsi

N

BAISHIQIAO LU

XUEYUAN NAN LU

WEIGONGCUN LU

5

NORTH OF THE CENTRE

Jiaotong University

XIZHIMEN BEI DAJIE

Boats To Summer Palace

Wanshou Si

National Library

Wuta Si   Beijing Aquarium   Xizhimen Zhan   DESHENGMEN XI DAJIE

Zizhuyuan Park   Long River

Capital Gymnasium   Carrefour Supermarket   Beijing Exhibition Theatre

English Corner   Zoo   Xizhimen   XIZHIMENNEI DAJIE

ZIZHUYUAN LU   XIZHIMENWAI DAJIE   XIZHIMENWAI DAJIE

Beijing Exhibition Centre   Dongwuyuan Wholesale Market   Xizhimen station

XIZHIMEN NAN DAJIE

BAITASI LU

CHEGONGZHUANG DAJIE   CHEGONGZHUANG DAJIE   PING'ANLI XI DAJIE   YUJIAO HUTONG

Chegongzhuang

ACCOMMODATION
Lama Temple
  Youth Hostel **C**
Lüsongyuan **F**
New Century **D**
Red Lantern House **B**
Sleepy Town Inn **A**
Xiyuan **E**

BAITAS LU

FUCHENG LU   Lu Xun Museum   Baita Si

FUCHENG LU   FUCHENGMENWAI DAJIE

FUCHENGMEN BEI DAJIE

Fuchengmen   FUCHENGMENWAI DAJIE

0   500 m

9

---

a coffee and a great place to stay. Two kilometres east of here, right next to the Yonghe Gong subway stop, the **Yonghe Gong** Tibetan lamasery is one of Beijing's most colourful (and popular) attractions. While you're in the vicinity, don't miss the peaceful, and unjustly ignored, **Kong Miao** (Confucius Temple) and **Ditan Park**, within easy walking distance of one another.

In the west of this area you'll find a number of little **museums** – the homes of two twentieth-century cultural icons, **Lu Xun** and **Xu Beihong** now hold exhibitions of their works, while the **Baita Si** functions as a museum of religious relics as well as a place of pilgrimage.

In the northwest of the city, around the transport hub of Xizhimen and easy to reach on the subway, are a couple of architectural oddities – the new **Exhibition Centre** and the old **Wuta Si** – plus the **zoo** and an enjoyable museum, the **Wanshou Si**, housed in a grand temple complex.

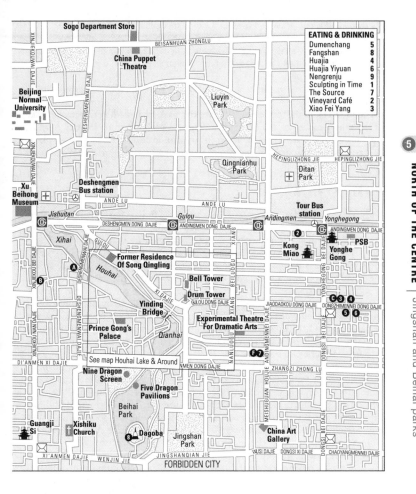

Map labels:
Sogo Department Store
BEISANHUAN ZHONGLU
China Puppet Theatre
Liuyin Park
Beijing Normal University
Qingnianhu Park
HEPINGLIZHONG JIE
Ditan Park
HEPINGLIZHONG JIE
Xu Beihong Museum
Deshengmen Bus station
ANDE LU
ANDE LU
Tour Bus station
Jishuitan
DESHENGMEN DONG DAJIE
Gulou
ANDINGMEN DONG DAJIE
Andingmen
Yonghegong
ANDINGMEN DONG DAJIE
Xihai
Kong Miao
Yonghe Gong
PSB
Houhai
Former Residence Of Song Qingling
Bell Tower
JIAODAOKOU DONG DAJIE
DONGZHIMENNEI DONG DAJIE
Yinding Bridge
Drum Tower
GULOU DONG DAJIE
Prince Gong's Palace
Qianhai
Experimental Theatre For Dramatic Arts
See map Houhai Lake & Around
NMEN DONG DAJIE
ZHANGZI ZHONG LU
DI'ANMEN XI DAJIE
Nine Dragon Screen
Five Dragon Pavilions
Beihai Park
Guangji Si
Xishiku Church
Dagoba
Jingshan Park
China Art Gallery
XI'ANMEN DAJIE
WENJIN JIE
JINGSHANQIAN JIE
NUSI DAJIE
DONGSI XI DAJIE
CHAOYANGMENNEI DAJIE
FORBIDDEN CITY

EATING & DRINKING
Dumenchang	5
Fangshan	8
Huajia	4
Huajia Yiyuan	6
Nengrenju	9
Sculpting in Time	1
The Source	7
Vineyard Café	2
Xiao Fei Yang	3

Jingshan and Beihai parks

A visit to **Jingshan Park** (daily 6am–9pm; ¥3) is a natural way to round off a trip to the Forbidden City, which most visitors exit from the north gate, just across the road from the park. Otherwise you can get here on bus #101 from Fuchengmen or Chaoyangmen subway stops. An artificial mound, the park was the byproduct of the digging of the palace moat, and served as both a windbreak and a barrier to keep malevolent spirits (believed to emanate from the north) from entering the imperial quarter of the city. Its history, most momentously, includes the suicide in 1644 of the last Ming emperor, **Chong Zhen**, who hanged himself here from a tree after rebel troops broke into the imperial palace. The spot, on the eastern side of the park, is easy to find as English-language signs for it appear everywhere (beneath those pointing the way to a children's playground), though the tree that stands here is not the original. Though he was a dissolute opium fiend, the suicide note pinned to his lapel was surprisingly noble:

My own insufficient virtue and wretched nature has caused me to sin against heaven above. I die knowing I am wholly unworthy to stand before my sacred ancestors... let the rebels tear my miserable body to pieces but let them touch not a single hair on the head of the least of my subjects.

Afterwards, the tree was judged an accessory to the emperor's death and as punishment was manacled with an iron chain.

The **views** from the top of the hill make this park a compelling target: they take in the whole extent of the Forbidden City and a fair swath of the city outside, a great deal more attractive than seen from ground level. To the west is a lake, Beihai; to the north the Bell and Drum towers; and to the northeast the Yonghe Gong.

Beihai Park

Only a few hundred metres west of Jingshan Park, **Beihai Park** (daily 6am–8pm, park buildings till 4pm; ¥5 for the park, ¥10 for the park and entry to all buildings), most of which is taken up by a lake, is a favourite skating spot in winter. Supposedly created by Kublai Khan, long before any of the Forbidden City structures were conceived, the park is of an ambitious scale: the lake was man-made, the island in its midst created with the excavated earth. Qing Emperor Qianlong oversaw its landscaping into a classical Chinese garden in the eighteenth century. Today its elegance is marred by funfairs and souvenir shops among the willows and red-columned galleries; still, it's a grand place to retreat from the city and recharge. Bus #101 passes Beihai Park's south gate en route between Fuchengmen and Chaoyangmen subway stops, while you can get to the park's north gate on bus #13 from Yonghe Gong subway stop.

Just inside the main gate, which lies on the park's southern side, the **Round**, an enclosure of buildings behind a circular wall, has at its centre a courtyard, where there's a large jade bowl, said to have belonged to Kublai Khan. The white-jade Buddha in the hall behind was a present from Burmese Buddhists. From here, a walkway provides access to the island, which is dotted with buildings – including the **Yuegu Lou**, a hall full of steles (stone slabs carved with Chinese characters); and the giant **dagoba** sitting on the crown of the hill, built in the mid-seventeenth century to celebrate a visit by the Dalai Lama. It's a suitable emblem for a park that contains a curious mixture of religious constructions, storehouses for cultural relics and imperial garden furniture. Nestling inside the *dagoda* is a shrine to the demon-headed, multi-armed Lamaist deity, Yamantaka. The island has a pier where you can rent a rowing boat or duck-shaped pedal boats for ¥20 an hour – also available from a pier near the south gate (same price).

On the north side of the lake stands the impressive **Nine Dragon Screen,** its purpose to ward off evil spirits. An ornate wall of glazed tiles, depicting nine stylized, sinuous dragons in relief, it's one of China's largest, at 27m in length, and remains in good condition. Nearby are the **Five Dragon Pavilions**, supposedly in the shape of a dragon's spine. Even when the park is crowded at the weekend, the gardens and rockeries over the other side of the lake remain tranquil and soothing – it's easy to see why the area was so popular with Qianlong. The park's north exit brings you out at the south end of the Shicha lakes.

▲ Nine Dragon Screen

Around the Shicha lakes

The area north of Beihai Park is the only district where the city's traditional street plan, a tangle of **hutongs**, has been preserved on any scale. These cluttered, grey alleyways show Beijing's other, private, face: here you'll see poky courtyards and converted palaces, and come across small open spaces where old men sit with caged pet birds. The network of *hutongs* centres on the two artificial **Shicha lakes**, Qianhai and Houhai. Created during the Yuan dynasty, they were once the terminus for a canal network that served the capital. Two giant old buildings, the Bell and Drum towers, are half hidden away to the east of the area.

Much of the district has been recast as a heritage area and is full of restaurants and cafés (see "Listings", p.144). All the public toilets have been spruced up and there's even a government sponsored rickshaw driver who gives free rides to the nearest convenience to any tourist who's caught short. Still, stray away from the lakeside and the showcasing vanishes quickly.

The best way to get around is by **bike**. Traffic within the *hutongs* is light, and you're free to dive into any alley you fancy, though you're almost certain to get lost – in which case cycle around until you come to a lake. You could walk here from Jishuitan or Gulou subway stop, though the best entry is opposite the northern entrance to Beihai Park – to get here by **bus**, take trolleybus #111 from Dongdan Bei Dajie, or bus #13 from the Yonghe Gong.

Regular **hutong tours** leave from 200m west of the north entrance to Beihai Park (daily 9am & 2pm, May–Oct also 7pm; ¥180; ☎010/66159097) and from outside the Drum Tower. More imaginative than most tours (visitors are biked about in rickshaws), they are very popular with tour groups. You can arrange a private trip for around ¥80 if you barter, though expect to be taken to a few shops where the driver gets commission.

Courtyard houses

Beijing's *hutongs* are lined with *siheyuans*, single-storey **courtyard houses** that are home to about a fifth of the city's population. These traditional Chinese dwellings follow a plan that has hardly changed since the Han dynasty, in essence identical to that of the Forbidden City.

A typical courtyard house has its entrance in the south wall. Just outside the front door stand two flat stone blocks – sometimes carved into lions – for mounting horses and to demonstrate the family's wealth and status. Step over the threshold and you are confronted with a freestanding wall; this is to keep out evil spirits, which can only travel in straight lines. Behind it is the outer courtyard, with the servants' quarters to the right and left. The entrance to the inner courtyard, where the family lived, would be in the north wall. The most important rooms, used by the elders, are those at the back, facing south.

With the government anxious to turn Beijing into a showcase for Chinese modernity, however, it seems unlikely that many of these houses will survive, and there are barely 100,000 courtyard houses left, the majority in Qianmen. A wander around the *hutongs* here shows the houses in their worst light; the dwellings are cramped and poorly maintained, the streets dirty, the plumbing and sanitation inadequate; it's only a matter of time before their inhabitants are rehoused in the new suburbs. But in the *hutongs* you'll also see how the system creates a neighbourliness absent from the new high-rises – here, you can't help knowing everyone else's business.

Responding to increasingly vocal complaints about the destruction of Beijing's architectural heritage, city planners point out that *hutongs* full of courtyard houses are unsuitable for contemporary living: besides the difficulty of providing them with proper plumbing, the houses are very cold in winter, and with only one storey they're an inefficient use of land. Anyway, they argue, the population of a modern city ought to live outside the centre. Ironically, the area around the Shicha lakes, where most of the city's other remaining courtyard houses are to be found, has become a fashionable area for high-ranking cadres to live, and some properties here have sold for more than a million dollars. The majority of the houses are in much better condition than in Qianmen, and many are earmarked for protection. A number of new luxury housing estates have been built in courtyard-house style – the best examples are around Deshengmen in the north of the city. They're very popular with foreigners.

Qianhai and Houhai

Just north of Beihai Park and across Di'anmen Xi Dajie is the pretty lake, **Qianhai**. It's an appealing place, removed from the traffic and with an easygoing feel. Having been dredged and cleaned up, the area around it has become a drinking and dining hotspot. Be warned that the lakeside bars and restaurants are over-designed and tacky, while the staff, annoyingly, hector passers by; for the really pleasant places, you'll need to head in from the shore – see p.144 for recommendations.

Heading north along Qianhai, look out for the hardy folk who swim here every day, all year round, cutting a hole in the ice in winter. You can hire pedalos from two jetties on the east bank (¥40/hr; ¥200 deposit). From the top of the cute humpback **Yinding Bridge**, spanning the lake's narrowest point and marking the divide between Qianhai and **Houhai,** you can see the western hills on (very rare) clear days. Here you can sit over a coffee at the *No Name Bar* (see p.149) and enjoy the scenery, something that can't be said about too many public places in Beijing. There's a famous restaurant just by the *No Name*, the *Kaorouji* (see p.145), that's been here for centuries.

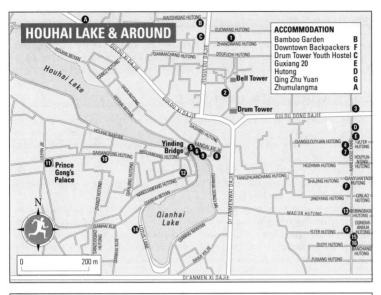

ACCOMMODATION

Bamboo Garden	B
Downtown Backpackers	F
Drum Tower Youth Hostel	C
Guxiang 20	E
Hutong	D
Qing Zhu Yuan	G
Zhumulangma	A

EATING & DRINKING

Bed Bar	1	Fish Nation	7	Mao Livehouse	3	Pass By Bar	16
Drum and Bell	2	Hutong Pizza	12	Mei Mansion	10	Sauveurs de Coree	4
Drum and Gong	15	Huxleys	8	No Name Bar	9	Sex and da City	14
Gong Wang Fu Restaurant	11	Kaorouji	5	Nuage	6	Xiaoxin's	13

Prince Gong's Palace and the courtyard museums

Situated on Liuyun Jie, the charming **Prince Gong's Palace** (daily 8.30am–5pm; ¥20) was once the residence of Prince Gong, the brother of Emperor Xianfeng and father of the last Qing emperor, Pu Yi. Its nine courtyards, joined by covered walkways, have been restored to something like their former elegance, and the landscaped gardens are attractively leafy. The largest hall now hosts **Beijing opera** performances, at around 11am and 4pm (for tour groups), and also at 7.30pm. Just north of the exit lies the excellent *Sichuan Restaurant* (see p.145).

You can get to Prince Gong's palace from Beihai Park by following the curving alley north that starts opposite the park's north entrance – Qianhai will be on the right as you walk along – then taking the first left onto Qianhai Xi Jie. Follow this as it bends round, until you reach an intersection with the music conservatory on your right; here you turn right into Liuyin Jie. There are plenty of other old palaces in the area, for this was once something of an imperial pleasure ground, and home to a number of high officials and distinguished eunuchs (see p.61). Head north up Liuyin Jie and you pass the former **Palace of Tao Beile**, now a school, after about 200m. It's one of a number of converted buildings in the area, some of which are identified by plaques.

Just behind Prince Gong's Palace you'll find a couple of old courtyard houses-turned-museums, perfect for a *hutong* stroll. The small **Mei Lanfang Musuem** (Tues–Sun 9am–4pm; ¥10; ⓦwww.meilanfang.com) was once the home of the greatest opera singer of the twentieth century, Mei Lanfang, whose tragic life was the basis for Chen Xiage's opulent movie *Farewell My Concubine* (see p.156). There are plenty of pictures of Mei Lanfang famously dressed up as a woman, playing female roles. Head back towards the lake and on Qianhai Xi Jie, behind Lotus Lane, you'll find **Guo Morou's Residence** (Tues–Sun 9am–4.30pm; ¥20). Guo (1892–1978) was a revered writer in his day though now he's considered a little stuffy. His elegantly furnished and spacious house is worth a peek around – not for the exhibits of dusty books and bric-a-brac – but for an insight into how snug courtyard houses could be.

Song Qingling's residence

On the northern shore of Houhai, **Song Qingling's** former **residence** at no. 46 Houhai Beiyan (Tues–Sun 9am–4.30pm; ¥20) is another Qing mansion, with an agreeable, spacious garden. The wife of Sun Yatsen, who was leader of the short-lived republic that followed the collapse of imperial China (see p.172), Song commands great respect in China, and the exhibition inside details her busy life. It's all pretty dry, but check out the revolver Sun Yatsen – obviously not a great romantic – gave his wife as a wedding gift.

More interesting is the interior, which gives a glimpse of a typical Chinese mansion from the beginning of the twentieth century – all the furnishings are pretty much as they were when she died, and her personal effects, including letters and cutlery, are on display. It's not much of a diversion from here to head west to the Xu Beihong Museum (see below), about 1km from Deshengmennei Dajie.

The Drum and Bell towers

The formidable two-storey **Gulou** (**Drum Tower**; daily 9am–4.30pm; ¥10), a squat, fifteenth-century Ming creation, sits at the eastern end of Gulou Xi Dajie, about 1km southeast of the Song Qingling residence. In every city in China, drums like these were banged to mark the hours of the day, and to call imperial officials to meetings. Nowadays, every half-hour between 10am and noon and from 2pm to 4pm a troupe of drummers in traditional costume whack cheerfully away at the giant drums inside. They're not, to be blunt, terribly artful, but it's still an impressive sight.

The building's twin, the **Zhonglou** (**Bell Tower**; same times and prices), at the other end of the small plaza, was originally Ming. Destroyed by fire and rebuilt in the eighteenth century, it still has its original iron bell which, until 1924, was rung every evening at 7pm to give an indication of the time.

It's easy to reach the lakes from the towers: take the first *hutong* you see on the right as you walk south along Di'anmenwai Dajie from the Drum Tower, then turn left for Yinding Bridge.

Xu Beihong Museum

Just outside the quarter of *hutongs*, but easily combined with a visit to the Shicha lakes, the **Xu Beihong Museum** at 53 Xinjiekou Bei Dajie (Tues–Sun 9–11am & 1.30–4.30pm; ¥5) is 500m south of the Jishuitan subway stop and definitely worth visiting. The son of a wandering portraitist, Xu Beihong (1895–1953) did for Chinese art what his contemporary Lu Xun did for literature – modernise an atrophied tradition. Xu had to look after his entire family from the age of 17 after his father died, and spent much of his early life labouring in semi-destitution and obscurity before receiving the acclaim he deserved. His extraordinary talent is well in evidence here in seven halls, which display a huge collection of his works. These include many ink paintings of horses, for which he was most famous, and Western-style oil paintings, which he produced while studying in France (and that are now regarded as his weakest works); the large-scale allegorical images also on display allude to tumultuous events in modern Chinese history. However, the pictures it's easiest to respond to are his delightful sketches and studies, in ink and pencil, often of his infant son.

Nanluogu Xiang

There aren't, to be frank, too many streets in Beijing that could be called appealing, so this north-south *hutong* is a little oasis. Dotted with laid-back cafés, boutiques and restaurants, it has become a playground for the city's *bobos* (bourgeois-bohemians). Still, there are enough open-air mahjong games, rickety mom and pop stores, and old men sitting out with their caged birds to maintain that ramshackle, backstreet Beijing charm. If there seem to be a surfeit of bright and beautiful young things, that's because of the drama school just around the corner. All in all, it's a great place to idle over a capuccino; *Xiao Xin's* (see p.141) is a recommended café venue. For a meal, try *Fish Nation* for English grub, *Saveurs* for Korean or the *Drum and Gong* for Sichuan (see p.144). At the north end of the street the grungy rock venue, *Mao's* (see p.156) is a good place to sample the live music scene. If you want to stay in the area, head for the *Downtown Backpackers*, or the upmarket *Lusongyuan* (see p.133).

Yonghe Gong and around

Though it is a little touristy, **Yonghe Gong** is well worth a visit (daily 9am–5pm; ¥25) – you won't see many bolder or brasher temples than this, built towards the end of the seventeenth century to be the residence of Prince Yin Zhen. In 1723, when the prince became Emperor Yong Zheng and moved into the Forbidden City, the temple was retiled in imperial yellow and restricted thereafter to religious use. It became a lamasery in 1744, housing monks from Tibet and Inner Mongolia. The temple has supervised the election of the Mongolian Living Buddha (the spiritual head of Mongolian Lamaism), who was chosen by drawing lots out of a gold urn. After the civil war in 1949, Yonghe Gong was declared a national monument and closed for the following thirty years. Remarkably, it escaped the ravages of the Cultural Revolution (see p.174), when most of the city's religious structures were destroyed or turned into factories and warehouses.

The temple couldn't be easier to reach; it's right next to the Yonghe Gong subway stop. There are five main **prayer halls**, arranged in a line from south to north, and numerous side buildings housing *bodhisattva* statues and paintings, where monks study scripture, astronomy and medicine. Visitors are free to wander through the prayer halls and pretty, ornamental gardens, the experience largely an aesthetic rather than a spiritual one nowadays. As well as the amazingly intricate mandalas hanging in side halls, the temple contains some notable statuary. The statues in the third hall, the **Pavilion of Eternal Happiness**, are *nandikesvras*, representations of Buddha having sex. Once used to educate emperor's sons, the statues are now completely covered by drapes. The chamber behind, the **Hall of the Wheel of Law**, has a gilded bronze statue of Gelugpa, the founder of the Yellow Hats (the largest sect within Tibetan Buddhism) and paintings which depict his life, while the thrones at its side are for the Dalai Lama (each holder of the post used to come here to teach). In the last, grandest hall, the **Wanfu Pavilion**, stands an eighteen-metre-high statue of the Maitreya Buddha, the world's largest carving made from a single piece of wood – in this case, the trunk of a Tibetan sandalwood tree. Gazing serenely out, the giant reddish-orange figure looms over you; details, such as his jewellery and the foliage fringing his shoulders, are beautifully carved. It took three years for the statue, a gift to Emperor Qianlong from the seventh Dalai Lama, to complete its passage to Beijing.

The lamasery also functions as an active Tibetan Buddhist centre. It's used basically for propaganda purposes, to show that China is guaranteeing and respecting the religious freedom of minorities. Nonetheless, it's questionable how genuine the monks you see wandering around are; at best, they're state-approved. After all, this was where the Chinese state's choice for Panchen Lama – the Tibetan spiritual leader, second only to the Dalai Lama in rank – was officially sworn in, in 1995. Just prior to that, the Dalai Lama's own choice for the post, the then 6-year-old Gedhum Choekyi Nyima, had "disappeared" – neither he nor his family have been heard of since.

If the temple leaves you hungry for more things Tibetan, visit the *Makye Ame* restaurant (see p.143).

Kong Miao

On the west side of Yonghegong Dajie, opposite the alley by which you enter Yonghe Gong, is a quiet *hutong* lined with shops selling incense, images and tapes of religious music. Down the alley and on the right, on Guozijian Dajie, **Kong Miao** (daily 8.30am–5pm; ¥10) is as restrained as the Yonghe Gong is gaudy. One of the best things to do here is sit on a bench in the peaceful courtyard among the ancient, twisted trees, and enjoy the silence, and there are also plenty of artefacts to seek out.

The dark main hall is the **museum**, holding incense burners and musical instruments that the souvenir vendors will play on the slightest pretext. Another, new museum in the side hall to the north holds a diverse range of objects – the Tang pottery, which includes images of pointy-faced foreigners, is the most diverting.

Ditan Park

Just 100m north of Yonghe Gong is **Ditan Park** (daily 6am–9pm), the northern member in the imperial city's original quartet of four parks (see p.70). As befits the park's name (*dì* means "ground" or "earth"), this was where the emperor once performed sacrifices to the earth god using using the huge, tiered stone platform in

---

Confucius

Confucius was born in 552 BC into a declining aristocratic family in an age of petty kingdoms where life was blighted by constant war and feuding. An itinerant scholar, he observed that life would be much improved if people behaved decently, and he wandered from court to court teaching adherence to a set of moral and social values designed to bring the citizens and the government together in harmony. Ritual and propriety were the system's central values, and great emphasis was placed on the five **"Confucian virtues"**: benevolence, righteousness, propriety, wisdom and trustworthiness. An arch-traditionalist, he believed that society required strict hierarchies and total obedience: a son should obey his father, a wife her husband, and a subject his ruler.

Nobody paid Confucius much attention during his lifetime, and he died in obscurity. But during the Han dynasty, six hundred years later, **Confucianism** became institutionalized, underscoring a hierarchical system of administration that prevailed for the next two thousand years. Seeing that its precepts sat well with a feudal society, rulers turned Confucianism into the state religion, and Confucius became worshipped as a deity. Subsequently, officials were appointed on the basis of their knowledge of the Confucian texts, which they studied for half their lives.

The great sage only fell from official favour in the twentieth century with the rise of the egalitarian communists, and today there are no functioning Confucian temples left in China. Ironically, those temples that have become museums or libraries have returned to a vision of the importance of **learning**, which is perhaps closer to the heart of the Confucian system than ritual and worship.

the park's northwest corner as an altar. A small museum (¥5) next to it holds the emperor's sedan chair – covered, of course, so that no commoner could glimpse the divine presence on his journey here. Wandering among the trees is probably the most diverting way to spend time here; at weekends the place is busy with old folk playing croquet, kids playing fishing games and *tai ji* practitioners hugging trees and the like. The park is at its liveliest during Chinese New Year, when it hosts a temple fair.

Around Fuchengmennei Dajie

East of Fuchengmen subway stop, **Fuchengmennei Dajie** is rather a pleasant street, lined with trees and equipped with a diverse range of shops, and a few sights all within walking distance of each other. Accessed through an alley off Fuchengmennei Dajie, the massive white dagoba of the **Baita Si** (daily 9am–5pm; ¥10) is visible from afar, rising over the rooftops of the labyrinth of *hutongs* that surround it. Shaped like an upturned bowl with an inverted ice-cream cone on top, the 35-metre-high dagoba, designed by a Nepalese architect, was built in the Yuan dynasty. It's a popular spot with Buddhist pilgrims, who ritually circle it clockwise. The temple is worth visiting simply for the collection of thousands of small statues of Buddha – mostly Tibetan – housed in one of its halls, very impressive en masse. Another hall holds bronze *luohans* (Buddha's original group of disciples), including one with a beak; small bronze Buddhas; and other, outlandish Lamaist figures. The silk and velvet priestly garments on display here were unearthed from under the dagoba in 1978. A shop beside it sells religious curios, such as Buddha images printed on dried leaves.

Nearly a kilometre east along Fuchengmennei Dajie is the **Guangji Si** (daily; free), headquarters of China's Buddhist Association and a working Buddhist temple with an important collection of painting and sculpture. Visitors can look around, though only academics with a specialist interest in the art are normally allowed to see the collection.

Lu Xun Museum

Just east of the giant Fuchengmen Bei Dajie intersection, Xisantiao Hutong leads north off Fuchengmennei Dajie to the **Lu Xun Museum** (Tues–Sun 9am–4pm; ¥10). A large and extensively renovated courtyard house, this was where Lu Xun (1881–1936), widely accepted as the greatest Chinese writer of the modern era, once lived. He gave up a promising career in medicine to write books, with the aim, so he declared, of curing social ills with his pithy, satirical stories. One of the most appealing and accessible of his tales is *The True Story of Ah Q*, a lively tragi-comedy written in the plain style he favoured as an alternative to the complex classical language of the era. Set in 1911, during the inception of the ill-fated republic, it tells the life story of a worthless peasant, Ah Q, who stumbles from disaster to disaster, believing each outcome to be a triumph. He epitomized every character flaw of the Chinese race, as seen by his creator; Ah Q dreams of revolution and ends up being executed, having understood nothing.

As someone who abhorred pomp, Lu Xun might feel a little uneasy in his house nowadays. His possessions have been preserved like treasured relics, giving a good idea of what Chinese interiors looked like at the beginning of the twentieth century, and there's a photo exhibition lauding his achievements. Unfortunately there are no English captions, though a bookshop on the west side of the compound sells English translations of his work.

The zoo and around

The area around **Xizhimen** is one of the city's transport hubs, and you're likely to pass through it on your way to the Summer Palaces or Haidian. If you head west from Xizhimen subway stop (buses #107 and #904, among others, pass by en route to Zizhuyuan Park), over the gargantuan traffic intersection, the first place of interest you come to on Xizhimenwai Dajie is the **Beijing Exhibition Centre,** easily distinguishable by its slim, star-topped spire. It's certainly worth inspection, and will stir anyone with a sense of historical irony. Built by the Russians in 1954, it's by far the city's best overtly communist construction, a work of grandiose Socialist Realism with great details, including heroic workers atop columns carved with acorns. Now it's badly maintained – the electric chandeliers are unlit and the escalators flanking the grand staircases lie still – and is used, in thoughtless affront, for the most banal forms of capitalism: the arches of the colonnade outside are hung with billboards and its twelve magnificent, cavernous halls host tacky clothes markets. The road on the east side leads to the dock for boats to the Summer Palace (see p.104). Head up the alley on the west side and you'll come to the city's oldest Western restaurant, the *Moscow* – the food is mediocre, but check out the grand decor if you're passing.

Next along Xizhimenwai Dajie, the **zoo** (daily 7.30am–5.30pm; ¥15), is worth visiting for the panda house (¥5). Here you can join the queues to have your photo taken sitting astride a plastic replica of the creature, then push your way through to glimpse the living variety – kept in relatively palatial quarters and familiar through the much-publicized export of the animals to overseas zoos for mating purposes. While the pandas lie on their backs in their luxury pad, waving their legs in the air, other animals, less cute or less endangered, slink, pace or flap around their miserable cells. However, the new **Beijing Aquarium** (adults ¥100, children ¥50, children under 1.2m free; @www.bj-sea.com) in the northwest corner of the compound, is surprisingly good. As well as thousands of varieties of fish, including sharks, it has a **dolphin show** every day at 10am and 2.30pm.

Past the zoo, head north up Baishiqiao Lu, take the first right and follow the canal, and ten minutes' walk will bring you to the **Wuta Si** (daily 9am–4.30pm; ¥10). The central hall is radically different from any other sacred building you'll see in the capital. Completed in 1424, it's a stone cube decorated on the outside with reliefs of animals, Sanskrit characters, and Buddha images – each has a different hand gesture – and topped with five layered, triangular spires. It's visibly Indian in influence, and is said to be based on a temple in Bodhgaya, where Buddha gained enlightenment. There are 87 steps to the top (¥5), where you can inspect the spire carvings at close quarters – including elephants and Buddhas, and, at the centre of the central spire, a pair of feet. The new halls behind the museum are home to statues of bulbous-eyed camels, docile-looking tigers, puppy-dog lions and the like, all collected from the spirit ways of tombs and long-destroyed temples. Outside is a line of seventeenth-century tombstones of Jesuit priests made in traditional Chinese style, with a turtle-like dragon at the base and text in Chinese and Latin.

From here it's a half-hour stroll following the river west back to Baishiqiao Lu, through the bamboo groves of **Zizhuyuan Park**, and out of the park's northwest exit to the **Wanshou Si** (daily 9am–4.30pm; ¥20). This Ming temple, a favourite of Cixi's, is now a small museum of ancient art, with five exhibition halls of Ming and Qing relics, mostly ceramics. There's nothing spectacular on view but it's worth a look if you are in the area. If you want to meet some locals, there's an "English corner" where students go to practise English.

6

The far northwest

T he northwest corner of the city is home to a cluster of attractions. The **Dazhong Si** (Great Bell Temple) and the pretty campus of **Beijing University** are worth a visit on the way to or from more alluring destinations, and the nearby districts of **Haidian** and **Zhongguancun** are known for hi-tech shopping and youth culture.

Yiheyuan, usually known in English as *the* **Summer Palace** (as opposed to Yuanmingyan, the old summer palace), is an excellent place to get away from the smog of the city, its grounds large enough to have an almost rural feel. This lavish imperial playground, once the private haunt of the notorious Empress Cixi, is today a lovely public park, two-thirds of which is taken up by Kunming Lake. During the hottest months of the year, the imperial court would decamp to this perfect location, the site surrounded by hills, cooled by the lake and sheltered by judicious use of garden landscaping.

Though it is rather eclipsed by its newer neighbour, **Yuanmingyuan**, also merits a visit, if only for the contrast, provided by the ruins. From here, it's not long by bus to Xiang Shan, the Botanical Gardens and other excursions to the west of Beijing – see p.115.

Dazhong Si

The **Dazhong Si** (Great Bell Temple; Tues–Sun 8am–4.30pm; ¥15) derives its name from the enormous bell hanging in the back; the temple halls now house one of Beijing's most interesting little exhibitions, showcasing several hundred bronze bells from temples all over the country. It's stuck out on Beisanhuan Lu, the north section of the third ring road, a long way from the centre; buses #302 and #367 go right past, or you can take the subway to Dazhong Si stop and walk 200m west. The best way to visit is on the way to or from the Summer Palace.

The bells here are considerable works of art, their surfaces enlivened with embossed texts in Chinese and Tibetan, abstract patterns, and images of storks and dragons. The odd, scaly, dragon-like creature shown perching on top of

Beijing University	北京大学	*běijīng dàxué*
Dazhong Si	大钟寺	*dàzhōng sì*
Haidian	海淀	*hǎidiàn*
Yiheyuan	颐和园	*yíhé yuán*
Yuanmingyuan	圆明园	*yuánmíng yuán*

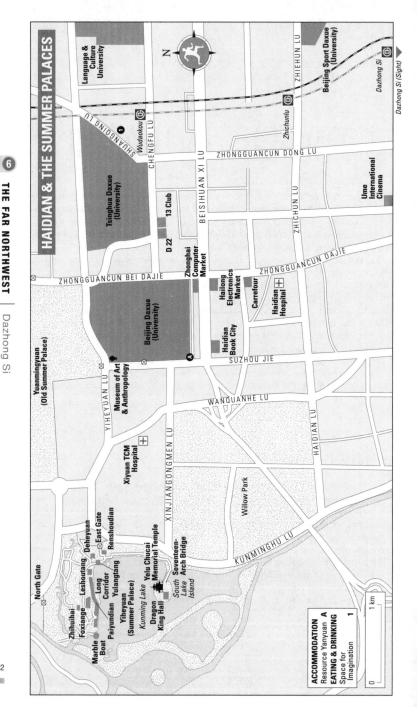

HAIDIAN & THE SUMMER PALACES

N

Language &
Culture
University

Tsinghua Daxue
(University)

13 Club

D 22

Zhonghai
Computer
Market

Hailong
Electronics
Market

Carrefour

Haidian Hospital

Haidian
Book City

Beijing Daxue
(University)

Museum of Art
& Anthropology

Yuanmingyuan
(Old Summer Palace)

Xiyuan TCM
Hospital

Beijing Sport Daxue
(University)

Dazhong Si (Sight)

Dazhong Si

Ume
International
Cinema

SHUANGQING LU

Wudaokou

CHENGFU LU

ZHIEHUN LU

ZHIHUN LU

Zhichunlu

ZHONGGUANCUN DONG LU

BEISIHUAN XI LU

ZHICHUN LU

ZHONGGUANCUN DAJIE

ZHONGGUANCUN BEI DAJIE

YIHEYUAN LU

SUZHOU JIE

WANQUANHE LU

XINJIANGONGMEN LU

HAIDIAN LU

Willow Park

KUNMINGHU LU

North Gate

Zhihuihai
Foxiange
Marble
Boat
Paiyundian

Leshoutang
Long
Corridor

Yulangtang

Yiheyuan
(Summer Palace)

Dragon
King Hall

Yelu Chucai
Memorial Temple

Deheyuan
East Gate
Renshoudian

South
Lake
Island

Seventeen-
Arch Bridge

Kunming Lake

ACCOMMODATION
Resource Yanyuan   A
EATING & DRINKING
Space for
Imagination   1

0   1 km

THE FAR NORTHWEST | Dazhong Si

6

102

each bell is a *pulao*, a legendary animal supposed to shriek when attacked by a whale (the wooden hammers used to strike the bells are carved to look like whales). The smallest bell here is the size of a goblet; the largest, a Ming creation called the King of Bells, is as tall as a two-storey house. Hanging in the back hall, it is, at fifty tonnes, the biggest and oldest surviving bell in the world, and can reputedly be heard up to 40km away. You can climb up to a platform above it to get a closer look at some of the 250,000 Chinese characters on its surface, and join visitors in trying to throw a coin into the small hole in the top. The method of its construction and the history of Chinese bell-making are explained by displays, with English captions, in side halls. The shape of Chinese bells dampens vibrations, so they only sound for a short time and can be effectively used as instruments: check out the audio tapes and CDs, which are on sale, of the bells in action.

Haidian

It's not an obvious tourist attraction – the only foreigners you're likely to see around here are students, and the area looks much like other parts of the city – but the **Haidian district** northwest of the Third Ring Road has a distinctive laidback atmosphere, courtesy of the local universities and the students, artists and intellectuals who have taken advantage of the area's low rents. You'll find plenty of internet cafés, and, on Zhongguancun Lu, a hi-tech zone of **computer shops** for tempting, if often warranty-free, bargains (see p.164). You can get here using Wudaokou subway stop or on bus #320 from Xi Zhan or bus #332 from the zoo.

In the north of the area, on the way to the Summer Palace, you'll pass **Beijing Daxue** (Beida, as it's referred to colloquially), the most prestigious **university** in China, with a pleasant campus – old buildings and quiet, well-maintained grounds make it nicer than most of the city's parks. Bring your passport if you want to poke around, as you may be required to fill out a visitor's form by the guard at the gate. Originally established and administered by Americans at the beginning of the twentieth century, the university stood on the hill in Jingshan Park before moving to its present site in 1953. Now busy with new contingents of students from the West, it was half-deserted during the Cultural Revolution (see p.174), when students and teachers alike, regarded as suspiciously liberal, were dispersed for "re-education". Later, in 1975–6, Beida was the power base of the radical left in their campaign against Deng Xiaoping, the pragmatist who was in control of the day-to-day running of the Communist Party's Central Committee during Mao's twilight years. The university's intake suffered when new students were required to spend a year learning Party dogma after 1989; now it's once again a centre for challenging political thought. The **lake** is a popular place to skate in the winter – skates can be hired for ¥10 an hour.

Just inside the university west gate you'll find the diverting Arthur M. Sackler **Museum of Art and Anthropology** (daily 9.30am–4pm; ¥20; ⓦwww.sackler. org/china/amschina.htm). Used as a teaching museum, it holds a well-presented permanent collection of ceramics and tools from prehistory to the present, with English captions throughout; check the website for details of frequent temporary exhibitions.

You can meet China's new **intellectuals** by hanging out in the bars clustered around the university's gates. The Wudaokou district nearby is regarded as the home of Beijing's alternative culture; it's a good place to catch the local rock bands, for example. See "Entertainment and art", p.155, for more on Haidian.

Yuanmingyuan

Beijing's original summer palace, the **Yuanmingyuan** (daily 9am–6pm; ¥15) was built by the Qing Emperor Kangxi in the early eighteenth century. Once nicknamed China's Versailles for its elegant, European-influenced design, the palace boasted the largest royal gardens in the world, containing some two hundred pavilions and temples set around a series of lakes and natural springs. Today there is precious little left; in 1860, the entire complex was burnt and destroyed by British and French troops, who were ordered by the Earl of Elgin to make the imperial court "see reason" during the Opium Wars (see p.172). The troops had previously spent twelve days looting the imperial treasures, many of which found their way to the Louvre and British Museum. This unedifying history is described in inflammatory terms on signs all over the park and it's a favoured site for nationalists to renew their ardour.

The site is easily accessible on bus #375 from Xizhimen subway stop, or #322 from the zoo, but probably the quickest way here is to take the subway to Wudaokou, then bus #331 or #375. If you happen to be visiting Beijing University (see p.103), the site is only a twenty-minute walk north. There are actually three parks here, the Yuanmingyuan (Park of Perfection and Brightness), Wanchunyuan (Park of Ten Thousand Springs) and Changchunyuan (Park of Everlasting Spring), all centred around the lake, Fuhai (Sea of Happiness). The best-preserved structures are the fountain and the **Hall of Tranquillity** in the northeastern section. The stone and marble fragments hint at how fascinating the original must once have been, with its marriage of European Rococo decoration and Chinese motifs.

Yiheyuan (Summer Palace)

There have been imperial summer pavilions at **Yiheyuan** (daily 8am–7pm, buildings close at 4pm; ¥40, plus additional charges of ¥5–10 to enter some buildings) since the eleventh century, although the present park layout is essentially eighteenth-century, created by the Manchu Emperor Qianlong. However, the key character associated with the palace is the **Dowager Empress Cixi** (see p.106), who ruled over the fast-disintegrating Chinese empire from 1861 until her death in 1908. Yiheyuan was very much her pleasure ground; it was she who built the palaces here in 1888 after Yuanmingyuan was destroyed, and determinedly restored them after another bout of European aggression in 1900.

The palace buildings, many connected by a suitably majestic gallery, are built on and around **Wanshou Shan** (Longevity Hill), north of the lake and west of the main gate. Many of these edifices are intimately linked with Cixi – anecdotes about whom are the stock output of the numerous tour guides – but to enjoy the site, you need know very little of its history: like Beihai (see p.92), the park, its lake and pavilions form a startling visual array, akin to a traditional Chinese landscape painting brought to life.

▲ Yiheyuan

The fastest route to Yiheyuan is via subway to Wudaokou, then a taxi (¥10) or bus #375 the rest of the way. Alternatively, bus #322 from the zoo terminates here; or you could take tourist bus #808 from Qianmen. There's also a **boat service** (daily 9am–3pm, leaving when full; 1hr; ¥40 one-way, ¥70 return) to Yiheyuan taking the old imperial approach, along the now dredged and prettified Long River; the trip embarks from a new dock at the back of the Exhibition Centre (see p.100). Your vessel is either one of the large, dragon-shaped cruisers or a smaller speedboat holding four people, passing the Wuta Si, Zizhuyuan Park, and a number of attractive bridges and willow groves en route.

The palace compound

The East Gate, by which most visitors enter, and where buses stop, is overlooked by the main palace compound. A path leads from the gate, past several halls (all signposted in English), to the lakeside. The strange bronze animal in the first courtyard is a *xuanni* or *kylin*, with the head of a dragon, deer antlers, a lion's tail and ox hooves. It was said to be able to detect disloyal subjects. The building behind is the **Renshoudian** (Hall of Benevolence and Longevity), a majestic, multi-eaved hall where the empress and her predecessors gave audience; it retains much of its original nineteenth-century furniture, including an imposing red sandalwood throne carved with nine dragons and flanked by peacock feather fans. The inscription on the tablet above reads "Benevolence in rule leads to long life". Look out, too, for the superbly well-made basket of flowers studded with precious stones.

A little way further along the main path, to the right, the **Deheyuan** (Palace of Virtue and Harmony) is dominated by a three-storey theatre, complete with trap doors in the stage for surprise appearances and disappearances by the actors. Theatre was one of Cixi's main passions – she even took part in performances sometimes, playing the role of Guanyin, the goddess of mercy. Today some of the halls function as a museum of theatre, with displays of costumes, props and waxworks of Cixi and attendants. The most unusual exhibit is a vintage Mercedes-Benz, a gift to the warlord Yuan Shikai (see p.172) in the early twentieth century and the first car to appear in China.

The next major building along the path is the lakeside **Yulangtang** (Jade Waves Palace). This is where the Emperor Guangxu, then still a minor, was kept in captivity for ten years while Cixi exercised his powers. A pair of decorative rocks in the front courtyard, supposed to resemble a mother and her son, were put there by Cixi to chastise Guangxu for insufficient filiality. The main hall contains a tablet of Cixi's calligraphy reading "The magnificent palace inspires everlasting moral integrity". One character has a stroke missing; apparently no one dared tell her.

North of here, behind Renshoudian, are Cixi's private quarters, three large courtyards connected by a winding gallery. The largest, the **Leshoutang** (Hall of Joy and Longevity), houses Cixi's hardwood throne. The large table in the centre of the main hall was where she took her infamous meals of 128 courses. The chandeliers were China's first electric lights, installed in 1903 and powered by the palace's own generator.

The Dowager Empress Cixi

The notorious Cixi entered the imperial palace at 15 as the **Emperor Xianfeng's concubine**, quickly becoming his favourite and bearing him a son. When the emperor died in 1861 she became regent, ruling in place of her infant boy. For the next 35 years she, in effect, ruled China, displaying a mastery of intrigue and court politics. When her son died of syphilis, she installed another puppet infant, her nephew, and retained her authority. Her fondness for extravagant gestures (every year she had ten thousand caged birds released on her birthday) drained the state's coffers, and her deeply conservative policies were inappropriate for a time when the nation was calling for reform.

With foreign powers taking great chunks out of China's borders on and off during the nineteenth century, Cixi was moved to respond in a typically misguided fashion. Impressed by the claims of the xenophobic **Boxer Movement** (whose Chinese title translated as "Righteous and Harmonious Fists") that their members were invulnerable to bullets, in 1899 Cixi let them loose on all the foreigners in China. The Boxers laid siege to the foreign legation's compound in Beijing for nearly two months before a European expeditionary force arrived and, predictably, slaughtered the agitators. Cixi and her nephew, the emperor, only escaped the subsequent rout of the capital by disguising themselves as peasants and fleeing the city. On her return, Cixi clung on to power, attempting to delay the inevitable fall of the dynasty. One of her last acts, the day before she died in 1908, was to oversee the murder of her puppet emperor.

The north shore of Kunming Lake

From Leshoutang, the **Long Corridor** runs to the northwest **corner** of **Kunming Lake**. Flanked by various temples and pavilions, the corridor is actually a seven-hundred-metre covered way, its inside walls painted with more than eight thousand restored images of birds, flowers, landscapes and scenes from history and mythology. Near the west end of the corridor is Cixi's ultimate flight of fancy, a magnificent lakeside pavilion in the form of a 36-metre-long **marble boat**, boasting two decks. Completed by Cixi using funds intended for the Chinese navy, it was regarded by her acolytes as a characteristically witty and defiant snub to her detractors. Her misappropriations helped speed the empire's decline, with China suffering heavy naval defeats during the 1895 war with Japan. Close to the marble boat is a jetty – the tourist focus of this part of the site – with rowing boats for hire (see box above).

Wanshou Shan

About halfway down the Long Corridor you'll see an archway and a path that leads uphill away from the lake. Head up the path and through two gates to the **Paiyundian** (Cloud Dispelling Hall), which was used by Cixi as a venue for her infamously extravagant birthday parties. The elegant objects on display here are twentieth-birthday presents to her from high officials (the rather flattering oil painting of her was a present from the American artist Hubert Vos). The largest building here, near the top of the hill, is the **Foxiangge** (Tower of Buddhist Incense), a charming three-storey octagonal pagoda built in 1750. It commands a panoramic view of the whole park and, deservedly, the area around it is a popular picnic spot.

The **Zhihuihai** (Sea of Wisdom) **hall**, on top of the hill, is strikingly different in style from the other buildings: there's not a single beam or column, and it sis tiled in green and yellow ceramic tiles and dotted with niches holding Buddha statues. At the foot of the hill on the far (north) side lies a souvenir market and the little-visited but very attractive back lake. Walk along the side of this lake for half a kilometre and you arrive at the **Garden of Harmonious Interests,** a pretty collection of lotus-filled ponds and pavilions connected by bridges. Cixi used to fish from the large central pavilion; to keep her sweet, eunuchs dived in and attached fish to her hook. The bridge up to the pavilion is called "Know the Fish Bridge" after an argument that took place here between two Ming dynasty philosophers: one declared that the fish he could see were happy; the other snorted, "How could you know? You're not a fish", whereupon the first countered, "You're not me, so how do you know I don't know?"

The south of the park

It's a pleasant fifteen-minute walk to the southern part of Kunming Lake, where the scenery is wilder and the crowds thinner. Should you need a destination, the main attraction to head for is the white **seventeen-arch bridge**, 150m long and topped with 544 cute, vaguely canine lions, each with a slightly different posture. The bridge leads to **South Lake Island**, where Qianlong used to review his navy, and which holds a brace of fine halls, most striking of which is the **Yelu Chucai Memorial Temple.** Yelu, an adviser to Genghis Khan during the Yuan dynasty, is entombed next to the temple, in the company of his wives and concubines, slaughtered for the occasion. The small, colourful **Dragon King Hall** nearby was used to pray for rain.

Around Beijing

Some great destinations, offering both countryside and culture, lie within a few hours of the capital. Most compelling is the **Great Wall**, whose remains, either crumbling or spruced up, can be seen in a number of places in the hills a few hours north and east of the city. The hilly, wooded landscape to the **west of Beijing,** called the **Western Hills,** is the most attractive countryside in the city's vicinity, and easily accessible from the centre. The **Botanical Gardens**, **Xiangshan Park** and **Badachu** – the last of these a collection of eight temples – make for an excellent day retreat; a little further out, the striking **Fahai, Tanzhe** and **Jietai temples** stand in superb rural isolation. All are at their quietest and best on weekdays.

Though less scenic than the Western Hills, the area **north of the city** contains a couple of sights of particular natural beauty, as well as the vast **Aviation Museum** and the much-visited **Ming Tombs**. Unfortunately though, these places are so spread out that it's impractical to visit more than one in a day.

The Great Wall

This is a Great Wall and only a great people with a great past could have a great wall and such a great people with such a great wall will surely have a great future.

Richard M. Nixon

The practice of building walls along China's northern frontier began in the fifth century BC, and continued until the sixteenth century. Over time, the discontinuous array of fortifications and ramparts came to be known as **Wan Li Changcheng** (literally, "Long Wall of Ten Thousand Li" – *li* being a Chinese measure of distance roughly equal to 500m), or the Great Wall to English speakers. Stretching from Shanhaiguan, where the wall meets the sea, to Jiayuguan Pass in the Gobi Desert, it's an astonishing civil engineering project.

Even the most-visited section at **Badaling**, constantly overrun by Chinese and foreign tourists, is still easily one of China's most spectacular sights. The section at **Mutianyu** is somewhat less crowded; distant **Simatai** much less so, and far more beautiful. To see the wall in all its crumbly glory, head out to **Jingshanling** or **Huanghua**, as yet largely untouched by development. For other trips to unreconstructed sections, check out @www.wildwall.com or contact Beijing Hikers (see p.166).

Aviation Museum	航空博物馆	*hángkōng bówùguǎn*
Badachu	八大处	*bādà chù*
Biyun Si	碧云寺	*bìyún sì*
Botanical Gardens	植物园	*zhíwù yuán*
Fahai Si	法海寺	*fǎhǎi sì*
Jietai Si	戒台寺	*jiètái sì*
Longqing Gorge	龙庆峡	*lóngqìng xiá*
Ming Tombs	十三陵	*shísān líng*
Miyun (Reservoir)	密云水库	*mìyún shuǐkù*
Tanzhe Si	潭柘寺	*tánzhē sì*
Western Hills	西山	*xī shān*
Wofo Si	卧佛寺	*wòfó sì*
Xiang Shan Park	香山公园	*xiāngshān gōngyuán*
Yanqing	延庆	*yánqìng*
Great Wall	长城	*chángchéng*
Badaling	八达岭	*bādálǐng*
Huairou	怀柔	*huáiróu*
Huanghua Great Wall	黄花长城	*huánghuā chángchéng*
Jinshanling Great Wall	金山岭长城	*jīnshānlǐng chángchéng*
Juyongguan Great Wall	居庸关长城	*jūyōngguān chángchéng*
Mutianyu	慕田峪	*mùtián yù*
Simatai	司马台	*sīmǎ tái*

Some history

Since the earliest times, the Chinese walled their cities and, during the Warring States period (around the fifth century BC), simply extended the concept by using walls to separate rival territories. The **Great Wall's origins** lie in these fractured lines of fortifications and in the vision of the first Emperor Qin Shi Huang, who, having unified the empire in the third century BC, joined and extended the sections to form one fairly continuous defence against barbarians. Under subsequent dynasties, whenever insularity rather than engagement drove foreign policy, the wall continued to be maintained and, in response to shifting regional threats, grew and changed course. It lost importance under the Tang, when borders were extended north, well beyond it. The Tang was in any case an outward-looking dynasty that kept the barbarians in check far more cheaply, by fostering trade and internal divisions. With the emergence of the insular Ming, however, the wall's upkeep again became a priority, and from the fourteenth to the sixteenth century, military technicians worked on its reconstruction.

The seven-metre-high, seven-metre-thick wall, with its 25,000 battlements, served to bolster Ming sovereignty, as it restricted the movement of the nomadic peoples of the distant, non-Han minority regions, preventing plundering raids. Signals made by gunpowder blasts, flags and smoke swiftly sent news of enemy movements to the capital: in the late sixteenth century, a couple of huge Mongol invasions were repelled, at Jinshanling and Badaling.

But a wall is only as strong as its guards, and by the seventeenth century the Ming royal house was corrupt and its armies weak; the wall was little hinderance to the invading Manchus, who, after they had established their own dynasty (the Qing), let the wall fall into disrepair. Slowly it crumbled away, useful only as a source of building material – recent demolitions of old *hutongs* in Beijing have turned up bricks from the wall, marked with the imperial seal.

Today, this great monument to state paranoia is big business – the restored sections are besieged daily by rampaging hordes of tourists – and is touted by the government as a source of national pride. Its image adorns all manner of products, from wine to cigarettes, and is even used – surely rather inappropriately – on visa stickers.

Badaling and Juyong Pass

The best-known section of the wall is at **Badaling**, 70km northwest of Beijing (daily 8am–4.30pm; ¥45). It was the first section to be restored (in 1957) and opened up to tourists. Here the wall is 6m wide, with regularly spaced watchtowers dating from the Ming dynasty. It follows the highest contours of a steep range of hills, forming a formidable defence, such that this section was never attacked directly but instead taken by sweeping around from the side after a breach was made in the weaker, low-lying sections.

Badaling may be the easiest part of the wall to get to from Beijing, but it's also the most packaged. At the entrance, a giant tourist circus – a plethora of restaurants and souvenir stalls – greets you. As you ascend to the wall, you pass a train museum (¥5), a cable car (¥30) and the **Great Wall Museum** (included in the main ticket). The wall museum, with plenty of aerial photos, models and construction tools, is worth a browse, though it's more useful visited on the way down.

Once you're up on the wall, flanked by guardrails, it's hard to feel that there's anything genuine about the experience. Indeed, the wall itself is hardly original here, as the "restorers" basically rebuilt it wholesale on the ancient foundations. To get the best out of this part of the wall you need to walk – you'll quickly lose the crowds and, generally, things get better the further you go. You come to unreconstructed sections after heading 1km north (left) or 2km south (right). That's as far as you are allowed to go; guards posted here will turn you back.

Country retreats

For the ultimate in **luxury breaks**, visit **Commune** (☎010/81181888; ⓦwww.communebythegreatwall.com; ⓐ), a "lifestyle retreat" at Shuiguan, at the base of the Great Wall and just east off the Badaling Expressway. Each of the eleven striking buildings was designed by a different architect (the complex won an architectural award at the 2002 Venice Biennale) and is run as a small boutique hotel. If you can't afford their rates – it's extremely expensive at more than US$800 a night – you can get a tour of the complex for ¥120, or pop in for lunch (around ¥400). As a result of poor occupancy rates, more affordable accommodation is now being added.

The **Goose and Duck Ranch** (☎010/65381691; ⓦwww.gdclub.net.cn; ⓖ–ⓐ), in Qiaozi near Hauirou, and run by the bar of the same name (see p.148), is rather more sensibly priced, with cabins starting at ¥300. It's a chirpy family holiday camp, with plenty of outdoor purusits on offer, including archery, go-karting and horseback riding. Their all inclusive weekend getaways (¥500 per person per day) are popular and convenient – turn up at the bar and they'll look after you from there. You'll have to book three days in advance.

For something much more restful, stay at the **Red Capital Ranch** (☎010/84018886; ⓦwww.redcapitalclub.com.cn/ranch; ⓐ), run by the Red Capital Club (see p.135). It's an idyllic boutique eco-lodge set in attractive countryside, a short walk from the Great Wall and two hours north of the city. Each of the ten traditional courtyard buildings was constructed from local materials; reckon on ¥1500 per person per night, including breakfast.

Practicalities

As well as CITS, all the more expensive Beijing hotels (and a few of the cheaper ones) run **tours** to Badaling, usually with a trip to the Ming Tombs thrown in. If you come with a tour you'll arrive in the early afternoon, when the place is at its busiest, spend an hour or two at the wall, then return, which really gives you little time for anything except the most cursory of jaunts and the purchase of an "I climbed the Great Wall" T-shirt. It's just as easy, and cheaper, to travel under your own steam. The easiest way to get here is on bus #919 from Deshengmen (a 2min walk east from Jishuitan subway stop) – there's an ordinary service (2hr; ¥3) and a much quicker a/c luxury bus (1hr; ¥10). Or there are plenty of tourist buses (outward journeys daily 6–10am; every 20min; ¥36–50): routes #1, #3 and #5 leave from Qianmen, #2 from the #103 terminus at Beijing Zhan, and #4 from outside the zoo. The journey to Badaling on one of these takes about an hour and a half, and the buses visit the Ming Tombs (see p.118) on the way back. Returning to Beijing shouldn't be a problem, as tourist buses run until about 6pm.

Juyong Pass

The closest section to Beijing, the wall at **Juyong Pass** (daily 8am–5pm; ¥45), only fifteen minutes' bus ride south of the Badaling section, has been rather over-restored by enthusiastic builders. That said, it's not too popular, so not crowded, and is easily reached on the ordinary bus #919 (not the luxury version) from Deshengmen bus station, or on tourist bus #1 from Qianmen. Strategically, this was an important stretch, guarding the way to the capital, only 50km away. From the two-storey gate, the wall climbs steeply in both directions, passing through modern copies of the mostly Ming fortifications. The most interesting structure, and one of the few genuinely old ones, is the intricately carved stone base of a long-vanished stupa just beyond here. Access to unreconstructed sections is blocked, but you can walk for about an hour in either direction.

Mutianyu

A two-kilometre section, the **Mutianyu Great Wall**, 90km northeast of the city (daily 8am–5pm; ¥35), is more appealing to most foreign visitors than Badaling, as it has rather fewer tourist trappings. Passing along a ridge through some lush, undulating hills, this part of the wall is well endowed with guard towers, built in 1368 and renovated in 1983.

From the entrance, steep steps lead up to the wall; you can get a cable car up (¥35) though it's not far to walk. The stretch of wall you can walk here is about 3km long (barriers in both directions stop you continuing any further). The atmospheric *Mutianyu Great Wall Guesthouse* (☎010/69626867; ❸), situated in a reconstructed watchtower 500m before the eastern barrier, is a good place for a quiet overnight stay, though be aware it has no plumbing. Call ahead to book.

Minibuses for Mutianyu leave from Dongzhimen and Xizhimen stations every morning (¥10 one way), but they take in photo stops and dubious amusement parks along the way. Alternatively, you can get tourist bus #6 (mid-April to mid-Oct, weekends only, outward journeys daily 7–8.30am; ¥50) from the south cathedral, near Xuanwumen subway stop, or the #42 bus station, just south of Dongsi Shitiao subway stop; they'll wait around at the site for an hour or two before heading back to Beijing. Returning by other means shouldn't be a hassle, provided you do so before 6pm; plenty of minibuses wait in the car park to take people back to the city. If you can't find a minibus back to Beijing, get one to the town of **Huairou**, from where you can get regular bus #916 back to the capital – the last bus leaves at 6.30pm.

Capital
cuisine

Forget spice, oil and rice; Beijing food is heavy and hearty, with steamed buns and noodles as a staple. It's delicious and nourishing, and fit for the harsh climate. The following are a selection of the capital's unmissable culinary delights, with recommended places to sample them.

Roasting the duck

Beijing duck

Succulent roast **duck** is Beijing's big hitter, and deservedly so. Locals love to debate the merits of convection roasters over peach-wood ovens and the like, and every venerable restaurant has a different preparation technique – but once it's been brought to your table and carved, the routine is always the same; slather dark tangy bean sauce onto pancakes, pop in a few scallions, add shreds of duck with your chopsticks, roll it up and prepare for the local taste sensation. Nothing is wasted; you finish off your meal with duck soup. Try it at *Lichun*, *Quanjude* or *Jiajingdu* restaurants.

Imperial cuisine

The royal birds' nest soup

Pity the poor emperor. At mealtimes he wasn't allowed to take more than one mouthful of any one dish, for fear that evidence of a preference would be of use to a poisoner. As a lowly citizen however, you are under no such compunction, and at places such as the *Fangshan* (see p.144) restaurant in Beihai Park and the *Red Capital Club* (see p.142), you can indulge in the **imperial cuisine** that originated in the Qing dynasty kitchens. As well as meticulously prepared dishes created with extravagant ingredients such as birds' nests and sharks' fins, imperial cuisine is noted for fish that's so fresh it's still flapping (it's all about keeping the nerves intact) and fine pastries such as pea-flour cakes and kidney bean-flour rolls. Thankfully, though, one element has been left out of all these dishes; imperial food always came with a strip of silver inside, as it was thought to turn black in the presence of poison.

Mongolian hotpot

Mongolian hotpot is Beijing's classic winter warmer, but makes for a fantastic communal meal at any time of year. The brass pot in the centre of the table has an outer rim around a chimney with a charcoal-burner underneath. Stock is boiled in the rim, and diners dip in slices of raw meat, vegetables, bean noodles, mushrooms and bean curd. Lamb is the traditional highlight, and it's sliced so finely it takes only a few seconds to cook up a slither between

Tucking into hotpot

your chopsticks. Shake to get rid of excess water, dunk into the sesame based dipping sauce, and it's ready to eat. *Dong Lai Shun Fan Zhuang* is a great place to try this, but there are hotpot restaurants all over town; just look for the steamed up windows.

A steamy breakfast

Beijing street snacks

Street snacks are the ultimate convenience food – cheap, tasty, available at all hours, and cooked in front of you in a few seconds.

Jiaozi are little dumplings of meat paste or vegetables, skilfully packaged in a thin skin of dough, and steamed or fried. They might seem unassuming but they constitute the heart of Chinese table culture, forming the staple of the family meal at Chinese New Year, partly as they are shaped like ingots – and so promise wealth for the coming months.

Savoury crêpes – *jianbing* – are by far the best breakfasts in the capital – and at ¥3, they're the cheapest, too.

Donghuamen Night Food market

Vendors put the whole thing together in a matter of seconds – first cooking up a pancake on a hotplate, then cracking an egg onto it, sprinkling cilantro and onion, adding a crunchy wedge of fried dough and a dash of bean paste, and finally folding the thing up while it's piping hot.

Street food vendors are common in the backstreets and the suburbs but rare in the centre. One great location to try street food is at the **Dong'anmen Night Market** (see p.140). Ignore the scorpions on sticks (strictly for the tourists) and get what the locals are eating – when it comes to food, Beijingers know their stuff.

Selling snacks and sharks' fin soup

Other Chinese cuisines

Of course, Beijing being the capital, you can try every kind of Chinese cuisine here. Boisterous **Sichuan** food, with its extravagant use of fiery chillies and pungent flavours, is a particular favourite. Try *mapo dofu* (beancurd with pork) *gongbao jiding* (chicken and peanuts), and *suan cai yu* (fish with pickles) for a classic spicy meal. Head to *The Source* (see p.146) or, if you're feeling adventurous, the *Sichuan Government Restaurant* (see p.143).

The joke that the Chinese will eat anything with four legs that isn't a table refers to **Cantonese** cuisine. Snake, dog and guinea pig are among the more unusual dishes here, but more conventionally, there's also plenty of lightly seasoned, fresh vegetables. *Dim sum* (*dianxin* in Mandarin), a meal of tiny buns, dumplings, and pancakes is a favourite for a long leisurely lunch. Beijing isn't short of Cantonese restaurants; *Fortune Garden* (see p.142) is one of the best.

Simatai

Peaceful and semi-ruined, **Simatai** (daily 8am–4pm; ¥40), 110km northeast of the city, is the most unspoilt section of the Great Wall around Beijing. The wall snakes across purple hills resembling crumpled velvet from afar, and blue mountains in the distance, fulfilling the expectations of most visitors more than the other sections – though it does get a little crowded at weekends. Most of this section is unrenovated, dating back to the Ming dynasty, and sports a few late innovations, such as slits for cannon, as well as inner walls at right angles to the outer wall to thwart invaders who breached the first defence.

From the car park, a winding path takes you up to the wall, where most visitors turn right. Regularly spaced watchtowers allow you to measure your progress uphill along the ridge. If you're not scared of heights you can take the **cable car** to the eighth tower (¥20).

The walk over the ruins isn't an easy one, and gets increasingly precipitous after about the tenth watchtower. The views are sublime, though. After about the fourteenth tower (2hr on), the wall peters out and the climb becomes quite dangerous, and there's no point going any further.

Turning left when you first reach the wall, you can do the popular hike to Jinshanling in three hours (see p.114). Most people though, do the walk in the other direction, as it's more convenient to finish up in Simatai.

Practicalities

The journey out from the capital to Simatai takes about three hours by private transport. **Tours** run from the backpacker hotels and hostels for around ¥150, generally once or twice a week in low season, daily in the summer, and sometimes offer overnight stays. Most other hotels can arrange transport, too (usually a minibus), though expect to pay a little more.

You can travel here independently, but considering the logistical hassles and expense, this is only worth doing if you want to stay for a night or two. To get

▲ The Great Wall around Simatai

At all the less visited places, each tourist, or group of tourists, will be followed along the wall, for at least an hour, by a villager selling drinks and postcards; if you don't want to be pestered make it very clear from the outset that you are not interested in anything they are selling – though after a few kilometres you might find that ¥5 of coke very welcome.

here under your own steam, catch a direct Simatai bus from Dongzhimen bus station (buses leave 7–9am; ¥40) or take bus #980 to **Miyun** and negotiate for a minibus or taxi to take you the rest of the way (you shouldn't have to pay more than ¥40). Between mid-April and mid-October tourist bus #12 heads to Simatai (6–8am; ¥50) from the #42 bus station south of Dongsi Shitiao subway stop, and from opposite Xuanwumen subway subway stop; buses return between 4 and 6pm. A rented **taxi** will cost about ¥350 return, including a wait.

To get from Simatai back to Beijing, you can either get a taxi from Simatai to Miyun, (¥70 or so, after some negotiaton; from Miyun, the last public bus back to Beijing is at 4pm), or wait at the Simatai car park for a tourist bus; they start to head back to the city at 4pm.

The *Simatai Youth Hostel*, by the entrance, has dingy rooms (¥160) and hard beds in an eight-bed dorm (¥70); there's hot water for two hours a day. You'll get rather better value if you head off with one of the locals who hang around the car park; they will charge ¥70 or so for a spare room in their house, though facilities will be simple, with only cold water on tap; ask, and your host will bring a bucket of hot water to the bathroom for you. As for **eating**, avoid the youth hostel's over-priced restaurant and head to one of the nameless places at the side of the car park, where the owners can whip up some very creditable dishes; if you're lucky, they'll have some locally caught wild game in stock.

Jinshanling

Jinshanling (¥30), 10km west of Simatai, is one of the least visited and best pre-served parts of the wall, with jutting obstacle walls and oval watchtowers, some with octagonal or sloping roofs. It's not easy to reach without your own transport, but there are plenty of tours out here from the hostels (¥180); they'll drop you off here in the morning and pick you up at Simatai in the afternoon. Otherwise, a taxi from Miyun (see above for routes) will cost around ¥100.

Turn left when you hit the wall and it's a three-hour walk to Simatai along an unreconstructed section. You won't meet many other tourists, and will experience something of the wall's magnitude; a long and lonely road that unfailingly picks the toughest line between peaks. Take the hike seriously, as you are scrambling up and down steep, crumbly inclines, and you need to be sure of foot. Watch, too, for loose rocks dislodged by your companions. When you reach Simatai there's a ¥30 toll at the suspension bridge.

Finally, if you head right when you get onto the wall at Jinshanling, you quickly reach an utterly abandoned and overgrown section. After about four hours' walk along here, you'll reach a road that cuts through the wall, and from here you can flag down a passing bus back to Beijing. This route is only recommended for the intrepid.

Huanghua

The section of the wall at **Huanghua** (¥25), 60km north of Beijing, is completely unreconstructed. It's a telling example of Ming defences, complete with wide ramparts, intact parapets and beacon towers. You can hike along the wall for as long as you like, though some sections are a bit of a scramble. It's not too hard to get here: backpacker hotels have started taking tours, otherwise take bus #916 from Dongzhimen bus station to Huairou (¥8), and catch a minibus taxi from there (around ¥10; agree the fare before setting off, as the driver may try to over-charge foreigners). You'll be dropped off on a road that cuts through the wall. The section to the left is too hard to climb, but the section on the right, past a little reservoir, shouldn't present too many difficulties for the agile; indeed, the climb gets easier as you go, with the wall levelling off along a ridge.

The wall here is attractively ruined – so watch your step – and its course makes for a pleasant walk through some lovely countryside. Walk the wall for about 2km, to the seventh tower, and you'll come to steps that lead south down the wall and onto a stony path. Follow this path down past an ancient barracks to a pumping station, and you'll come to a track that takes you south back to the main road, through a graveyard and orchards. When you hit the road you're about 500m south of where you started. Head north and after 150m you'll come to a bridge where taxis (¥10) and buses to Huairou congregate. The last bus from Huairou to Beijing leaves at 6.30pm.

The Western Hills

Like the Summer Palace (see p.104), the **Western Hills** are somewhere to escape urban life for a while, though they're more of a rugged experience. Thanks to their coolness at the height of summer, the hills have long been favoured as a rest-ful retreat by religious men and intellectuals, as well as politicians in the modern times – Mao lived here briefly, and the Politburo (Political Bureau) assembles here in times of crisis.

The hills are divided into three parks, the nearest to the centre being the **Botani-cal Gardens**, 3.5km due west of the Summer Palace. Two kilometres farther west, **Xiangshan** is the largest and most impressive of the parks, but just as pretty is **Badachu**, its eight temples strung out along a hillside 2.5km to the south of Xiangshan.

About 20km from the centre, the hills take roughly an hour to reach on public transport. You can explore two of the parks in one day, but each deserves a day to itself. For a weekend escape and some in-depth exploration of the area, the *Xiangshan Hotel*, close to the main entrance of Xiangshan Park, is a good base (T010/62591155; ❾). A startlingly incongruous sight, the light, airy hotel looks like something between a temple and an airport lounge. It was designed by Bei Yuming (more usually known as I.M. Pei in the West), who also designed the pyra-mid at the Louvre in Paris and the Bank of China building at Xidan (see p.73).

The Botanical Gardens

Beijing's **Botanical Gardens** (daily 8am–6pm; ¥5) boast two thousand varieties of trees and plants, arranged in formal gardens that are particularly attractive in spring, when most of the flowers are in bloom. Plants are labelled in English; some varieties have whole gardens dedicated to them – the peony and cherry-tree gardens are worth seeking out. There's also a huge new hothouse which boasts tropical and desert environments (¥50), and has a lot of fleshy flora from Yunnan province in southwest China.

▲ Botanical Gardens

The path from the main gate, where the buses drop visitors (you can get here on bus #333 from outside the Yuanmingyuan or #360 from the zoo), leads after 1km to the **Wofo Si** (daily 8am–4.30pm; ¥5), housing a huge reclining Buddha, over 5m in length and cast in copper. Calm in repose, with two giant feet protruding from the end of his painted robe, and a pudgy baby-face, he looks rather cute, although he isn't actually sleeping, but dying – about to enter nirvana. Suitably huge shoes, presented as offerings, are on display around the hall. Behind the temple is a bamboo garden, from which paths, signposted in English, wind off into the hills. One heads northwest to a pretty cherry valley, just under 1km away, where Cao Xueqiao is supposed to have written *The Dream of Red Mansions* (see p.180).

Xiangshan Park

Two kilometres west of the gardens lies **Xiangshan Park** (Fragrant Hills; daily 7am–6pm; ¥5; same buses as for the Botanical Gardens, stopping at the main entrance), a range of hills dominated by Incense Burner Peak in the western corner. It's at its best in the autumn (before the sharp November frosts), when the leaves turn red in a massive profusion of colour. Though busy at weekends, the park is too large to appear swamped, and is always a good place for a hike and a picnic.

Just northeast of the main entrance, on the eastern side of the park, is the **Zhao Miao** (Temple of Clarity), one of the few temples in the area to escape being vandalized by Western troops in 1860 and 1900. Built in 1780 by Qing Emperor Qianlong in Tibetan style, it was designed to make visiting lamas feel at home. From here, it's worth following the path west up to the peak (an easy 1hr walk) from where, on clear days, there are magnificent views down towards the Summer Palace and as far as distant Beijing. For those equinely minded, you can hire a horse to ride down (¥20), though you're not free to go where you please; the horse will be led by a lackey to the park's north entrance, which is also where the cable car (¥20) from the summit sets you down.

Just outside the park gate here is the superb **Biyun Si** (Azure Clouds Temple; daily 7.30am–4.30pm; ¥10). A striking building, it's dominated by a bulbous dagoba and topped by extraordinary conical stupas. The giant main hall is now a maze of corridors lined with statues of *arhats* – five hundred of these Buddhist saints in all. The benignly smiling golden figures are all different – some have two heads or sit on animals (one is even pulling his own face off); you might see monks moving among them and bowing to each. The temple also contains a tomb containing the hat and clothes of Sun Yatsen (president of the short-lived republic founded in 1911; his body was stored here for a while before being moved to Nanjing in 1924. Unfortunately, the tomb isn't open to public view.

Badachu

A forested hill 10km south of Xiangshan Park, **Badachu** (Eight Great Sites; daily 8am–5pm; ¥10) derives its name from the presence of eight temples here. Fairly small affairs, lying along the path that curls around the hill, the temples and their surroundings are nonetheless quite attractive, at least on weekdays; don't visit at weekends when the place is swamped. Bus #347 comes here from the zoo, or you can take the east–west subway line to the westernmost stop, Pingguoyuan, and get a taxi the rest of the way (¥10).

At the base of the path is a pagoda holding what's said to be one of Buddha's teeth, which once sat in the fourth temple, about halfway up the hill. The third temple is a nunnery, and is the most pleasant, with a relaxing teahouse in the courtyard. There's a statue of the rarely depicted, boggle-eyed thunder deity inside the main hall. The other temples make good resting points as you climb up the hill.

Inevitably, there's a cable car which you can ride to the top of the hill (¥20); you'll see it as you enter the park's main (north) gate. To descend, there's also a metal sled which you can use to slide down the hill (¥40). You'll whizz to the bottom in a minute.

Fahai Si

Though its exterior is unremarkable, the **Fahai Si** (daily 9am–5pm; ¥20) is worth a visit for its beautiful, richly detailed Buddhist frescoes. Lying west of the capital, the easiest way to get here is to take subway line 1 to the last stop, Pingguoyuan, then take a cab (¥10). The halls where the frescoes are painted are rather dark; you're issued with a small torch at the entrance, but if you've got a decent one of your own, take it along. The lively, expressive images, painted in the 1440s, depict the pantheon of Buddhist deities travelling for a meeting. Look out for the elegant God of Music, Sarasvati, whose swaying form seems appropriately melodic, and the maternal-looking God of children, Haritidem, with her attendant babies. There are plenty of animals, too; as well as the rather doglike lions, look out for the six-tusked elephant – each tusk represents a quality required for the attainment of enlightenment.

Tanzhe Si and Jietai Si

Due west of Beijing, two splendid temples sit in the wooded country outside the industrial zone that rings the city. Though **Tanzhe Si** and **Jietai Si** are relatively little-visited by tourists, foreign residents rate them as among the best places to escape the city smoke. Take a picnic and make a day of it, as getting there and back can be time-consuming.

Tourist bus #7 from Fuchengmen visits both temples (mid-April to mid-Oct outward journeys 7–8.30am; ¥38 return), giving you ninety minutes at each, before returning to Qianmen. Otherwise, you could ride the east–west subway line all the way to its western terminus at Pingguoyuan, then catch bus #931 (¥3; this bus has two routes so make sure the driver knows where you're going) to Tanzhe Si. From here you'll be able to find a taxi on to Jietai Si (¥20) – get one back to the city from here as well. Or you can save yourself some hassle by hiring a taxi to visit both temples, which should cost around ¥250 if you start from the city centre.

Tanzhe Si

Forty kilometres west of Beijing, **Tanzhe Si** (daily 8am–6pm; ¥35) has the most beautiful and serene location of any temple near the city. The site is the largest of Beijing's temples, too, and one of the oldest, first recorded in the third century as housing a thriving community of monks. Wandering through the complex, past terraces of stupas, you reach an enormous central courtyard, with an ancient, towering gingko tree that's over a thousand years old (christened the "King of Trees" by Emperor Qianlong) at its heart.

Across the courtyard, a second, smaller gingko, known as "The Emperor's Wife", was once supposed to produce a new branch every time a new emperor was born. From here you can take in the other temple buildings, arrayed on different levels up the hillside, or look around the lush gardens, whose bamboo is supposed to cure all manner of ailments. Back at the temple entrance, the spiky *zhe* trees nearby (*Cudrania tricuspidata*, sometimes called the Chinese mulberry), after which the temple is named, "reinforce the essence of the kidney and control spontaneous seminal emission", so a sign here says.

Jietai Si

In complete contrast to the Tanzhe Si, the **Jietai Si** (daily 8am–6pm; ¥35), sitting on a hillside 12km east, looks more like a fortress than a temple, surrounded by forbiddingly tall, red walls. It's an extremely atmospheric, quiet place, made slightly spooky by its dramatically shaped pines, eccentric-looking venerable trees growing in odd directions. Indeed, one, leaning out at an angle of about thirty degrees, is pushing over a pagoda on the terrace beneath it.

In the main hall is an enormous tenth-century platform of white marble at which novice monks were ordained. At three metres high, it's intricately carved with figures – monks, monsters (beaked and winged) and saints. The chairs on top are for the three masters and seven witnesses who oversaw ordinations. Another, smaller side hall holds a beautiful wooden altar that swarms with dragon reliefs.

The Ming Tombs (Shisan Ling)

After their deaths, all but three of the sixteen Ming-dynasty emperors were entombed in giant underground vaults, the **Shisan Ling** (Thirteen Tombs, usually referred to as the **Ming Tombs** in English). Two of the tombs, Chang Ling and Ding Ling, were restored in the 1950s; the latter was also excavated.

The tombs are located in and around a valley 40km northwest of Beijing. The location, chosen by the third Ming emperor, Yongle, for its landscape of gentle hills and woods is undeniably one of the loveliest around the capital, the site marked above ground by grand halls and platforms. That said, the fame of the tombs is overstated in relation to the actual interest of their site, and unless you've a strong archeological bent, a trip here isn't worth making for its own sake. The tombs are, however, very much on the tour circuit, being conveniently placed on the way to Badaling Great Wall (see p.111). The site also makes a nice place to picnic, especially if you just feel like taking a break from the city and its more tangible sights. To get the most out of the place, it's better not to stick to the tourist route between the car park and Ding Ling, but to spend a day here and hike around the smaller tombs further into the hills. You'll need a map to do this – you'll find one on the back of some Beijing city maps, or you can buy one at the site (¥2).

The easiest way to get to the Ming Tombs is to take any of the **tourist buses** that go to Badaling (see p.112), which visit the tombs on the way to and from Beijing. You can get off here, then rejoin another tourist bus later, either to continue to Badaling or to return to the city. To get there on ordinary public transport, take bus #845 from Xizhimen to the terminus at Changping, then get bus #345 the rest of the way. All buses drop you at a car park in front of one of the tombs, Ding Ling, where you buy your ticket (¥35).

The Spirit Way and Chang Ling

The approach to the Ming Tombs, the seven-kilometre **Spirit Way**, is Shisan Ling's most exciting feature, well worth backtracking along from the ticket office. The road commences with the **Dahongmen** (Great Red Gate), a triple-entranced triumphal arch, through the central opening of which only the emperor's dead body was allowed to be carried. Beyond, the road is lined with colossal stone statues of animals and men. Alarmingly larger than life, they all date from the fifteenth century and are among the best surviving examples of Ming sculpture. Their precise significance is unclear, although it is assumed they were intended to serve the emperors in their next life. The animals depicted include the mythological *qilin* – a reptilian beast with deer's horns and a cow's tail – and the horned, feline *xiechi*; the human figures are stern, military mandarins. Animal statuary reappears at the entrances to several of the tombs, though the structures themselves are something of an anticlimax.

At the end of the Spirit Way stands **Chang Ling** (daily 8.30am–5pm; ¥35), which was the tomb of Yongle himself, the earliest at the site. There are plans to excavate the underground chamber – an exciting prospect since the tomb is contemporary with some of the finest buildings of the Forbidden City in the capital. At present, the enduring impression above ground is mainly one of scale – vast courtyards and halls, approached by terraced white marble. Its main feature is the Hall of Eminent Flowers, supported by huge columns consisting of individual tree trunks which, it is said, were imported all the way from Yunnan in the south of the country.

Ding Ling

The main focus of the area is **Ding Ling** (daily 8.30am–5pm; ¥35), the underground tomb-palace of the Emperor Wanli, who ascended the throne in 1573 at the age of 10. Reigning for almost half a century, he began building his tomb when he was 22, in line with common Ming practice, and hosted a grand party within on its completion. The mausoleum, a short distance east of Chang Ling, was opened up in 1956 and found to be substantially intact, revealing the emperor's coffin, flanked by those of two of his empresses, and floors covered with scores of trunks containing imperial robes, gold and silver, and even the imperial cookbooks. Some of the treasures are displayed in the tomb, a huge musty stone vault, undecorated but impressive for its scale; others have been replaced by replicas. It's a cautionary picture of useless wealth accumulation, as the tour guides are bound to point out.

Other sights north of Beijing

Heading north out of the city, you'll see vast swathes of new tree growth – the **Great Green Wall** (see p.176). There are some areas of great natural beauty in the rugged landscape beyond, notably Longqing Gorge and Shidu, and, oddly, the rather good Aviation museum. There's public transport to all these areas but having a car and driver makes it easier.

Aviation Museum

Out in the sticks 60km north of the city, the **Aviation Museum** is a fascinating place (daily 8.30am–5.30pm; ¥40; bus #912 from Andingmen subway stop). This enormous museum contains over three hundred aircraft, displayed in a giant hangar inside a hollow mountain and on a concourse. These range from the copy of the Wright brothers' plane flown by Feng Ru, a pioneering Chinese aviator, in 1909, to Gulf War helicopter gunships. As well as plenty of fighter planes, many of which saw action in the Korean War, the bomber that flew in China's first atom-bomb test is here, as is Mao's personal jet (with his teacup and frilly cushions still inside) and the plane that scattered the ashes of the deceased Zhou Enlai, which is covered with wreaths and tributes. But unless you have a special interest in aircraft, it's the sight of archaic downed machines en masse – like the setting for a J.G. Ballard story – that makes the place memorable.

Longqing Gorge

Longqing Gorge (¥40) is a local recreation spot at the edge of a reservoir some 90km northwest of the capital, known as the place to come for outdoor pursuits such as canoeing, horse riding and rock climbing, all of which can be arranged when you arrive, for between ¥60 and ¥120. The main attraction, though, is the **Ice Festival** held on the shore of the reservoir (late Jan & Feb, sometimes into March), at which groups of sculptors compete to create the most impressive ice sculpture. The enormous resulting carvings depict cartoon characters, dragons, storks and figures from Chinese popular culture; with coloured lights inside for a gloriously tacky psychedelic effect, they look great at night.

There are two ways to reach the gorge by public **transport**: either tourist bus #8 (mid-April to mid-Oct; approx 3 hrs) from the #328 bus terminus near Andingmen subway stop, or train #575 from Xizhimen Zhan (daily at 8.30am; 2hr 30min). Unfortunately, the **hotels** around the reservoir are expensive and a bit dirty, and their rooms are especially pricey during the festival – though you needn't feel compelled to stay, as there are buses back to Beijing until at least 10pm. The nearest decent hotel in this area is the *Yanqing Guesthouse* in **Yanqing**, a few kilometres to the south (☏010/69142363; ❸).

Shidu

The "wilderness area" of **Shidu** (Ten Bends), around 90km north of the city, is Bejing's equivalent to Guilin; the Juma river twists between steep karst peaks to create a landscape that resembles a classical Chinese painting. The trip here on bus #917 from Tianqiao will take two hours or so. As at Longqing Gorge, you can go horse riding, boating, fishing and rock climbing – all of which cost ¥120 or so, can be organized on your arrival, and are aimed at the novice. There's even a bungee jump (¥150). But perhaps it's most rewarding simply as a place to **hike** – pick up a map at the entrance and set off. Though it can get crowded, few visitors seem to get much further than the restaurants that line the only road, so the experience rather improves the further into the resort you go.

Chengde

CHENGDE, a country town 250km northeast of Beijing is a quiet, unimportant place, but on its outskirts are some of the most magnificent examples of imperial architecture in China, remnants from its glory days as the **summer retreat** of the Manchu emperors. Gorgeous temples punctuate the cabbage fields around town, and a palace-and-park hill complex, **Bishu Shanzhuang**, covers an area nearly as large as the town itself.

Some history

Originally called "Rehe", the town was discovered by the Qing-dynasty emperor **Kangxi** at the end of the seventeenth century, while marching his troops to the Mulan hunting range to the north. He was attracted to the cool summer climate and the rugged landscape, and built small lodges here from which he could indulge in a fantasy Manchu lifestyle, hunting and hiking like his northern ancestors. The building programme expanded when it became diplomatically useful to spend time north of Beijing, to forge closer links with the troublesome Mongol tribes. Kangxi, perhaps the ablest and most enlightened of his dynasty, was known more for his economy – "The people are the foundation of the kingdom; if they have enough then the kingdom is rich" – than for such displays of imperial grandeur. Chengde, however, was a thoroughly pragmatic creation, devised as an effective

Chengde	承德	chéngdé
Anyuan Miao	安远庙	ānyuǎn miào
Arhat Hill	罗汉山	luóhàn shān
Bishu Shanzhuang	避暑山庄	bìshǔ shānzhuāng
Palace	正宫	zhèng gōng
Pule Si	普乐寺	pǔlè sì
Puning Si	普宁寺	pǔníng sì
Puren Si	溥仁寺	pǔrén sì
Putuozongcheng Miao	普陀宗乘之庙	pǔtuō zōngchéng zhīmiào
Shuxiang Si	殊像寺	shūxiàng sì
Xumifushouzhi Miao	须弥福寿之庙	xūmí fúshòu zhīmiào
Shanzhuang	山庄宾馆	shānzhuāng bīnguǎn
Xinhua	新华饭店	xīnhuá fàndiàn
Yunshan	云山饭店	yúnshān fàndiàn

means of defending the empire by overawing Mongol princes with splendid audiences, hunting parties and impressive military manoeuvres.

Construction of the first palaces started in 1703. By 1711 there were 36 palaces, temples, monasteries and pagodas set in a great walled park, its ornamental pools and islands dotted with beautiful pavilions and linked by bridges. Craftsmen from all parts of China were invited to work on the project; Kangxi's grandson, **Qian-**

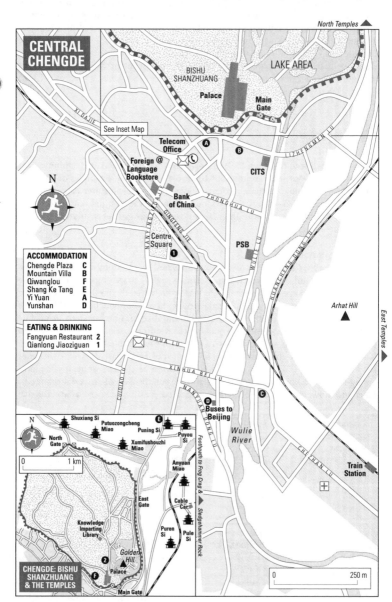

CENTRAL CHENGDE

BISHU SHANZHUANG

LAKE AREA

Palace

Main Gate

North Temples

XI DAJIE

See Inset Map

Telecom Office

Foreign @ Language Bookstore

CITS

LIZHENGMEN LU

N

Bank of China

ZHONGHUA LU

NANYINGZI LU

QINGFENG JIE

Centre Square

PSB

HUANCHENG DONG LU

Arhat Hill

East Temples

ACCOMMODATION

Chengde Plaza	C
Mountain Villa	B
Qiwanglou	F
Shang Ke Tang	E
Yi Yuan	A
Yunshan	D

EATING & DRINKING

| Fangyuan Restaurant | 2 |
| Qianlong Jiaoziguan | 1 |

YUHUA LU

XINHUA BEI LU

CHUIYUN LU

NANYUAN LU

Buses to Beijing

Wulie River

CHEHAN LU

Train Station

CHENGDE: BISHU SHANZHUANG & THE TEMPLES

N

Shuxiang Si

Putuozongcheng Miao

Puning Si

Puyou Si

North Gate

Xumifushouzhi Miao

0   1 km

Anyuan Miao

East Gate

Cable Car

Knowledge Imparting Library

Puren Si

Pule Si

Golden Hill

Palace

Footpath to Frog Crag & Sledgehammer Rock

Main Gate

0   250 m

long (1736–96), added another 36 imperial buildings during his reign, which was considered to be the heyday of Chengde.

The first **British Embassy** to China, under Lord Macartney, visited Qianlong's court here in 1793. Qianlong, at the height of Manchu power, was able to hold out against the British demands, refusing to grant any of the treaties requested and remarking, in reply to a request for trade: "We possess all things. I set no value on objects strange or ingenious, and have no use for your country's manufactures." His letter to the British monarch concluded, magnificently, "O king, Tremblingly Obey and Show No Negligence!"

Chengde gradually lost its imperial popularity when the place came to be seen as unlucky after emperors Jiaqing and Xianfeng died here in 1820 and 1860 respectively. The buildings were left empty and neglected for most of the twentieth century, but largely escaped the ravages of the Cultural Revolution. Restoration, in the interests of tourism, began in the 1980s and is ongoing.

Arrival and transport

The train journey from Beijing to Chengde takes four hours on the fastest trains (¥75) through verdant, rolling countryside, hugging the Great Wall awhile before arriving at the **train station** in the south of town. Travelling from Beijing by **bus** takes about the same time, though you run greater risk of traffic and weather delays. Buses from Beijing Zhan (¥50) terminate just outside the Yunshan Hotel.

Getting around Chengde by public transport isn't easy, as **local buses** are infrequent and always crammed. Buses #5 and #11, which go from the train station to Bishu Shanzhuang, and bus #6, from there to the Puning Si, are the most useful. **Taxis** are easy to find, but the drivers are often unwilling to use their meters – a ride around town should cost ¥5, or ¥10 to an outlying temple. At peak hours during the summer, the main streets are so congested that it's quicker to walk. The town itself is just about small enough to cover on foot.

If your time is limited, consider a minibus **tour** to cram in all the sights. It's occasionally possible to arrange an English-speaking day-tour through CITS, though it's much easier to go through one of the larger hotels. Chinese tours, which leave sporadically from outside the train station, are slightly cheaper. A day-long organized tour is something of a trial of endurance, however, and the tours tend to overlook the less spectacular temples, which are also the most peaceful. Probably the best way to see everything in a short time is to take a minibus or a bike around the temples one day and explore the mountain resort the next. If you're travelling in a group you can charter a taxi or a minibus for around ¥150 a day (bargain hard) and create your own itinerary.

Accommodation

There are plenty of hotels in Chengde town itself, plus a couple of expensive places inside Bishu Shanzhuang. Rates are highly negotiable; the price codes below apply to the peak summer season and weekends. At other times you can get discounts of up to two-thirds.

Chengde Plaza Chezhan Lu ☎0314/2088808, ℱ2024319. This recently renovated fifteen-storey block is convenient for the station, but in an uninteresting area of town. ❽
Qiwanglou Around the corner and uphill from the Bishu Shanzhuang main entrance ☎0314/2024385. A well-run hotel in a pleas-

ing imitation Qing-style building, the grounds make for an interesting walk even if you're not staying here. ❽
Mountain Villa 127 Xiaonanmen (entrance on Lizhengmen Lu) ☎0314/2025588. This grand, well-located complex has huge rooms, high ceilings and a cavernous, gleaming lobby,

and is extremely popular with tour groups. The large rooms in the main building are nicer but a little more expensive than those in the ugly building round the back, and there are some very cheap rooms in the basement. Buses #5 or #11 from the train station will get you here. ❺

Shang Ke Tang Puning Si
ⓣ0314/2058888. This interesting hotel's staff wear period clothing and braided wigs befitting the adjoining Puning temple, and glide along the dim bowels of the complex to lead you to appealingly rustic rooms. ❼

Yi Yuan Lizhengmen Lu. Just around the corner from the Mountain Villa, this sprawling complex has gloomy rooms but is cheap year-round and extremely convenient for Bishu Shanzhuang. ❷

Yunshan 2 Banbishan Lu ⓣ0314/2055588, ⓕ20558855. This modern block was once popular with tour groups, before being trumped by the Mountain Villa. The second-floor restaurant is good, the plushest in town, and not too expensive. A 10min walk from the train station. ❽

The Town

Bishu Shanzhuang lies in the north of the town, while farther north and to the east, on the other side of the river, stand Chengde's eight imposing **temples**.

Bishu Shanzhuang

Surrounded by a ten-kilometre wall and larger than the Summer Palace in Beijing, **Bishu Shanzhuang** (also referred to as the Mountain Resort) occupies the northern third of the town's area (daily: summer 7am–5.30pm; winter 8am–4.30pm; ¥90 combined ticket for the park and the palace). This is where, in the summer months, the Qing emperors lived, feasted, hunted, and occasionally dealt with affairs of state. The palace buildings just inside the main entrance are unusual for imperial China as they are low, wooden and unpainted – simple but elegant, in contrast to the opulence and grandeur of Beijing's palaces. It's said that Emperor Kangxi wanted the complex to mimic a Manchurian village, to show his disdain for fame and wealth, though with 120 rooms and several thousand servants he wasn't exactly roughing it. The same principle of idealized naturalness governed the design of the park. With its twisting paths and streams, rockeries and hills, it's a fantasy re-creation of the rough northern terrain and southern Chinese beauty spots that the emperors would have seen on their tours of inspection. The whole is an attempt to combine water, buildings and plants in graceful harmony. Lord Macartney noted its similarity to the "soft beauties" of an English manor park of the Romantic style.

The palace

The **main gate**, Lizhengmen, is in the south wall, off Lizhengmen Lu. The **palace quarter**, just inside the complex to the west of the main gate, is built on a slope, facing south, and consists of four groups of dark wooden buildings spread over an area of 100,000 square metres. The first, southernmost group, the **Front Palace**, where the emperors lived and worked, is the most interesting, as many of the rooms have been restored to their full Qing elegance, decked out with graceful furniture and ornaments. Even the everyday objects are impressive: brushes and ink stones on desks, ornate fly whisks on the arms of chairs, little jade trees on shelves. Other rooms house displays of ceramics, books and exotic martial-art weaponry. The Qing emperors were fine calligraphers, and examples of their work appear throughout the palace.

There are 26 buildings in this group, arranged south to north in nine successive compounds, which correspond to the nine levels of heaven. The main gate leads into the **Outer Wumen**, where high-ranking officials waited for a single peal of a large bell, indicating that the emperor was ready to receive them. Next is the **Inner Wumen**, where the emperor would watch his officers practise their archery. Directly behind, the **Hall of Frugality and Sincerity** is a dark, well-appointed room made of cedar wood, imported at great expense from south of the Yangzi River by Qianlong, who had none of his grandfather Kangxi's scruples about conspicuous consumption. Topped with a curved roof, the hall has nine bays, and patterns on the walls include symbols of longevity and good luck. The **Four Knowledge Study Room**, behind, was where the emperor did his ordinary work, changed his clothes and rested. A vertical scroll on the wall outlines the knowledge required of a gentleman, as written in the Chinese classics: he must be aware of what is small, obvious, soft and strong. It's more spartanly furnished, a little more intimate and less imposing than the other rooms.

The main building in the **Rear Palace** is the **Hall of Refreshing Mists and Waves**, the living quarters of the imperial family, and beautifully turned out in period style. It was in the west room here that Emperor Xianfeng signed the humiliating Beijing Treaty in the 1850s, giving away more of China's sovereignty and territory after their defeat in the Second Opium War. The **Western Apartments** are where the notorious Cixi, (see p.106), lived when she was one of Xianfeng's concubines. A door connects the apartments to the hall, and it was through here that she eavesdropped on the dying emperor's last words of advice to his ministers, intelligence she used to force herself into power. The courtyard of the Rear Palace has a good **souvenir shop**, inside an old Buddhist tower reached by climbing a staircase by the rockery.

The other two complexes are much smaller. The **Pine and Crane Residence**, a group of buildings parallel to the front gate, is a more subdued version of the Front Palace, home to the emperor's mother and his concubines. In the **Myriad Valleys of Rustling Pine Trees**, to the north of here, Emperor Kangxi read books and granted audiences, and Qianlong studied as a child. The group of structures southwest of the main palace is the **Ahgesuo**, where male descendants of the royal family studied during the Manchurian rule; lessons began at 5am and finished at noon. A boy was expected to speak Manchu at 6, Chinese at 12, be competent with a bow by the age of 14, and marry at 16.

The grounds

The best way to get around the **lake area** of the park – a network of pavilions, bridges, lakes and waterways – is to rent a **rowing boat** (¥20 an hour). Much of the architecture here is a direct copy of southern Chinese buildings. In the east, the **Golden Hill**, a cluster of buildings grouped on a small island, is notable for a hall and tower modelled after the Golden Hill Monastery in Zhenjiang, Jiangsu province. The **Island of Midnight and Murmuring Streams**, roughly in the centre of the lake, holds a three-courtyard compound which was used by Kangxi and Qianlong as a retreat, while the compound of halls, towers and pavilions on **Ruyi Island**, the largest, was where Kangxi dealt with affairs of state before the palace was completed.

Just beyond the lake area, on the western side of the park, is the grey-tiled **Wenjinge**, or Knowledge Imparting Library, surrounded by rockeries and pools for fire protection. From the outside, the structure appears to have two storeys. In fact there are three – a central section is windowless to protect the books from the sun. A fine collection is housed in the building, including *The Four Treasures*, a 36,304-volume Qing-dynasty encyclopedia, but sadly you can't go inside.

A vast expanse of **grassland** extends from the north of the lake area to the foothills of the mountains, comprising Wanshun Wan (Garden of Ten Thousand Trees) and Shima Da (Horse Testing Ground). Genuine Qing-dynasty **yurts** sit here, the largest an audience hall where Qianlong received visiting dignitaries from ethnic minorities.

The temples

The **temples** (daily 8am–5.30pm) in the foothills of the mountains around Chengde were built in the architectural styles of different ethnic nationalities, so that wandering among them is rather like being in a religious theme park. This isn't far from the original intention, as they were constructed by Kangxi and Qianlong less to express religious sentiment than as a way of showing off imperial magnificence, and also to make envoys from anywhere in the empire feel more at home. Though varying in design, all the temples share **Lamaist features** – Qianlong found it politically expedient to promote Tibetan and Mongolian Lamaism as a way of keeping these troublesome minorities in line.

The temples are now in varying states of repair, having been left untended for decades. Originally there were twelve, but two have been destroyed and another two are dilapidated. Present restoration work is being paid for by the high entrance fees charged in the large temples.

The best way to see the temples is to **rent a bicycle** (ask at your hotel; the *Qiwanglou* and *Mountain Villa* have bikes to rent): the roads outside the town are quiet, it's hard to get lost and you can dodge the tour groups.

The northern temples

Just beyond the northern border of Bishu Shanzhuang are five temples that were once part of a string of nine. Three of these deserve special attention but the **Puning Si** (Temple of Universal Peace; ¥40) is a must, if only for the awe-inspiring statue of Guanyin, the largest wooden statue in the world. This is the only working temple in Chengde, with shaven-headed Mongolian monks manning the altars and trinket stalls, though the atmosphere is not especially spiritual. There are rumours that the monks are really paid government employees working for the tourist industry, though the vehemence with which they defend their prayer mats and gongs from romping children suggests otherwise.

The Puning Si was built in 1755 to commemorate the Qing victory over Mongolian rebels at Junggar in northwest China, and is based on the oldest Tibetan temple, the Samye. Like traditional Tibetan buildings, it lies on the slope of a mountain facing south, though the layout of the front is typically Han, with a gate hall, stele pavilions, a bell and a drum tower, a Hall of Heavenly Kings, and the Mahavira Hall. In the **Hall of Heavenly Kings**, the statue of a fat, grinning monk holding a bag depicts Qi Ci, a tenth-century character with a jovial disposition, who is believed to be a reincarnation of the Buddha. Four gaudy *devarajas* (guardian demons) glare at you with bulging eyeballs from niches in the walls. In the **West Hall** are statues of Buddha Manjusri, Avalokiteshvara and Samantabhadra. In the **East Hall**, the central statue, flanked by *arhats*, depicts Ji Gong, a Song-dynasty monk who was nicknamed Crazy Ji for eating meat and being almost always drunk, but who was much respected for his kindness to the poor.

The rear section of the temple, separated from the front by a wall, comprises 27 Tibetan-style rooms laid out symmetrically, with the **Mahayana Hall** in the centre. Some of the buildings are actually solid (the doors are false), suggesting that the original architects were more concerned with appearances than function. The hall itself is dominated by the 23-metre-high wooden **statue of Guanyin**, the Goddess of Mercy. She has 42 arms with an eye in the centre of each palm, and three eyes on her face, which symbolize her ability to see into the past, present and future. The hall has two raised entrances, and it's worth looking at the statue from these upper viewpoints as they reveal new details, such as the eye sunk in her belly button, and the little Buddha sitting on top of her head.

Recently restored, the **Xumifushouzhi Miao** (Temple of Sumeru Happiness and Longevity; ¥40), just southwest of Puning Si, was built in 1780 in Mongolian style for the sixth Panchen Lama when he came to Beijing to pay his respects to the emperor. Though he was lavishly looked after – contemporary accounts describe Qianlong invited the Lama to sit with him on the Dragon Throne – he went home in a coffin, dead from either smallpox or poison.

The temple centrepiece is the **Hall of Loftiness and Solemnity**, its finest feature the eight sinuous gold dragons sitting on the roof, each weighing over a thousand kilograms.

The Putuozongcheng Miao and Shuxiang Si

Next door to the Xumifushouzhi Miao, the magnificent **Putuozongcheng Miao** (Temple of Potaraka Doctrine; ¥30) was built in 1771 and is based on the Potala Palace in Lhasa. Covering 220,000 square metres, it's the largest temple in Chengde, with sixty groups of halls, pagodas and terraces. The grand terrace forms a Tibetan-style facade screening a Chinese-style interior, although many of the windows on the terrace are fake, and some of the whitewashed buildings around the base are merely filled-in shapes. Inside, the West Hall is notable for holding a rather comical copper statue of the Propitious Heavenly Mother, a fearsome woman wearing a necklace of skulls and riding side-saddle on a mule. According to legend, she vowed to defeat the evil demon Raksaka, so she first lulled him into a false sense of security – by marrying him and bearing him two sons – then swallowed the moon and in the darkness crept up on him and turned him into a mule. The two dancing figures at her feet are her sons; their ugly features betray their paternity. The **Hall of All Laws Falling into One**, at the back, is worth a visit for the quality of the decorative religious furniture on display. Other halls hold displays of Chinese pottery and ceramics and Tibetan religious artefacts, an exhibition slanted to portray the gorier side of Tibetan religion and including a drum made from two children's skulls. The roof of the temple has a good view over the surrounding countryside.

The eastern temples

The three **eastern temples** are easily accessible off a quiet road that passes through dusty, rambling settlements, 3–4km from the town centre. From Lizhengmen Lu, cross over to the east bank of the river and head north.

The **Puren Si** (Temple of Universal Benevolence) is the first one you'll reach and the oldest in the complex, but it has been closed to tourists. It was built by Kangxi in 1713, as a sign of respect to the visiting Mongolian nobility, who came to congratulate the emperor on the occasion of his sixtieth birthday.

The **Pule Si** (Temple of Universal Happiness; ¥30) farther north was built in 1766 by Qianlong as a place for Mongol envoys to worship, and its style is an odd mix of Han and Lamaist elements. The Lamaist back section, a triple-tiered terrace and hall, with a flamboyantly conical roof and lively, curved surfaces, steals the show from the more sober, squarer Han architecture at the front. The ceiling of the back hall is a wood and gold confection to rival the Temple of Heaven in Beijing. Glowing at its centre is a mandala of Samvara, a Tantric deity, in the form of a cross. The altar beneath holds a Buddha of Happiness, a life-size copper image of sexual congress; more cosmic sex is depicted in two beautiful mandalas hanging outside. In the courtyard, prayer flags flutter while prayer wheels sit empty and unturned. Outside the temple, the view from the car-park is spectacular, and just north is the path that leads to **Sledgehammer Rock** and the cable car.

Recently renovated, the less interesting **Anyuan Miao** (Temple of Appeasing the Borders; ¥30) is the most northerly of the group. It was built in 1764 for a troop of Mongolian soldiers who were moved to Chengde by Qianlong, and has a delightful setting on the tree-lined east bank of the Wulie River.

Eating and drinking

Chengde is located in Hebei's most fertile area, which mainly produces maize and sorghum but also yields excellent local chestnuts, mushrooms and apricots. This fresh produce, plus the culinary legacy of the imperial cooks, means you can eat very well here. The town is also noted for its wild game, particularly deer (*lurou*), hare (*yetou*) and pheasant (*shanji*), and its medicinal juice drinks: almond juice is said to be good for asthma; date and *jujube* juice for the stomach; and *jinlianhua* (golden lotus) juice for a sore throat. Date and almond are the sweetest and most palatable. Local cakes, such as the glutinous Feng family cakes, once an imperial delicacy but now a casual snack, can be found in the stalls on Yuhua Lu and Qingfeng Jie. Rose cakes – a sweet, crisp pastry cake and a particular favourite of Qianlong – are sold in Chengde's department stores.

There are plenty of **restaurants** catering to tourists on Lizhengmen Lu, around the main entrance to Bishu Shanzhuang. The small places west of the *Mountain Villa* hotel are fine, if a little pricey, and lively on summer evenings, when rickety tables are put on the pavement outside. A meal for two should cost about ¥60, and plenty of diners stay on drinking well into the evening. The best *jiaozi* in town are served at *Qianlong Jiaoziguan*, just off Centre Square, a park at the heart of the shopping district. Nearby, **Qingfeng Jie** is an old, charmingly seedy street of restaurants and salons, and is a great place to have a satisfying *shaguo* – a veggie clay-pot costs ¥6, a meat-based one ¥10. Inside Bishu Shanzhuang itself, the *Fangyuan* offers imperial cuisine, including such exotica as "Pingquan Frozen Rabbit", in an attractive environment.

Listings

Listings

8

Accommodation

eijing hotels were once largely impersonal concerns, with standardized, rather nondescript, modern interiors. But newer accommodation options are placing more emphasis on design and character, the established places are sprucing themselves up, and now, whatever your budget, it's possible to stay somewhere that's not just functional but memorable. For information on finding long-term accommodation in the city, see p.40.

Central Beijing – anywhere within or just off the second ring road – has plenty of luxury and a few mid-range hotels, while budget options have sprung up, including a number of good youth hostels. Beijing being the size it is, proximity to a subway stop is an enormous advantage, so accommodation on or near the second ring road – and therefore the loop line – are often the most convenient. **Out of the centre**, the vast majority of hotels are on or near the third ring road, a long way out in what is rather a dull area, though there are usually good transport connections to the centre. These hotels are mainly mid-range and comfortable, without many frills; all have a business centre.

The glitzy, expensive hotels are in or around the **Chaoyang** district, in the **east** of the city. Though anonymous architecturally, it's a cosmopolitan area with lively restaurants and nightlife: this is the place for international style and comfort.

The **north** of the city (south of the second ring road) has some charmingly ramshackle (and newly fashionable) areas, particularly around Nanluogu Xiang and the Drum Tower. Head for this area if you want to stay in traditional Beijing; you'll also find the best budget and mid-range places.

The **west** and **south** of the city are, on the whole, less interesting, and likely to become even duller in the midst of the new building – though there are plenty of accommodation options here, few are included below for this reason.

At all but the cheapest hotels, rack rates should not be taken literally; it's almost always possible to **bargain** the rate down, sometimes by as much as two-thirds in

ACCOMMODATION

Accommodation price codes

The accommodation in this book has been graded according to the price codes below, indicating the price of the **cheapest double room** available to foreigners. Most places have a range of rooms: staff will usually offer you the more expensive ones – it's always worth asking if they have anything cheaper. Some upmarket establishments have separate high- and low-season rates, in which case the price code represents the cost in high season (April–Sept).

❶ Up to ¥150	❹ ¥350–500	❼ ¥900–1100
❷ ¥150–250	❺ ¥500–700	❽ ¥1100–1500
❸ ¥250–350	❻ ¥700–900	❾ Over ¥1500

low season. If you're on a tight budget, a little searching should turn up a bed in a clean dormitory for about ¥60 a night, or an en-suite double room for less than ¥250.

Reservations can be made by phone – generally someone on reception will speak English. You can reserve rooms from a counter at the airport (on the left as you exit customs), and they will usually offer a small discount – though you'll get a much better deal if you book the same room yourself. **Online** reservations are simple, don't require a credit-card payment and often propose a sizeable discount: try Ⓦ www.hotelschina.net, Ⓦ www.elong.com or Ⓦ www.sinohotel.com.

Checking in involves filling in a form and paying a deposit. Remember to grab a few hotel business cards when you check in; the symbols on these are vital for letting taxi drivers know where you're staying. Whatever type of place you're in, you can rely on the presence of plastic slippers and a giant thermos flask of hot water.

All hotels have **tour offices** offering trips to the obvious sights: the Great Wall, acrobatics and Beijing opera shows. These trips are usually good value, and the most convenient way to get to remote destinations such as Simatai Great Wall. Most hotels will book train and plane tickets for you, for a small commission.

Youth hostels

On the whole, Beijing's **hostels** are clean and professionally run and, unless otherwise mentioned, will feature a lounge, free washing machine or cheap laundry service (¥15 or so), bike rental (around ¥20 a day), free or cheap Internet access and wi-fi. They'll often pick up from the train station too. Don't be put off if you don't fit the backpacker demographic; they also have inexpensive double and some single rooms, (though sometimes with shared bathrooms). An added bonus is that they are actually rather better located than most of the larger mid-range hotels, in quiet neighbourhood *hutongs*.

Note that any place billing itself a "youth hostel" will give you a ¥10 per night discount if you have a youth-hostel (ISIC) card which they can sell you for ¥50.

South of the centre

The hostel reviewed here is marked on the map on pp.66–67.

Far East International Youth Hostel
远东国际青年旅舍
yuǎndōng guójì qīngnián lǚshè
90/113 Tieshuxie Jie ☏ 010/63018811. Walk south from Hepingmen subway stop and take the second alley on the left after Liulichang's pedestrian overpass. Then it's left at the T-junction, first right, left, and the hostel is 50m up here. This popular budget place consists of two buildings opposite each other deep in the *hutongs* of Qianmen, off Nanxinhua Jie. The rooms in the new building are faded – you can do better elsewhere – but the four-bed dorms in the traditional courtyard house on the west side are good, and the courtyard itself is a great place to linger over a beer. Staff are friendly if bumbling. It's tough to find first time, and cab drivers never know where it is – see above for directions. Dorm beds ¥60 in the courtyard; new building ➌

East of the centre

The hostel reviewed below is shown on the map on pp.80–81.

Saga Youth Hostel
实佳国际青年旅舍
shíjiā guójì qīngnián lǚshè
9 Shijia Hutong, off Chaoyangmen Nan Xiao Jie ☏ 010/65272773. In a quiet *hutong* off a busy street, and walkable from the airport bus stop (the terminus of Route B) and the main train station. It's signposted off Chaoyangmen Nan Xiao Jie, just beyond the stop for bus #24. The hostel is clean and utilitarian, but ask to see a few rooms as standards vary. Unusually, some of the dorms have TVs. Dorm beds ¥60, rooms ➋

Sanlitun and the northeast

The hostels reviewed below are shown on the map on p.88.

Youyi Youth Hostel
友谊饭店
yǒuyí fàndiàn
Off Sanlitun Lu ☎010/64172632 or 64156866, ⓦwww.poachers.com.cn. Tidy and well run, with a good location – Sanlitun's bars and some classy restaurants are within short walking distance, and it's not as noisy as you might expect. Head north up Sanlitun Lu and turn left after 200m, at the sign for Cross Bar. Take the first left and the hotel will be on the right, next to the Poachers Inn. There are a few four-bed dorms but most of the rooms are doubles. The bathrooms, all communal, are spotless, and there's free Internet access and laundry service. Rate includes breakfast. Dorms ¥70, rooms ❸

Zhaolong International Youth Hostel
兆龙国际青年旅舍
zhàolóng guójì qīngnián lǚshè
2 Gongrentiyuchang Bei Lu ☎010/65972299, ⓦwww.zhaolonghotel.com.cn. Behind the swanky Zhaolong Hotel – follow the cars right round from the glitzy facade to the shabby car park behind. Staying so near to glamour isn't likely to sap morale though, as the hostel is clean and ably managed, and only a short stumble from the bars on Sanlitun Lu. Dorms ¥60–70, rooms with shared bathroom ❶; without ❷

North of the centre

The hostels reviewed here are marked on the map on pp.90–91.

Lama Temple Youth Hostel
雍和国际青年旅舍
yōnghé guójì qīngnián lǚshè
56 Beixinqiao Toutiao ☎010/64028663. Well-located courtyard hostel just south of Yonghe Gong. Rooms are spacious but dark, though at the price you can't really complain, and there's a large common room with a DVD collection. Staff are keen and friendly. Close to both Ghost Street and Nanluogu Xiang, it's handy for restaurants and nightlife. To get there, take the first *hutong* north of the Dongzhimennei and Yonghegong Dajie intersection, a few minutes south of Yonghe Gong subway stop; look for the yellow sign at the *hutong* entrance. Dorms ¥60, rooms ❷

Red Lantern House
仿古园
fǎnggǔ yuán
5 Zhengjue Hutong, Xinjiekou Nan Dajie ☎010/66115771. The main feature here is an extraordinary courtyard overloaded with ornament, including two water features and a forest of red lanterns. Hidden amongst the jungle of kitsch is a cat, a dog and a receptionist. Rooms are good value and their plain white walls come as some relief. It's a 15min walk to Jishuitan subway stop. Six-bed dorms ¥60, rooms with shared bathroom ❷

Sleepy Town Inn
丽舍什刹海国际青年旅店
lìshěshíshāhǎi guójì qīngnián lǚdiàn
103 Deshengmennei Dajie ☎010/64069954, ⓦwww.sleepyinn.com.cn. This homely place has a great location, beside a canal just off Houhai Lake, but little in the way of facilities; there's no restaurant, for example. A good terrace and pleasant staff make up for slightly over priced rooms. Dorms are good value though. It's a 10min walk from Jishuitan subway station. Four- to eight-bed dorms ¥60; rooms ❷

Houhai Lake

See the map on p.95 for the locations of the hostels reviewed below.

Downtown Backpackers
dōngtáng qīngnián lǚshè
东堂青年旅舍
85 Nanluogu Xiang ☎010/84002429. Possibly the best backpackers, with a location on artsy Nanluogu Xiang, Beijing's trendiest *hutong*; you won't be short of eating and nightlife options. Graffiti all over the walls extol the virtues of the staff, though perhaps they've let it go to their heads. There are a couple of single and double rooms, which get rapidly booked up. Light sleepers might find the gurgling plumbing in winter annoying. Six-bed dorms ¥60; double without windows ¥130, rooms ❷

Drum Tower Youth Hostel
鼓楼青年旅舍
gǔlóu qīngnián lǚshè
51 Jiugulou Dajie ☎010/64037702. This three-storey hostel is in a good area, though on a noisy main road. Rooms are spartan but clean, staff are friendly and there's a mellow rooftop patio. There's a self-service kitchen and all the facilities you might expect but no free Internet (¥8/hr). It's a 10min walk south from Gulou subway station. Dorms ¥50, rooms ❷

Hotels

The capital's **upmarket** hotels (❼–❾) are legion, and more are appearing all the time. They offer amenities such as gyms, saunas, and business centres. These establishments are comparable to their counterparts elsewhere in the world, though the finer nuances of service might be lacking. Even if these hotels are beyond your budget, you can still avail yourself of their lavish facilities, such as the lobby toilets featuring uniformed attendants who wipe the seat for you.

If nothing else, these hotels make useful landmarks, and some have pretty good restaurants that are, by Western standards at least, inexpensive. Some of the hotels in this bracket offer **off-season discounts** of up to seventy percent.

Mid-range hotels (❹–❻) are well equipped and comfortable, offering spacious double rooms, but are generally anonymous and unstylish – except for a few hotels converted from old courtyard houses, which have quiet gardens, period furniture, and an ambience that is recognizably Chinese. Breakfast apart, it's recommended to eat out rather than in the hotel restaurant: hotel food is mediocre and expensive at this level.

Budget hotels (❶–❸) boast little in the way of facilities; you can expect your room to be clean, but it might be pokey.

Most hotels have few **single rooms**; if you're on your own you might be able to persuade the receptionist to let you have a double room for half price. **Breakfast** is not usually included in the rate except in the classier places, where a choice of Western and Chinese fare is available.

South of the centre

These hotels are marked on the map on pp.66–67.

Hademen
哈德门饭店
hādémén fàndiàn

2a Chongwenmenwai Dajie ☎010/67012244. This place is a little rambling and the staff don't speak much English, but given that it's close to Chongwenmen subway and the train station, it's a sensible option. Rooms are en suite and quite comfy. ❹

Jianguo Qianmen
建国前门饭店
jiànguóqiánmén fàndiàn

175 Yong'an Lu ☎010/63016688. Bus #14 south from Hepingmen subway stop comes here – get off at the third stop. This huge hotel has at least a glimmer of character: the architecture is po-faced Soviet style, but the interiors are stylishly decorated. It's well located, close to the Temple of Heaven. The theatre, where nightly performances of Beijing opera are shown (see p.152), is an added bonus. ❺

Rainbow
新北纬饭店
xīnběiwěi fàndiàn

Xijing Lu ☎010/63012266, ⊛www.rainbowhotel.com.cn. Bus #20 from Beijing Zhan will get you to Yongdingmennei Dajie, from where the hotel is a 1km walk west. This efficiently run Sino-Japanese joint venture consists of two buildings, to separate the riffraff from the high rollers: the budget building to the west resembles a barracks, the eastern building a cruise liner. Facilities – open to guests in both buildings – include a gym and a large basement health centre, and there's a good Japanese restaurant. Western building ❸, eastern building ❻

West of the centre

See the map on pp.74–75 for location of this hotel.

Minzu
民族饭店
mínzú fàndiàn

51 Fuxingmen Dajie ☎010/66014466; ⊛www.minzuhotel.com. Built in 1959, this Chinese-run hotel has a rather dated feel. There are more than 600 rooms, plus a gym, a billiards room and a good first-floor restaurant, and the Sanwei teahouse (see p.151) over the road is an added attraction. The hotel is midway between Fuxingmen and Xidan subway stops, and not too far from some attractive parts of the city. Rooms ❼

East of the centre

The establishment reviewed at the start of this section is marked on the map on p.86.

Red House
瑞秀宾馆
ruìxiù bīnguǎn

10 Chunxiu Jie ☎010/64167500, ⊛www.red-house.com.cn. An inexpensive and friendly hotel offering discounts for long-term guests. There are plenty of good-value singles. To get there from Dongzhimen subway stop, head east along Dongzhimenwai Dajie and take the turning opposite Pizza Hut, and you can't miss the place – it's a deep red colour. ④; single rooms ②

🏃 Red Capital Residence
新红资客栈
xīnhóngzī kèzhàn

9 Dongsi Liu Tiao; ☎010/84035308, ⊛www.red-capitalclub.com. Formerly a state guesthouse, this discreet *hutong* hotel now has five rooms tricked out with Cultural Revolution artefacts. The courtyard rock formation hides the entrance to a bomb shelter-turned-bar and Madame Mao's old Red Flag limousine is available for tours. It's more a novelty than a luxury experience, but as Beijing's most original boutique hotel it's very popular; you'll have to book in advance. It's neatly hidden away: look for the red doors and the little "9". ⑧

Wangfujing

See the map on p.83 for the locations of the hotels reviewed below.

Beijing
北京饭店
běijīng fàndiàn

33 Dongchang'an Jie ☎010/65137766, ⊛www.chinabeijinghotel.com.cn. **Wangfujing subway stop.** One of the most recognizable buildings in Beijing, this mansion just east of Tian'anmen Square was built in 1900. The view from the top floors of the west wing, over the Forbidden City, is superb. After the addition of a new wing in 1974, an office block had to be constructed nearby so that top-floor guests couldn't see into Zhongnanhai. Unfortunately, the hotel rested on its laurels for decades, and even though it's now trying to catch up with the competition, this is still more the home of cadres on junkets than businessmen. ⑦

Cote Cour SL

🏃 **70 Yanyue Hutong, Dongcheng Qu**
☎010/65128021 ⊛www.hotelcote-coursl.com. **Wangfujing subway stop.** This new fourteen-room courtyard-style boutique hotel is bang in the middle of the city but in a quiet *hutong*, skilfully decorated in lavish oriental chic (though oddly it doesn't have the Chinese name you'd expect). Recommended, if you would rather pay for style and character than lavish facilities. Reserve in advance. ⑥

Grand Hotel Beijing
北京贵宾楼饭店
běijīng guìbīnlóu fàndiàn

35 Dongchang'an Jie ☎010/65130057, ⊛www.grandhotelbeijing.com.cn. A central, five-star palace next to the Beijing, with splendid views over the Forbidden City. Rooms feature period rosewood furniture, and there's plenty of elegant calligraphy around. **Wangfujing subway stop.** Doubles start at US$275. ⑨

🏃 Haoyuan
好园宾馆
hǎoyuán bīnguǎn

53 Shijia Hutong ☎010/6512 5557. **Beijing Zhan subway stop.** Down a quiet alley off Dongsi Nan Dajie – look for the gates with two red lanterns hanging outside. This characterful, converted courtyard house features rooms kitted out with imitation Qing furniture, including four-poster beds. Recommended, but it's very small and often booked up. ⑥

🏃 Holiday Inn Crowne Plaza
北京国际艺苑皇冠饭店
běijīng guójìyìyuàn huángguàn fàndiàn

48 Wangfujing Dajie ☎010/65133388, ⊛www.crowneplaza.com. **Wangfujing subway stop.** Well-established hotel with arty pretensions (there's an on-site gallery), and a location handy for the shops. The best of a number of pricey hotels in the area. ⑧

🏃 Peninsula Palace
王府半岛饭店
wángfǔbàndǎo fàndiàn

Jingyu Hutong ☎010/6512 8899, ⊛www.peninsula.com. **Wangfujing subway stop.** A discreet, very upmarket place (doubles start at US$300) with an extremely good reputation. It's well located, within walking distance of the Forbidden City, but if you need to get around quickly by taxi, be aware of the traffic snarls around here during rush hour, which might delay you. ⑨

Jianguomen

The hotels reviewed here are marked on the map on p.86.

International
北京国际饭店
běijīng guójì fàndiàn

9 Jianguomenwai Dajie ☎010/65126688. Just north of the train station, and next to the airport bus stop, this stern-looking black edifice attracts a lot of tired travellers. It's old-fashioned, with dim, cavernous rooms, and as they don't need to try very hard for custom, it's overpriced and the staff are slack. Handy for the airport bus and the CITS ticket office on the ground floor, though. ❻

Jianguo
建国饭店
jiànguó fàndiàn

5 Jianguomenwai Dajie ☎010/65002233, ⓦwww.hoteljianguo.com. Yong'an Li subway stop. Deservedly very popular, as it's well run and attractive; many of the rooms are arranged around cloistered gardens. The restaurant, *Justine's*, has the best French food in the city (see p.143). ❽

New Otani
长富宫饭店
chángfùgōng fàndiàn

26 Jianguomenwai Dajie ☎010/65125555. Jianguomen subway stop. Get seriously pampered in this five-star Japanese-managed modern mansion, although the fee for the privilege is hefty. There's a decent-sized swimming pool, saunas and a squash court. ❽

🏃 **St Regis**
国际俱乐部饭店
guójì jùlèbù fàndiàn

21 Jianguomen Wai Dajie, ☎010/6460668. ⓦwww.luxurycollection.com. The plushest hotel in the city, though with double rooms from £110/US$225 it's not the most expensive. It features real palm trees in the lobby, and there's a personal butler for guests. ❾

Sanlitun and the northeast

The hotels reviewed here are shown on the map on p.88.

Great Wall Sheraton
长城饭店
chángchéng fàndiàn

6 Dongsanhuan Bei Lu ☎010/65005566. ⓦwww.sheraton.com. A modern compound out on the third ring road towards the airport. Built around a seven-storey atrium, it's not only architecturally impressive but also very comfortable, with a good ground-floor teahouse that hosts jazz performances. There are plenty of excellent restaurants and some lively bars nearby. ❽

Kempinski
凯宾斯基饭店
kǎibīnsijī fàndiàn

Lufthansa Centre, 50 Liangmaqiao Lu ☎010/64653388. On the third ring-road, this luxurious business hotel is a little out of the way, though the huge attached shopping complex means there's no shortage of diversions on site. Doubles from US$270. ❾

North of the centre

The hotels reviewed here are marked on the map on pp.90–91, except for the *Resource Yanyuan* in Haidian, which appears on the map on p.102.

▼ Lüsongyuan

🏃 **Lüsongyuan**
侣松园宾馆
lǚsōngyuán bīnguǎn

22 Banchang Hutong, off Jiaodaokou Nan Dajie ☎010/64040436. A charismatic hotel converted from a Qing dynasty mansion, with a wide range of stylish, elegant rooms, quiet gardens and even a teahouse. It's popular with tour groups, so book ahead in season. To get there from Beijing Zhan, take bus #104 and get off at the Beibingmasi stop. Walk 50m south and you'll find a sign pointing you down an alley to the hotel. Dorm beds ¥60–100. ❺

New Century
新世纪饭店
xīnshìjì fàndiàn

6 Xizhimenwai Dajie ☎010/6846200, ⓦwww.

newcenturyhotel.com.cn. 1km from Xizhimen subway stop. A substantial, swanky, efficient business hotel with all mod cons, but in a rather noisy area by the Capital Gymnasium. ❼

Resource Yanyuan
资源燕园宾馆
zīyuányànyuán bīnguǎn

Haidian Lu ☎010/62757199. Run by nearby Beijing University, this is a reasonably priced small hotel far from the centre in lively Haidian, on the route of bus #320 from Chegongzhuang subway stop. Besides rooms, they have one- to three- bedroom apartments, which offer the best value (¥400–600). ❺

Xiyuan
西苑饭店
xīyuàn fàndiàn

1 Sanlihe Lu ☎010/68313388. This large, agreeable hotel would be a lot more enticing if it wasn't stuck out near the zoo in an area that's most notable for heavy traffic. At least the staff try hard to please, and it's not too far to Xizhimen subway stop. ❽

Houai Lake

The hotels reviewed below on marked on the map on p.95.

🏃 Bamboo Garden
竹园宾馆
zhúyuán bīnguǎn

24 Xiaoshiqiao Hutong, Jiugulou Dajie ☎010/64032299. This very pleasant hotel was converted from the residence of a Qing official, and the courtyards, elegant facades and gardens full of bamboo are its best features. There's a wide range of

▼ Bamboo Garden

rooms, the more expensive suites boasting period furniture. It's well located too, in an agreeable part of the city near Houhai. Head south from Gulou subway for about 250m down Jiugulou Dajie and take the fourth alley to the right; continue along for 100m, turn left and you're there. ❻

🏃 Guxiang 20
古巷20号商务会
gǔxiàngèrshíhào shāngwùhuì

20 Nanluogu Xiang, ☎010/64005566. A promising new hotel, well located on trendy Nanluogu Xiang, done out in that discreet, Orientalist style perennially popular in restaurants – dark, red, minimal. The best doubles have four-poster beds and there's a tennis court on the roof too. It doesn't maintain much presence on the street and looks rather like a club; hence, presumably, the English sign outside announcing that there's no entrance fee. Rooms are surprisingly inexpensive, making this a great mid-range choice; though they may put their prices up as they become established. ❸–❼

🏃 Hutong
胡同人文化旅馆
hútóngrén wénhuà lǚguǎn

71 Xiaoju'er Hutong ☎010/84025238. Like many others, this hotel takes advantage of the area's gentrification. This courtyard just off Nanluogu Xiang is quiet and cosy, and unlike some similar hotels, just about gets enough natural light. There's a small bar and free wi-fi. Some of the best cheap rooms in the city. ❷

Qing Zhu Yuan
青竹园
qīngzhú yuán

113 Nanluogu Xiang ☎010/64013961. No frills cheap rooms but that's forgiven as it's on party central Nanluogu Xiang – you won't want to stay in much. Great for when the Downtown Backpackers is booked out, or if you find their demographic tiresome. Doubles without bathroom ❶, with ❷

Zhumulangma
珠穆朗玛宾馆
zhūmùlǎngmǎ bīnguǎn

149 Gulou Xi Dajie ☎010/64018822. Bus #5 from Qianmen Dajie passes by. This was once a Lamaist temple, though there's little evidence of that now. It's home to the Beijing office of the Tibetan administration and the restaurant is Tibetan. A great location, well inside the northern section of the second ring road and close to some of the nicest *hutongs* in the city, makes this hotel a good bet. ❹

9

Eating

The Chinese love eating. Even pleasantries revolve around the subject; a way of asking "how are you?" – *nǐ chīfàn ma*? – translates literally as "have you eaten rice yet?", and they talk about food as much as the British talk about the weather. From market-stall buns and soup through to intricate varieties of regional cooking, China boasts one of the world's most complex cuisines.

The culinary wealth of Beijing is unique; it encompasses every style of Chinese food available, along with just about any Asian fare and most world cuisines. It's no surprise that, for some visitors, eating becomes the highlight of their trip. Prices are low in comparison with the West, and it's possible to eat well for less than ¥50 a head, although you can spend a lot more if you fancy dining lavishly in palatial surroundings. Meals are considered social events, and the Chinese like their restaurants to be *renao* – hot and noisy.

Restaurant hours are long, but the Chinese tend to eat early, sitting down to lunch at noon and dinner at six, so by 2pm most restaurants are empty and the staff impatient to begin their afternoon break. Late evening meals should present no problems, though some restaurants are closed by ten (those that see a lot of foreigners stay open much later). **Tipping** isn't expected; if there is a service charge, it will be on the bill. Chopsticks aren't obligatory: all restaurants have knives (*da-ozi*) and forks (*cha-zi*). Tofu dishes should be eaten with a spoon.

Among China's varied cuisines (see colour section), **Sichuan cooking** and **hot-pot meals** are perhaps the most popular in Beijing. As for cuisines from elsewhere in Asia, Japanese and Korean food are widely available and well worth trying, and Thai food has recently become popular. You'll also find Indian, Russian and Middle Eastern cooking, generally in upmarket areas.

There's also ample opportunity to eat **Western food** in the city, though this generally costs a little more than a Chinese meal in a comparable restaurant. If you really want the home comforts, try international fast-food chains, many of which are well established here.

Many visitors find the Chinese **breakfast** of dumplings and glutinous rice bland and unappealing, but the classic Beijing breakfast snack *jianbing guozi* (seasonal vegetables wrapped in an omelette wrapped in a pancake), deftly made in thirty seconds by street vendors, is definitely worth trying (¥2). Most large hotels offer some form of Western breakfast; alternatively, head to a branch of *Delifrance* for cheap croissants, *Dunkin' Donuts* for muffins or there are plenty of international coffee shops where you can pick up a coffee, croissant or a muffin. Coffee is generally a drink of the westernized elites, so coffee shops tend to cluster in expensive areas.

Beijing is well stocked with **supermarkets**, especially useful if you want to get a picnic, or have self-catering facilities (see p.160 for details). Finally, note that you can forgo the whole tedious business of leaving your room by contacting Beijing

Goodies (☎010/64167676; ⓦ www.beijinggoodies.com) who deliver from many of the city's popular restaurants, for a small service charge.

Fast food and street food

The Chinese version of fast food (found in department stores or at street stalls), is usually a serving of noodles or dumplings, or rice with meat, in a polystyrene carton. The best Asian fast-food restaurants are Yoshinoya (for noodles), Dayang Dumplings and Viva Curry (fusion curries).

Street food, sold by stalls parked by the roadside, is widely available, though not right in the city centre, where vendors are shooed away by the police. The best place to try street fare is at one of the designated night markets (see p.140), which begin operating around 5pm and start to shut down around 10pm; they're at their busiest and best in the summer. Generally, what's on offer is hygienic – you can feel confident of food cooked in front of you. Most popular are the skewers of heavily spiced, barbecued meat, often served up by Uyghurs from Xinjiang, China's far west. For cheap and filling suppers, try huntun (wonton) soup; xianer bing, savoury stuffed pancake; or the plentiful varieties of noodles. However, you should avoid anything that's eaten cold, such as homemade ice cream, which is often of a dubious standard.

It's also worth knowing that every shopping centre and plaza also holds a **food court** – either in the basement or on the top floor – which offers inexpensive meals from a cluster of outlets. Food courts are good places to start sampling simple Chinese food – the environment may not be very atmospheric but it's clean, and prices are fixed. Paying can be a little confusing at first; you have to buy a plastic card at a central booth (¥20 is the lowest denomination), which is debited at the food counters when you order. There's always a good range of dishes, and as the food is displayed on the counter it's easy to make your selection. Good, substantial food

▲ Tasty *huntun* soup

courts can be found at the Parkson Building on Fuxingmennei Dajie (see p.74); in the Xidan stores (see p.73); and, on Wangfujing, on the sixth floor of the Sun Dong'an Plaza or the basement of the Oriental Plaza (see p.82).

Dong'anmen night market
东安门夜市

dōng 'ānmén yèshì

Dong'anmen Dajie, off Wangfujing Dajie. Set up along the street, the red-canopied stalls here offer xiǎ"o chī – literally, "little eats" – from all over China. Nothing costs more than a few yuan, except the odd delicacy, such as chicken hearts.

Goubuli
狗不理包子铺

gǒubùlǐ bāozipù

155 Di'anmenwai Dajie, just south of the Drum Tower. Delicious steamed buns with various fillings (the original fast food) for a few yuan. You can eat them here – the downstairs canteen is cheaper than upstairs – or take away, as most customers do.

Kempi Deli

1st floor, *Kempinski Hotel* **(see p.136),** Lufthansa Centre, 50 Liangmaqiao Lu. Produces the city's best bread and pastries. It's not cheap (a croissant is ¥12) but prices halve after 8pm. Daily 7am–11pm.

Subway
赛百味

sàibǎiwèi

Jianguomenwai Dajie, just east of the Jinglun Hotel; China World Trade Centre Jianguomenwai Dajie; east side of the Henderson Centre, Jianguomennei Dajie (opposite the International Hotel); 52 Liangjiu Lu (opposite the Kempinski Hotel); opposite the north gate of the Workers' Stadium, Gongrentiyuchang Bei Lu. An American chain offering filling, if pricey, sandwiches. Stays open till midnight.

Xiaochi Jie
小吃街

xiǎochī jiē

Xiagongfu Jie, running west off the southern end of Wangfujing. This alley is lined with stalls where pushy vendors sell exotic food – take the plunge and try skewers of fried scorpions, silkworm pupae, crickets and sparrows; all available for less than ¥10, and not as alarming as you might think. You can also get noodles and seafood for a few yuan.

Yoshinoya

4th floor of the Sun Dong'an Plaza, Wangfujing; outside the main gate of the Yiheyuan (Summer Palace); and in the New World Plaza, Jianguomennei Dajie. A Japanese chain offering bowls of rice topped with slices of meat or fish and vegetables – healthy fast food that's cheap, clean and tasty.

Cafés

As well as those places listed below, note that some bars are also great spots to linger over a cappuccino, notably *Pass By Bar* (see p.149), *Drum and Gong* (see p.144) and *Stone Boat* (see p.148). The places below all have wi-fi.

Bookworm
书虫

shū chóng

Sanlitun Nan Jie, back of building 4 ⓦwww.chinabookworm.com. This classy bistro-cum-café-cum-library stands out in this area. There are regular literary events and lectures; check the website. A good place to muse.

Sculpting In Time
雕刻时光

diāokè shíguāng

7 Weigongcun Lu, outside the southern gate of the Beijing Insititute of Technology ⓦwww.sitcafe.com. A relaxed, attractive café with a largely student clientele. Follow by example and sip on lattes, browsing the book collection and gazing thoughtfully out of the window. They serve good muffins and pasta dishes here, too.

Starbucks

1st floor, China World Trade Centre, Jianguomenwai Dajie; 1 Jianguomenwai Dajie (east side of the Friendship Store); COFCO plaza, 8 Jianguomennei Dajie; Chaoyangmenwai Dajie, opposite the Dongyue Temple; Sun Dong'an Plaza (basement) and Oriental Plaza (1st floor, A307) on Wangfujing Dajie; north side of Xidan Plaza, Xidan. The coffee colonizers have overtaken McDonald's as the most potent symbol of westernization. A medium-sized cup of their caffeinated mud is ¥15.

Vineyard Café
葡萄院儿
pútáoyuànér
31 Wudaoying Hutong, south of Yonghe Gong Bridge. Good western wine and food, including pizzas, makes this popular with the local French community. Cross the second ring-road onto Yonghe Gong Dajie and take the first hutong on the right. Serves good brunches, a perfect combination with a trip to the Yonghe Gong. Closed Mon.

Xiaoxin's
小新的店
xiǎoxīndediàn
103 Nanluogu Xiang. A cosy staple of artsy Nanluogu Xiang with a limited menu; but there is a tasty cheesecake (¥18).

Restaurants

The estimated prices for meals in the reviews are calculated on the basis of each person ordering a couple of dishes plus rice, or a main course and dessert.

All the expensive **hotels** have several well-appointed restaurants, where the atmosphere is sedate and prices are sometimes not as high as you might expect. Look out for their special offers – set lunches and buffets, usually – advertised in the city's listings magazines.

South of the centre

See the map on pp.66–67 for the locations of the restaurants below.

Gongdelin
功德林素菜馆
gōngdélín sùcàiguǎn
158 Qianmen Nan Dajie. This vegetarian restaurant serves Shanghai fake meat dishes. It's rather hit and miss – try the imitation fish dishes, the "dragons' eyes", made of tofu and mushrooms, and the "meatballs". It's partly owned by the government, so service is old-fashioned – meaning lacklustre, at best – though meals are cheap at around ¥50 a head.

Lichun
利群烤鸭店
lìqún kǎoyādiàn
11 Bei Xiang Hutong ☎010/67025681. Deep in a *hutong*, this place is tough to find but offers decent duck at half the price of the chains (¥80). From Qianmen subway stop walk east along Qianmen Dong Dajie, take the first right into Zhengyi Lu, and turn right at the end. Then follow the English sign to the "Lijun Roast Duck Restaurant" and it's on the left. If in doubt, ask a passer-by. The restaurant is in an old courtyard house, and it's small, so you'd be wise to reserve.

Quanjude Roast Duck
全聚德烤鸭店
quánjùdé kǎoyādiàn
32 Qianmen Dajie ☎010/67011379; **14 Qianmen Xi Dajie** ☎010/63018833; ⓦwww.quanjude. com.cn. "The Great Wall and Roast Duck, try both to have a luck", announces a ditty by the entrance to the Qianmen Dajie premises of this Beijing institution, operated by the same family since 1852 and sometime host to luminaries such as Fidel Castro. Though it's touristy, there's nothing inauthentic about the food, and the experience – the bustle and noise, the chef carving at your table – is a memorable one. At Qianmen Dajie, tour groups are herded upstairs, though the ground floor is livelier. Takeaway duck from the same kitchen can be bought next door. The branch on Qianmen Xi Dajie earned its local moniker, "Super Duck", thanks to its size: it seats over 2000. Though it tends to be the haunt of large groups, there are more intimate side rooms with smaller tables. Prices are the same at both locations: a whole duck is ¥170. Not cheap, but worth experiencing once.

East of the centre

The restaurants below are marked on the map on pp.80–81.

Afunti
阿凡提
āfántí
2A Houguaibang Hutong, off Chaoyangmennei Dajie ☎010/65272288, ⓦwww.afunti.com.cn. A boisterous place serving Xinjiang food – kebabs, naan and the like – and featuring belly dancing, an Uigur band, and even a bit of kung fu. Popular with tour groups. Around ¥60 per person.

Golden Thaitanium
泰合金
tàihéjīn
Dongsanhuan Bei Lu, next to the Chaoyang Theatre. Tasty, spicy and inexpensive Thai food in a relaxed setting. There's a picture menu to order from. For an enjoyable evening out, combine a meal here with a trip to the acrobatics show at the theatre next door (see p.154); the restaurant stays open after the performance finishes at 9pm.

🏃 **Jiajingdu Peking Duck**
嘉靖都烤鸭店
jiājìngdū kǎoyā diàn
8 Hot Spring Chamber, Chaoyang Park West Gate, east of Zhanghong Qiao, near Jingchao Building. Go south, past Suzie Wong's bar, turn right after 50m and you'll see a building standing alone; the restaurant is on its north side ☏010/65918008; ⓦ www.afunti.com.cn. This place is pure theatre; your chair is a throne, located in what looks like an Imperial hall, while the emperor and his concubines come out to greet you. It might be bizarre but the Imperial fantasy is impressively authentic and the banquets are pretty good – the duck is the last of many courses, so arrive hungry. Only set meals, starting at ¥200.

Red Capital Club
新红资俱乐部
xīnhóngzī jùlèbù
66 Dongsijiu Tiao; ⓦ **www.redcapitalclub.com. cn.** Imperial cuisine in an environment of pure Communist kitsch, including Mao pictures on the wall and a red-flag limo parked out front. All this irony and decadence will set you back about ¥250 a head.

Wangfujing and around

The restaurants below are marked on the map on p.83.

Fortune Garden
福景轩港式茶餐厅
fújǐngxuān gǎngshì chácāntīng
Palace Hotel (see p.135), Jingyu Hutong ☏010/65128899. Upmarket Cantonese restaurant, popular with Cantonese businessmen. Try the *cha shao bao* – barbecued pork buns. Eating here isn't cheap; it's around ¥150 per person, though at lunchtime there's a delicious *dim sum* buffet for ¥100 per person. Daily 11.30am–2.30pm & 6–10pm.

Green Tianshi Vegetarian Restaurant
绿色天食餐厅
lǜsètaīnshí cāntīng

57 Dengshi Xikou, just off Wangfujing Dajie ☏010/65242349, ⓦ www.greentianshi.com. All dishes in this bright, modern restaurant are tuber-, legume- or grain-based, low in calories and cholesterol-free. This being China, most of this healthy veggie fare is presented as meat imitations. Try "chicken" or "eel" and wash them down with fruit juice – no booze is served. A decent meal will cost about ¥50 per person. The downstairs shop has pricey Western and Chinese health food. Daily 10am–10pm.

Hong Kong Food City
香港美食城
xiānggǎng měishíchéng
18 Dong'anmen Dajie ☏010/65136668. A big, bright Cantonese restaurant with a good seafood menu. Popular with Chinese tourists, and can get noisy. Reasonably priced at around ¥60 per person – if you avoid the sharks' fin.

Muslim Fast Food
Off Dongsixi Dajie. This tackily decorated canteen might not look like much, but it serves cheap and delicious food with lots of vegetarian options. Point to the dishes that take your fancy from the wide selection on display at the counters. The sticky sweets are especially good. Head north up Wangfujing Dajie and just past the crossroads with Wusi Dajie; you'll see a *hutong* full of clothes stalls on the east side of the road. Walk down here about 200m and you'll come to a little square. The restaurant is on the south side, opposite a McDonald's – look for the white lettering on a green background. Bus #102 from Chaoyangmen subway stop.

🏃 **The Courtyard**
四合院
sìhéyuàn
95 Donghuamen Dajie, outside the east gate of the Forbidden City ☏010/65268883, ⓦ www. courtyardbeijing.com. Listed as one of the world's fifty best restaurants, this elegant, modish place specializes in fusion cuisine – continental food with a Chinese twist – which will set you back ¥250 or so. There's a contemporary art gallery downstairs (see p.158) and a cigar lounge upstairs. Daily 6pm–1am.

Wangfujing Quanjude Roast Duck
王府井全聚德烤鸭店
wángfǔjǐng quánjùdé kǎoyādiàn
13 Shuaifuyuan Hutong ☏010/65253310. Smaller than the others in the Quanjude chain (see p.141) – this one earned its unfortunate nickname, "Sick Duck", thanks to its proximity to a hospital. Daily 11am–1.30pm, 4.30–9pm.

Jianguomen and around

See the map on p.86 for the locations of these restaurants.

 Dong Lai Shun Fan Zhuang
东来顺饭庄
dōngláishùn fànzhuāng
Xiaoyangmao Jie, just off Jianguomennei Dajie. A great place to sample hotpot; it's inexpensive, has a very good reputation among locals and an English menu. Stick to the staples – glass noodles, vegetables, tofu and lots of thinly sliced meat – for a plentiful feed. It's just around the corner from the ancient observatory. Around ¥50 per person.

▼ Beijing hotpot

Justine's
Jianguo Hotel (see p.136) 5 Jianguomenwai Dajie. An exclusive French restaurant with the best wine list in the capital. Try the lobster soup or grilled lamb. Service is attentive. Around ¥150 per person.

Makye Ame
玛吉阿米
mǎjí āmǐ
2nd floor, Ā1 Xiushui Nan Jie ☎010/65069616. Hale and hearty Tibetan food in a cosy atmosphere, rather more upscale than anywhere in Tibet. Try the *tashi delek* (a meat lasagne) and wash it down with butter tea. Tibetan singing and dancing on Wed & Fri nights. It's behind the Friendship Store – head north past the Starbucks and take the first alley to the left.

Nadaman
滩万日餐厅
tānwànrì cāntīng
3rd floor, China World Hotel, China World Trade Centre ☎010/65052266. Discreet, minimalist and seriously expensive Japanese restaurant with a three- or four-course set menu priced at ¥300 per person. Most of the ingredients are flown in from Japan. Take someone you want to impress.

Phrik Thai
泰辣椒餐厅
tàilàjiāo cāntīng
Gateway Building, 10 Yabao Lu ☎010/65925236. Smart Thai restaurant popular with expats; try the delicious red curry and chicken satay. There are nightly Thai song and dance performances. Around ¥70 per person.

Rotary Sushi
福助回转寿司
fúzhùhuízhuàn shòusī
Jianguomenwai Dajie. Cheap and idiot-proof Japanese fast-food restaurant just outside the Friendship Store. Choose dishes from the conveyor belt as they glide past (¥5–25, colour-coded according to price). Great for a light lunch.

 Sichuan Government
川京办餐厅
chuānjīngbàn cāntīng
5 Gongyun Tou Tiao, off Jianguomennei Dajie. A fantastic find, serving homesick bureaucrats the best Sichuan food in the capital. Head north up the alley that passes the east side of the Chang'an Theatre, and after 200m there's an alley to the right with a public toilet opposite. Around 50m down the alley a set of green and gold gates on the left mark the entrance to the Sichuan government building. Pass through these into the compound and you'll see the restaurant on the left. No English menu, no concessions to wimpy palettes, no fancy decor – just fantastic, inexpensive food.

Steak and Eggs
喜来中
xǐláizhōng
Xiushui Nan Jie, behind the Friendship Store; ☎010/65928088; ⓦwww.steakeggs.com.cn. Good-value American-diner fare has made this an expat favourite, especially for Sunday brunch.

EATING | Restaurants

Xiheya Ju
義和雅居餐厅
xīhéyǎjū cāntīng

Ritan Park ☎010/65067643. Food from all over China served in an imitation Qing-dynasty mansion. Try the *ganbian rou si* – dried beef fried with celery and chilli, or the spicy Sichuan chicken or shredded lamb. Deservedly popular with locals and expats. ¥60 per head.

Sanlitun and the northeast

See the map on p.88 for the locations of the restaurants reviewed here.

🏃 Ai Yao Hunan Restaurant
爱谣湘菜馆
àiyáo xiāngcàiguǎn

9 Liangmaqiao Lu, opposite the Hilton Hotel. Bus #18 from Dongzhimen subway stop. An excellent little place that gets very busy, so arrive early or late to be sure of getting a table. It serves some of the best *shui zhu roupian*, or boiled spicy pork, in the capital; like many other Hunan dishes, it's spicy, but with a sweet aftertaste. Other dishes to try are Hunan favourites *luobogan larou*, dried turnip with pork; and *rou mo chao suan dou jiao*, sour green beans with mince. ¥40 per head.

Alameda
散步道路
sànbùdàolù

Sanlitun Bei Jie, inside Tongli Studios ☎010/64178084. This bright and cheery Brazilian restaurant is a firm expat place, so be sure to reserve. Set lunches (¥60) are good value, but watch out for that little dish of olives – they aren't complimentary.

Berena's Bistro
柏瑞娜中国菜
bórùinà zhōngguócài

6 Gongrentiyuchang Dong Lu, at the southern end of Sanlitun Nan Jiu Ba Jie ☎010/92262865. Bus #118 from Dongsi Shitiao subway stop.** Foreigner-friendly but a little pricier than elsewhere, serving foreigner friendly Sichuan food (so not too spicy, unless you insist). Try their *gongbao jiding* or the sweet-and-sour pork. Reckon on ¥70 per head.

🏃 Old Character Hakka Restaurant
老汉子客家菜馆
lǎohànzi kèjiā càiguǎn

Qianhai Nanyan; ☎010/64042259. Harassed, shouty staff reveal how popular this place is, and deservedly so – it's cramped but

atmospheric, and the food, Hakka dishes from the south, is delicious and not expensive. Try the "three cup duck".

One Thousand and One Nights
一千零一夜
yīqiānlíngyīyè

21 Gongrentiyuchang Bei Lu ☎010/65324050. Bus #118 comes here from Dongsi Shitiao subway stop.** Beijing's first Middle Eastern restaurant, this place is very popular, a favourite both with Western big wigs who come here to fill up on kebabs before or after hitting the bars, and with homesick diplomats who puff on hookahs on the pavement outside. There's nightly belly dancing. It's open till late but some dishes sell out early on: try the hummus as a starter and the baked chicken for a main course, and leave enough room for some baklava (which can also be bought separately at their sweet shop, 100m east of the restaurant). About ¥60 per head. Daily 11am–2am.

Serve the People
为人民服务
wéirénmínfúwù

1 Sanlitun Xiwujie ☎010/64153242. Trendy Thai restaurant, going for a postmodern Soviet look, presumably ironically. Thai staples such as green curry, pork satay with peanut sauce and *tom yam* seafood soup are all worth trying, and you can ask them to tone down the spices. The stylish T-shirts worn by the staff are available to buy. About ¥70 per person.

North of the centre

The maps on pp.90–91 and p.95 show the places reviewed below.

Drum and Gong
锣鼓洞天
luógǔdòngtiān

104 Nanluogu Xiang. Foreigner friendly, cheap Sichuan and fusion fare. Always busy.

Fangshan
仿膳饭店
fǎngshàn fàndiàn

Beihai park, near the east gate ☎010/64011879 Superbly situated in an ancient building on the central island in Beihai Park, this venue is a great place to sample Imperial cuisine. It's all magisterially kitsch and good for a splurge. Arrive hungry; fixed price meals start at ¥150 per person for fourteen courses. Dishes on offer include chicken pate wrapped in seaweed and egg, camel's

Ghost Street (鬼街, guǐ jiē)

Dongzhimennei Dajie, nicknamed "Ghost Street" (Gui Jie) is lined with hundreds of restaurants – one after the other, and all festooned with red lanterns and neon lights – creating a colourful and boisterous scene, particularly on weekends. Take the subway to Yonghe Gong and walk south for ten minutes.

Many venues specialize in **hotpot** and **shuishuyu** (spicy Sichuan-style fish served in oil on a heated metal tray). Note that staff will likely speak little or no English; though few establishments have an English menu, plenty have a picture menu. You can't go too far wrong just picking somewhere busy, but recommended is famous hotpot brand **Xiao Fei Yang** (209 Dongzhimen Neidajie, north side) and duck restaurant **Huajia** (235 Dongzhimen Neidajie, north side). For spicy fish, try **Dumenchang** (208 Dongzhimen Neidajie, south side).

paw with scallion and turtle soup. The place closes early in the evening; booking is recommended – ask for a lake view.

Fish Nation
鱼邦
yú bāng

31 Jiaodaokou, Nanluogu Xiang You wouldn't guess from the decor, but this is an English restaurant, with a surprisingly authentic fish "n" chips for ¥40. Shame about the lacklustre service but there's a good balcony.

Gong Wang Fu Sichuan Restaurant
恭王府四川饭店
gōngwángfǔ sìchuān fàndiàn

14 Liuyin Jie, just north of Prince Gong's Palace ☎010/66156924. Fiery Sichuan food in a lavishly re-created traditional setting with bamboo chairs and a lot of rosewood – but with pop art on the walls. Sees plenty of tourist traffic, so there's an English menu and they'll tone down the spices if asked. Around ¥60 per head.

Huajia Yiyuan
花家怡园
huājiā yíyuán

Beixinqiao Toutaio, first hutong north of the Dongzhimennei and Yonghegong Dajie intersection; follow the yellow signs for the Lama Temple Youth Hostel, and the restaurant is 50m east of the hostel. This secluded courtyard restaurant, with songbirds and pleasant outdoor seating, is an excellent place to sample Beijing duck, a bargain at ¥88. It's a few doors east of the Lama Temple Youth Hostel.

Hutong Pizza
胡同批萨
hútóng pīsà

9 Yindingqiao ☎010/66175916. A charming little courtyard restaurant serving up delicious, square pizzas. It's hidden

away in an alley; go to the *hutong* directly opposite *Kaorouji* and follow the signs.

Kaorouji
烤肉季
kǎoròu jì

14 Qianhai Dong Yuan ☎010/64045921. **From the Drum Tower, continue south down Di'anmenwai Dajie, then take the first hutong on the right; the restaurant is a short walk down here, just before the lake bridge**. In the *hutongs* close to the Drum Tower, this Muslim place, run by the same family for 150 years, takes advantage of its great lakeside location with big windows and, in summer, balcony tables. The beef and barbecued lamb dishes are recommended. Around ¥50 a head. Daily 11am–2pm & 5–8.30pm.

Mei Mansion
梅府家宴
méifǔjiāyàn

24 Daxiangfeng Hutong, Houhai ☎010/66126845. You can expect to pay ¥400 a head, but if you're really set on impressing a date, this courtyard deep in a *hutong* is the place to take them. The private dining rooms are elegantly furnished with antiques and the meals are lavish.

Nengrenju
能仁居饭庄
néngrénjū fànzhuāng

5 Taipingqiao Dajie, close to Baita Si. From Fuchengmen subway stop, head east for about 500m, then turn right (south) down Taipingqiao Dajie. A neat little place to sample Mongolian hotpot. There's a lot on the menu, including the classic ingredients – mutton, cabbage, potato and glass noodles. With all those boiling pots, it gets quite hot and steamy here in the evening. The place is very popular with middle-class locals – you'll just have to tolerate the mobile phones.

Nuage
庆云楼
qìngyún lóu
Just east of Kaorouji, at 22 Qianhai Dong Zhao ☎ **010/64019581.** Decent Vietnamese food and a smart but cozy upstairs bar-restaurant. Try steamed garlic prawns and battered squid, and finish with super-strong Vietnamese coffee if you don't intend to sleep in the near future. ¥100 per head. Don't forget to visit the extraordinary tropical fantasy toilets. Daily 10am–9.30pm; bar open till 2am.

Sauveurs de Coree
韩香馆
hánxiāng guǎn
29 Nanluogu Xiang; ☎ **010/64016083.** A comfortable Korean bistro, with keen-to-please staff. If you're new to spicy Korean cuisine, go for one of the set meals, which start at ¥50 for *bibimbap* (rice, vegetables, egg and beef). Finish with iced cinnamon tea.

The Source
都江源
dūjiāng yuán
14 Banchang Hutong; ☎ **010/64003736,** ⊛ **www. yanclub.com** Foreigner-friendly Sichuan set-meals, starting at ¥120 per person, in a courtyard restaurant next to the *Lusongyuan Hotel.* They'll go easy on the spices if you ask.

Supermarkets

All supermarkets sell plenty of Western food alongside all the Chinese, though few have a decent range of dairy products. The CRC Supermarket in the basement of the China World Trade Centre is impressive, though Western goods cost a little more here than they would at home. Park'n'Shop, in the basement of the COFCO Plaza on Jianguomen Dajie, is a little cheaper. The supermarket on the first floor of the Friendship Store, Jianguomenwai Dajie, is very pricey but a good place to find imported cheese and canned goods. The Parkson Store, Lufthansa Centre and CVIC Plaza also have large basement supermarkets, and Carrefour have stores at 6 Dongsanhuan Bei Lu, just west of the zoo, and on Xizhimenwai Dajie.

But for the best range of Western produce, including hard-to-find items such as oregano and hummus, head for **Jenny Lou's** outside the west gate of Chaoyang Park in the east of the city, where prices are half those of the Friendship Store.

Beijing's large population of Korean expats are amply catered for in the strip of restaurants, shops and bars at "**Koreatown**", in Wudaokou, Haidian District, outside the Beijing Language and Culture Insititute. Prices for meals are pretty inexpensive, around ¥30 per head. The other Koreatown, opposite the *Kempinski Hotel* (see p.000), is more upmarket. At either, pick any restaurant that looks busy and order *nayng myon*, cold noodles; *bibimbap*, a clay pot of rice, vegetables, egg and beef; or *pulgoki* barbecued beef, which you cook yourself on the table grill.

Drinking and nightlife

eijing's nightlife scene has well and truly recovered from the moral clampdown of the 1960s and 70s, when "bourgeois" bars and teahouses disappeared. They were replaced by an enforced emphasis on traditional Chinese culture (especially opera and formal theatre), which was often worthy to the point of tedium, and at its worst when addressing the subject matter of the revolution. Nowadays, modern Beijingers, who find themselves with rising disposable incomes, living through comparatively liberal times, just want to have a good time.

In 1995, **Sanlitun Lu** in the east of the city had just one bar, and it was losing money. A new manager bought it, believing the place had potential but that the *feng shui* was wrong – the toilet was opposite the door and all the wealth was going down it. He changed the name, moved the loo, and – so the story goes – the city's bar scene took off from there. Now the area is choked with drinking holes, and new bars open all the time. Many mimic their popular neighbours; if one does well, a couple more will open around it, and before you know it, the original will have closed down.

Most **clubs** these days have embraced a slickly international style, and import their DJs from abroad. The city's **indie music** scene is thriving – for more, see p.155.

Bars

Beijing bars appear quickly, multiply, then die suddenly. For the latest information, check one of the expat magazines (see p.45).

Despite recent demolitions, Sanlitun Lu remains as popular as ever. Head up the main strip (avoiding the touts, beggars, neon and sleaze); just off it lie a fascinating array of diverse venues, from cheap and cheerful pick-up joints to exclusive jazz bars.

A mellow scene exists around attractive **Houhai**, where venues are laid-back, with ambient music and no dancefloors. For a really civilised drink, join the artsy crowd at the heritage district Nanluogu Xiang. A group of new expat-oriented bars around the west gate of **Chaoyang Park** in the far east of the city is increasingly popular. For something a bit edgier – and the heart of the rock scene – head to Wudaokou; the student clientele means these places tend to be cheaper and trendier.

Bar **hours** are flexible – a bar tends to close only when its last barfly has lurched off – though all bars open till at least midnight (and well into the early hours at weekends). We've listed the phone numbers of bars that can be tough to find (just get your cabbie to ring them) or have regular gigs; usually there's a cover charge to get in (around ¥30) when a band is playing.

Though Chinese **beer** can be cheaper than bottled water if bought in a shop, a 350ml bottle of Tsingtao or the local Yanjing at a bar will usually cost ¥15–25. Many bars also sell Western draught beers such as Guinness and Boddingtons, which cost at least ¥40. The *Tree* (see below) has an impressive collection of Belgian brews.

East of the centre

Just inside the northeast section of the third ring road, this busy area can be reached by taking the subway to Dongsi Shitiao, then bus #113 east; get off at the third stop. The main strip – **Sanlitun Lu** – is sometimes called **Jiuba Jie**, literally "bar street".

We've listed the best bars below, but there are plenty more in this area from which to choose. In addition to drinks, a few offer Western food, and there are plenty of decent places to eat in the area too (see p.144). Venues with a cover charge are listed under discos. The places listed here are marked on the maps on pp.80–81, p.86 and p.86.

Browns
红磨坊
hóngmò fǎng
Nan Sanlitun Lu The punters, it would appear, just can't get enough of this joint: many get so excited they cannot restrain themselves from dancing on the bar. Good pub grub, lots of shots and draught beer at ¥40. It's neither big nor clever but it does the job.

Bus Bar
车吧
chē bā
On the edge of the parking lot by the north gate of the Workers' Stadium. A cheap and cheerful bar made out of two buses welded together and decorated with graffiti. ¥5 tequilas and gangster rap bring in plenty of passengers.

Centro
炫酷酒廊
xuànkù jiǔláng
1st floor, *Kerry Centre Hotel*, **1 Guanghua Lu.** Slinky lounge bar whose lavish cocktails will cost the best part of a red bill. Dress up.

Jazz Ya
爵士屋
juéshì wū
18 Sanlitun Bei Lu ☎**010/64151227.** This mellow place, with its rough-hewn wooden tables and moody music, has a better drinks menu than most of its neighbours. It's set back from the road; look for the yellow sign down an alley next to *Bella Coffee*. Occasional live jazz.

Kai
开吧
kāi bā
Sanlitun Bei Jie, behind 3.3 Mall. An unpretentious little bar, popular with foreigners for the ¥10 beers.

Public Space
阿尔卑斯酒屋
āěrbēisī jiǔwū
50 Sanlitun Lu. Though the exterior looks like every other watering hole on the strip, this is actually Sanlitun's first bar, perennially popular and one of the liveliest in the area. Draught beer is ¥20, a gin and tonic ¥30.

Stone Boat
石舫酒吧
shífǎng jiǔbā
Southwest corner of Ritan Park, by the lake ☎65019986. A stubby pier shaped like a boat – the sort of thing you would expect to find in the Summer Palace – has been sympathetically converted into a great little venue, with a good tea and wine list and live music on summer evenings. Recommended at any time of day.

Tree
树酒吧
shù jiǔbā
43 Sanlitun Nan Lu, behind 3.3 Mall; ☎64151954; ⊛www.treebeijing.com Cosy, relaxed and unassumingly fashionable, with a good selection of Belgian white beers and great pizza. Free wi-fi.

Around Chaoyang Park

Bus #113 comes here from Dongsi Shitiao subway – get off at the fourth stop.

Goose and Duck
鹅和鸭酒吧
éhéyā jiǔba
Outside the park's west gate ⊛www.gdclub.net. cn A faux British pub run by an American, this

is the place to play pool and darts, and watch sports on TV. Good Guinness and shepherd's pie. Two drinks for the price of one 4–8pm.

World of Suzie Wong
苏西黄酒吧
sūxīhuáng jiǔbā

Outside the park's west gate, above the Mirch Masala restaurant – look for the discreet yellow neon sign outside ⓦ www.suziewong.com.cn Striking neo-Oriental decor – think lacquer and rose petals. Dancing downstairs and a cocktail bar above. Though named after a fictional Hong Kong prostitute, this is a classy place, so dress up.

▼ World of Suzie Wong

North of the centre

As well as the obvious strip that runs alongside of **Houhai**, there are plenty of chilled out venues sunk in the *hutongs* all around.

To reach the area, take bus #107 from Dongzhimen subway stop, get off at the north entrance to Beihai Park and walk north around the lake. The places listed here are marked on the map on p.95.

Bed Bar
床
chuáng

17 Zhangwang Hutong ☏ 010/84001554 Good looking, courtyard night spot, rather hidden away from the action and all the better for it. Serves good tapas.

Drum and Bell
鼓钟咖啡馆
gǔzhōng kāfēiguǎn

41 Zhonglouwan Hutong; ☏ 010/84033600 With a great location between the drum and bell towers and welcoming staff this little place is always popular. The rooftop patio is an added bonus in summer.

Huxleys
德比酒吧
débǐ jiǔbā

Yandai Xiejie. Cheap booze, no attitude and approachable staff make this a winner with the "wild young expat" demographic.

No Name Bar

3 Qianhai Dongyuan, just east of the Kaorouji restaurant. A hippy-ish café bar that thinks it's special because it doesn't have a sign. Look for the red walls and the out of control foliage. This was the first lakeside bar, and its trendy anonymity and bric-a-brac-style interior design has informed every other one in the area. They also serve Yunnan cuisine.

Pass By Bar
过客酒吧
guòkè jiǔbā

108 Nan Luo Guo Xiang, off Di'anmen Dong Dajie ☏ 010/84038004. A renovated courtyard house turned comfortable bar/restaurant, popular with backpackers and students. There are lots of books and pictures of China's far-flung places to peruse, and well-travelled staff to chat to – if you can get their attention. Pretty good pizzas too.

Sex and da City
欲望都市
yùwáng dūshì

Houhai, Lotus Lane. A pick-up joint with bartop dancing; Carrie Bradshaw might not approve but Samantha probably would.

Nightclubs

Gone are the days when everything stopped at 10pm for a raffle; Chinese clubs are pretty slick these days, with hip hop and house music proving enduringly popular. There's a dense concentration of clubs around the west side of the Workers' Stadium, and on Saturday night the car park here is full of white Mercedes dropping off the *dakuans* (big moneys) and their *xiaomis* (little honeys). African guys work the crowds, selling the shaky head drug (ecstasy). Welcome to the new China.

All places listed here have a cover charge, given in our reviews, which generally increases at weekends. Note that if you just want to dance, and aren't too prissy about the latest music, see the bar reviews above for venues with their own dance-floor; *World of Suzie Wong* is a popular choice.

East of the centre

Sanlitun and the northeast

These venues are labelled on the maps on p.88.

▼ Vics nightclub

Vics 威克斯
wēikèsī
Inside the Workers' Stadium's north gate, next to the *Outback* **steakhouse.** Eighties LA decor, a sweaty dancefloor and a Less Than Zero-ambience of numb dissipation. The low cover charge and cheapish drinks (bottled beer ¥15) make it popular with students and embassy brats. Women get in free on Wednesdays and get free drinks till midnight. Thursday is ragga/reggae night. Hip-hop, R&B and techno all weekend. ¥30 except Thurs, when it's free to get in.

Babyface
娃娃脸
wáwáliǎn
6 Gongti Xi Lu, Workers' Stadium West Gate.
Big, brash and bold, for those who need lasers and breakbeat in their life. The dancefloor practically steams. Regularly hosts international DJs and has just been ranked as one of the world's top fifty clubs. ¥40 cover, more on weekends.
China Doll
中国娃娃
zhōngguó wáwá
Tongli Studios 2nd floor, Sanlitun Jie.
Despite the name, this slinky place has an undersea theme; popular with sharks, exotic tropicals and bottom feeders. No cover, but pricey drinks.

Jianguomen

Club Banana
赛特饭店
sàitè fàndiàn
Scitech Hotel, **22 Jianguomenwai Dajie.** Huge and in-your-face, this mega club has three sections – techno, funk and chill-out – and features go-go girls, karaoke rooms and an enthusiastic, young clientele. Mon–Thurs & Sun 8.30pm–4am, Fri & Sat 8.30pm–5am. ¥20, except weekends ¥40.

Gay Beijing

Official **attitudes** towards homosexuality have softened of late – it's been removed from the official list of psychiatric disorders and is no longer a national crime, though gay men have occasionally been arrested under public disturbance statutes. That's unlikely to happen in cosmopolitan Beijing however, where pink power is a big influence on fashion and the media.

The **gay scene** is vibrant but discreet, with gay bars no longer required to hand out pamphlets urging clients to go home to their wives. *Destination* (see map on p.000) at 7 Gongti Xi Lu, opposite the Worker's Stadium West Gate, is one of the livelier revues, with a busy dance floor (ⓦwww.bjdestination.com). *Drag-On* , at Deshengmen Tower, Sanhuan Bei Lu (ⓣ010/62019110), is fun, with weekend amateur pole dancing and other activities for the *tongzhi* (literally, comrades). *Club Banana* (see above) is popular with the young gay crowd.

⑪

Entertainment and art

M ost visitors to Beijing make a trip to see **Beijing opera** and the superb Chinese **acrobatics displays** – both of which remain timeless arts. Fewer investigate the equally worthwhile contemporary side of the city's entertainment scene – the new music, theatre and art events. There are also a number of **cinemas** where you can check out the provocative movies emerging from new, underground film-makers.

For mainstream cultural events – visiting ballet troupes, large-scale concerts and so forth – check the listings in the *China Daily*, available at most hotels; but for a more in-depth view and comprehensive listings, including gigs and art happenings and the like, check an expat magazine (see p.45).

Tickets for all big shows are available at the venue's box office or from China Ticket Online (☎010/64177845, ⓦwww.piao.com.cn).

Traditional opera

Beijing opera (*jingxi*) is the most celebrated of China's 350 or so regional operatic styles – a unique combination of song, dance, acrobatics and mime. Highly stylized, to the outsider the performances can often seem obscure and wearying, as they are punctuated by a succession of crashing gongs and piercing, discordant songs.

Shows at teahouses

Beijing has a small number of teahouse theatres, where you can sit and snack and watch performances of Beijing opera, sedate *zither* music and martial arts, though all are aimed at tourists rather than locals.

You can watch a ninety-minute variety show – comprising all three genres – at the **Lao She Teahouse**, 3rd floor, Dawancha Building, 3 Qianmen Xi Dajie (daily 2.30pm & 7.40pm; ¥40–130, afternoon performances are cheaper; ☎010/63036830, ⓦwww.laosheteahouse.com). Popular with tour groups, the show gives a gaudy taste of traditional Chinese culture.

The **Tianqiao Theatre**, set in a mock-traditional building at 113 Tianqiao Nan Dajie (☎010/63040617), aims to create an authentic atmosphere, right down to the Qing costumes of the staff. Performances begin at 7pm and last two hours, and are mostly segments of traditional opera with a little acrobatics in between. The ticket price of ¥180 includes tea and snacks; for ¥330, you get a duck dinner, too. Buying tickets a day in advance is advised as the place is sometimes booked out with tour groups.

The **Sanwei Bookstore**, at 60 Fuxingmennei Dajie (opposite the *Minzu Hotel*; ☎010/66013204) has jazz on Fridays and Chinese folk music on Saturdays (both 8.30–10pm).

ENTERTAINMENT AND ART | Traditional opera

But it's worth seeing once, especially if you can acquaint yourself with the story beforehand. Most of the plots are based on historical or mythological themes – two of the most famous sagas, which any Chinese will explain to you, are *The White Snake* and *The Water Margin* – and full of moral lessons. An interesting, if controversial, variation

▲ Painting faces before opera

on the traditions are operas dealing with contemporary themes – such as the struggle of women to marry as they choose. Apart from checking out the venues below, you can visit a teahouse for your opera fix (see p.151). Teahouse performances are short and aimed at foreigners; you can also slurp tea or munch on snacks – often Beijing duck as well – while being entertained.

The **colours** used on stage, from the costumes to the make-up on the players' faces, are highly symbolic: red signifies loyalty; yellow, fierceness; blue, cruelty; and white, evil.

Chang'an Theatre
长安大剧院
cháng'ān dàjùyuàn
7 Jianguomennei Dajie ☎010/65101309. A modern, central theatre putting on nightly performances at 7.15pm. ¥40–150.

Huguang Guild Hall
湖广会馆
húguǎng huìguǎn
3 Hufang Lu, a 20min walk south from Hepingmen subway stop ☎010/63518284, ⑩www.beijinghuguang.com. This reconstructed theatre with a fine performance hall also has a small opera museum on site, with costumes and pictures of famous performers, though no English captions. Nightly performances at 7.15pm. ¥150–¥280.

Liyuan Theatre
梨园剧场
líyuán jùchǎng
1st floor of the Jianguo Qianmen Hotel (see p.134), 175 Yong'an Lu. Take bus #66 from Hepingmen subway stop ☎010/63016688 ext 8860. Pricey, but perhaps the best place to see opera, with an emphasis on accessibility; as you go in you pass the actors putting on their make-up – a great photo op. The opera itself is a visitor-friendly bastardization, lasting an

hour and jazzed up with some martial arts and slapstick. A display board at the side of the stage gives an English translation of the few lines of dialogue. Nightly performances are at 7.30pm; tickets can be bought from the office in the front courtyard of the hotel (daily 9–11am, noon–4.45pm & 5.30–8pm; ¥70–180). The more expensive seats are at tables at the front, where you can sip tea and nibble pastries during the performance.

Prince Gong's mansion
恭王府
gōngwáng fǔ
Liuyun Jie ☎010/66186628. Opera is put on every night for tour groups in the grand hall at the Prince Gong mansion (see p.95). Call to book a seat. Performances start at 7.30pm and cost ¥80–120.

Zhengyici Theatre
正义祠剧场
zhèngyìcí jùchǎng
220 Qianmen Xiheyan Jie ☎010/63189454. The genuine article, performed in the only surviving wooden Beijing opera theatre and worth a visit just to check out the architecture. Duck dinners cost an additional ¥110. Performances nightly at 7.30pm (2hr; ¥150).

Drama and dance

Spoken **drama** was only introduced into Chinese theatres in the twentieth century. The People's Art Theatre in Beijing became the best-known company and, prior to the Cultural Revolution, staged Chinese-language translations of European plays – Ibsen and Chekhov were among the favourite playwrights. But in 1968, Jiang Qing, Mao's third wife, declared that "drama is dead". The company, along with most of China's cinemas and theatres, was almost completely out of action for nearly a decade afterwards, with a corpus of just eight plays (deemed socially improving) continuing to be performed. Many of the principal actors, directors and writers were banished, generally to rural hard labour. In 1979 the People's Art Theatre reformed and quickly re-established its reputation.

Most evenings you can catch Chinese **song and dance** simply by turning on the TV, though there's plenty of opportunity to see it live. One revue not to miss is the regularly staged Red Detachment of Women, a classic piece of retro communist pomp that celebrates a revolutionary women's fighting outfit – the dancers wear guerilla uniform and carry hand grenades and rifles. Some venues, such as the Beijing Exhibition Theatre (see below), occasionally stage performances, in the original language, of imported musicals like The Sound of Music, which, with tickets at ¥50–100, are a lot cheaper to watch here than at home.

Dance is popular in Beijing, generally more so at the traditional end of the spectrum, though a few small venues purvey more contemporary forms. Besides the venues listed below, the Poly Theatre (see p.155) is another place where you can watch theatrical and dance performances.

Beijing Exhibition Theatre
北京展览馆剧场
běijīng zhǎnlǎnguǎn jùchǎng
135 Xizhimenwai Dajie ℡010/68354455, ⓦwww.bjexpo.com. This giant hall stages classical concerts and large-scale song-and-dance revues.

Beijing Modern Dance Company Theatre
北京现代舞团实验剧场
běijīng xiàndàiwǔtuán shíyàn jùchǎng
8 Majiabao Dongli, in the south of the city beyond the third ring road ℡010/67573879. A small but dedicated dance troupe performing modern pieces. Tickets are cheap at around ¥40.

Capital Theatre
首都剧场
shǒudū jùchǎng
22 Wangfujing Dajie ℡010/65253677. Look out for the People's Art Theatre company here – displayed in the lobby is their photo archive, documenting their history. Tickets generally start at ¥40 and can cost as much as ¥300.

Experimental Theatre For Dramatic Arts
中央实验话剧院小剧场
zhōngyāng shíyànhuàjùyuàn xiǎojùchǎng
45 Mao'er Hutong, Di'ananmen Dajie ℡010/64031099. This is known for putting on modern, avant-garde performances, in Chinese.

Puppet Theatre
中央木偶剧院
zhōngyāng mùǒu jùyuàn
Ā, Section 1, Anhua Xi Li, Bei Sanhuan Lu (third ring road), opposite the Sogo Department Store ℡010/64254798, ⓦwww.puppetchina.com. Once as important for commoners as opera was for the elite, Chinese puppetry usually involves hand puppets and marionettes. Occasionally, shadow puppets made of thin translucent leather and supported by rods are used. Beijing opera, short stories and fairy tales, aimed at kids. Shows daily at 6.30pm. ¥20.

Acrobatics and martial arts

Certainly the most accessible and exciting of the traditional Chinese entertainments, **acrobatics** covers anything from gymnastics through to magic tricks and juggling. The tradition of professional acrobatics has existed in China for two thousand years and continues today at the country's main training school, Wu Qiao in Hebei province, where students begin training at the age of 5. The style may be vaudeville, but performances are spectacular, with truly awe-inspiring feats of dexterity – sixteen people stacked atop a bicycle and the like. Just as impressive are martial-arts displays, which usually involve a few mock fights and feats of strength, such as breaking concrete slabs with one blow.

Chaoyang Theatre
朝阳剧场
cháoyáng jùchǎng
36 Dongsanhuan Bei Lu ☎010/65072421. If you want to see acrobatics, come to one of the shows here. At the end, the Chinese tourists rush off as if it's a fire drill, leaving the foreign tour groups to do the applauding. There are plenty of souvenir stalls in the lobby – make your purchases after the show rather than during the interval, as prices reduce at the end. Shows nightly (1hr 15min); tickets cost ¥180, though they can work out cheaper if you arrange them through your hotel.

Red Theatre
红剧场
hóng jùchǎng
44 Xingfu Dajie, east of the Temple of Heaven ☎010/67142473. A lively kung fu routine, taking place daily at 7.30pm. Tickets ¥180–680.

Wansheng Theatre
万胜剧场
wànshèng jùchǎng
95 Tianqiao Market, at the eastern end of Beiwei Lu and west of Tiantan Park ☎010/63037449. Performances at this oddly unkempt theatre are lighter on glitz than elsewhere. Nightly performances at 7.15pm. ¥100–150.

Xinrong Theatre
金融剧院
jīnróng jùyuàn
16 Baizhifang Xi Jie, the street leading west off the southern end of Niu Jie ☎010/63543344. A popular kung fu show with a story about two competing schools used as an excuse for a monumental choreographed rumble. Nightly performances at 7.30pm. ¥70–280.

Live-music venues

Traditional Han Chinese music is usually played on the *erhu* (a kind of fiddle) and *qin* (a seven-stringed *zither*). Contemporary compositions tend to be in a pseudo-romantic, Western-influenced style; easy on the ear, they can be heard live in upmarket hotels and restaurants. To hear traditional pieces, visit the concert halls, the Sanwei Bookstore on a Saturday (see p.151) or the *Tianhai Teahouse*. Western classical music is popular – the best place to catch it is the Beijing Concert Hall – as is jazz, which you can hear at a few venues, notably *Jazz Ya* (see p.148) and the Sanwei Bookstore on Fridays.

Mainstream **Chinese pop** – mostly slushy ballads sung by Hong Kong or Taiwanese heartthrobs – is hard to avoid; it pumps out of shops on every street and can be heard live at the Workers' Stadium (see p.155). Beijing also has a thriving underground scene of edgy rock (see box opposite).

Beijing Concert Hall 北京音乐厅
běijīng yīnyuètīng
1 Beixinhua Jie, just off Xichang'an Jie ☎010/66057006. South of Zhongnanhai, this hall seats 1000 people and hosts regular concerts of Western classical and Chinese traditional music by Beijing's resident orchestra and visiting orchestras from the rest of China and overseas. Tickets, usually priced in the ¥30–150 range, can be bought here, at the CVIK Plaza (see p.85), and at the Parkson Department Store (see p.74).

Century Theatre

世纪剧院

shìjì jùyuàn

At the Sino-Japanese Youth Centre, 40 Liang-maqiao Lu, 2km east of the Kempinski Hotel ☎010/64663311. An intimate venue for soloists and small ensembles. Mostly Chinese modern and traditional classical compositions. Evening performances. ¥120–150.

Forbidden City Concert Hall

北京中山公园音乐堂

běijīng zhōngshāngōngyuán yīnyuètáng

Inside Zhongshan Park, Xi Chang'an Jie ☎010/65598285. A stylish new hall, with regular performances of Western and Chinese classical music. Tickets from ¥20.

Poly Theatre

保利大厦国际剧场

bǎolìdàshà guójìjùchǎng

Poly Plaza, 14 Dongzhimen Nan Dajie, near Dongsi Shitiao subway stop ☎010/65001188 ext 5127, ⓦwww.polyculture.com.cn. A gleaming hall that presents diverse performances of jazz, ballet, classical music, opera and modern dance for the enjoyment of Bei-

jing's cultural elite. Tickets start at around ¥100 and performances begin 7.15pm.

Workers' Stadium

工人体育场

gōngrén tǐyùchǎng

In the northeast of the city, off Gongren Tiy-uchang Bei Lu ☎010/65016655. This is where giant gigs are staged, mostly featuring Chinese pop stars, though the likes of Björk have also played here.

2 Kolegas

两个好朋友

liǎnggè hǎopéngyǒu

21 Liangmaqiao, inside the drive-in movie cinema park ☎010/81964820, ⓦwww.2kolegas.com. This dive bar is great for checking out the indie rockers and their fans. In summer the crowd spill out onto the lawn.

D22

242 Chengfu Lu; come out of Wudaokou Subway and walk towards the Beijing University East Gate ☎010/62653177, ⓦwww.d22beijing.com. In-your-face bar in Wudaokou that attracts an energetic student crowd. Try and catch house band

The Beijing music scene

Controversial local legend **Cui Jian**, a sort of Chinese Bob Dylan, was China's first real rock star, giving up a job as a trumpeter in a Beijing orchestra to perform gravel-voiced guitar rock with lyrics as risky as he could get away with. Look out for his albums *Power to The Powerless* and *Egg Under the Red Flag*.

Cui Jian is now seen as the granddaddy of Beijing's thriving **indie music** scene. Nobody makes any money, as venues and bands struggle to survive against all-pervasive pop pap, and when an act does take off, piracy eats up any profits the recordings might have made – but fierce dedication keeps the scene alive. Most bands of note are on the Scream, Badhead or Modern Sky labels and the best new electronic music is on Shanshui Records.

Many **bands** perform in English, or have a mixed set. Currently, Beijing's best live bands are the Rolling Stones-wannnabies Joyside, who have made venue D22 their own; pouty Joy Division fans, the Retros, Mongolian rockers Voodoo Kungfu, indie noise merchants Last Chance of Youth, and the grungey Hedgehog. Veteran punks Brain Failure are still going strong, though the mantle of nuttiest punks has passed to younger bands like Demerit (now fronted by Chun Sue, see p.000). For electronica, look out for iLoop and Sulumi.

Not so well represented is **hip hop**, (odd, as it has made plenty of inroads in fashion) though old favourites CMCB carry it off pretty well.

The **Midi Rock Music** festival is held at the beginning of May in Haidian Park, just west of Beijing University campus (ⓦwww.midifestival.com). In 2007 there were four stages and almost two hundred bands played. Plenty of local talent is on display along with a few foreign acts, and the audience is enthusiastic. You can even camp, for the full on "Chinese Glastonbury" experience. Tickets are ¥100 for the four-day event, ¥50 for one day.

The above venues are a line-up of the best live music venues; there will generally be a cover of around ¥30.

Joyside to observe Chinese crowd surfing. Rival rock venue, Club 13 (ⓦ www.myspace .com/13clubinchina), is two doors down.

Mao Live

光芒

guāngmáng

111 Gulou Dong Dajie, at the north end of Nan-luogu Xiang ☎ 010/64025080, ⓦ www.maolive. com. With perhaps the best sound system around, this great venue hosts all the best local rock and punk bands; the crowd could be more animated though. Management know their stuff.

What Bar

什么酒吧

shénme jiǔbā

72 Beichang Jie, north of the Forbidden City west gate ☎ 13341122757. Oddly, this rock and punk gig venue is within spitting distance of the Forbidden City. It's so small you could reach out and play the instruments (though it's not advised).

Yugong Yishan

愚公移山

yúgōngyíshān

Gongti Bei Lu, opposite the north gate of the Workers' Stadium ☎ 010/64150687. With a big dance floor, an up-for-it crowd and an eclectic mix of live acts, this has to be the all round best venue in town. There are rumours of a relocation, so ring to check.

Cinemas

There are plenty of **cinemas** showing Chinese and dubbed Western films, usually action movies. Just ten Western films are picked by the government for release every year. Despite such restrictions, these days most Beijingers have an impressive knowledge of world cinema, thanks to the prevalence of cheap, pirated DVDs.

Some of the largest screens in Beijing, showing mainstream Chinese and foreign films, are the old Dahua Cinema at 82 Dongdan Bei Dajie (☎ 010/65274420, ⓦ www.dhfilm.cn), Star City in the Oriental Plaza Mall (BB65, 1 Dongchang'an jie;

Beijing on film

Chinese film is enjoying something of a renaissance. Foreigners are likely to be familiar with acclaimed "fifth generation" films such as **Chen Kaige's** *Farewell My Concubine*, the epic tragedy of a gay Beijing opera singer, and **Zhang Yimou's** hauntingly beautiful *Raise the Red Lantern*.

However, these films were criticized at home as being overly glamourous and made only for foreigners. The new "sixth generation" of directors subsequently set out to make edgier work. Their films, usually low-budget affairs, shot in black and white – and difficult to catch in China – depict what their makers consider to be the true story of modern urban life: cold apartments, ugly streets, impoverished people. The most well-known of these films is *Beijing Bastards*, the story of apathetic, fast-living youths, which included a role for rebel rocker Cui Jian (see p.000). The satirical *In The Heat of The Sun* was scripted by **Wang Shuo**, the bad boy of Chinese contemporary literature (see p.000), and perfectly captures the post-revolutionary ennui of 1970s Beijing in its tale of a street gang looking for kicks.

Commercial films have been influenced by this social-realist aesthetic; look out for *Beijing Bicycle*, the story of a lad trying to get his stolen bike back, and **Liu Fendou's** *Spring Subway*, which employs the capital's gleaming new underground stations as a backdrop to the main character's soul-searching.

The biggest box office director is **Feng Xiaogang**. Sadly, he's started making overwrought historical confections like *The Banquet*, but his early works – *Be There or Be Square*, *Sorry Baby*, *A World Without Thieves* and *Big Shot's Funeral* – are his best: light, clever comedies set in Beijing.

85186778, ⓦ www.xfilmcity.com); the Xin Dong'an Cinema on the fifth floor of the Sun Dong'an Plaza in Wangfujing (ⓣ 010/65281988, ⓦ www.xfilmcity.com) and the UME Huaxing Cinema at 44 Kexueyuan Nan Lu, Haidian, next to the Shuang Yu Shopping Centre, just off the third ring road (ⓣ 010/62555566) – which has the biggest screen. **Tickets** cost ¥50 or more. There are usually two showings of foreign movies; one dubbed into Chinese, the other subtitled. Ring to check.

Space for Imagination at 5 Xi Wang Zhuang Xiao Qu, Haidian, opposite Qinghua University's east gate, (ⓣ 010/62791280) is a sleek cineastes' bar that shows avant-garde films every Saturday at 7pm.

The best **art-film** venue though, is Cherry Lane Movies, usually housed at the Peking Opera Photo Studio, Kent Centre 29 Liangmaqiao Lu, 2km east of the Kempinski Hotel. (ⓣ 010/65224046, ⓦ www.cherrylanemovies.com.cn; check as the venue changes occasionally). Their screenings, which include obscure and controversial underground Chinese films, usually with English subtitles, take place every Friday at 7.30pm (¥50), followed by a discussion, often featuring the director or cast members.

Art galleries

Chinese **painting** has an ancient history. The earliest brush found in China, made out of animal hairs glued to a hollow bamboo tube, dates from about 400 BC. The Chinese used silk for painting on as early as the third century BC, with paper being used as early as 106 AD. **Traditional** Chinese paintings are light and airy, with empty spaces playing an important element in the design, and rich in symbolism; they're decorated with a few lines of poetry and several names in the form of seals – the marks of past owners.

The best place to see fine **classical** Chinese paintings is the gallery in the Forbidden City (see p.62); examples from the Sui, Song and Tang dynasties are the highlights. Respectable examples of Chinese painting are for sale at the Traditional Painting Store, at 289 Wangfujing Dajie. However, be wary in general of private art galleries selling classical-looking paintings. They're aimed at tourists, and almost all the images are worthless prints or produced en masse in art sweatshops.

Contemporary art is flourishing in Beijing, and worth checking out. Chinese art schools emphasize traditional crafts, but many students have been quick to plug themselves into international trends. At its best, this leads to art that is technically proficient and conceptually strong. Artists and photographers have fewer problems with censorship and counterfeiting than writers or musicians and the scene has been nurtured by considerable foreign interest – the best galleries are owned by expats, and Chinese art is seen as an attractive investment by foreign buyers.

The arty stomping ground is **798**, an old electronics factory in the north east of the city that's been redeveloped as a sprawl of studios and over a hundred galleries (see p.87 for more information). Some of the most reputable galleries here are the Beijing Commune (ⓣ 010/86549428, ⓦ www.beijingcommune.com), White Space (ⓣ 010/84562054, ⓦ www.alexanderochs-galleries.de), Star Gallery (ⓣ 010/84560591, ⓦ www.stargallery.com) and Beijing Tokyo Art Projects (ⓣ 010/84573245, ⓦ www.tokyo-gallery.com).

China Art Gallery
中国美术馆
zhōngguó měishùguǎn
1 Wusi Dajie. Bus #2 from Qianmen or trolleybus

#104 from Beijing Zhan. At the northern end of Wangfujing Dajie, this huge, recently renovated building usually holds a couple of shows at once. There's no permanent display; past exhibitions have included specialist women's and minority people's exhibitions, even a show of Socialist-Realist propaganda – put up not to inspire renewed zeal but as a way to reconsider past follies. Once regarded as a stuffy academy it now reluctantly embraces modern trends such as installation and video art. In July, the art colleges hold their degree shows here. Tues–Sun 9am–4pm; entrance fee varies from ¥2 up to ¥50.

Courtyard Gallery
四合院画廊
sìhéyuàn huàláng
95 Donghuamen Dajie ⊤010/65268882, Ⓦwww.courtyard-gallery.com. In an old courtyard house by the east gate of the Forbidden City, this is a great venue for contemporary art, with frequent shows; it's something of a meeting point for the cultural elite. There's also a cigar lounge and restaurant (see p.142). Mon–Sat 11am–7pm, Sun noon–7pm.

Red Gate Gallery
红门画廊
hóngmén huàláng
Dongbianmen watchtower, Chongwenmen Dong Dajie ⊤010/65251005, Ⓦwww.redgategallery. com. Commercial gallery, run by a Western curator, inside one of the last remnants of the old city wall. A little more adventurous than other Beijing galleries, it's used as a resource for foreign museum directors. Daily 10am–5pm.

Soka Art Centre
索卡艺术中心
suǒkǎ yìshù zhōngxīn
North end of Xiushui Dong Jie, behind the British embassy and east of Ritan Park ⊤010/65860344, Ⓦwww.soka-art.com. Small, chic space with a good stable of contemporary figurative painters. Tues–Sun 10am–9pm.

Wanfung
云峰画苑
yúnfēng huàhyuàn
136 Nanchizi Dajie, in the old archive building of the Forbidden City ⊤010/65233320, Ⓦwww.wanfung.com.cn. Shows the work – generally at the traditional end of modern – of established contemporary artists, sometimes from abroad. Two viewing spaces, one for group Chinese work, one for solo shows.

12

Shopping

Beijing has a good reputation for its shopping, much of it concentrated in four main shopping districts: Wangfujing has mostly mid-range shops and malls, and famous Chinese brands; Xidan hosts giant department stores; Dongdan sells mainly brand-name clothes; and Qianmen has a few quirky outlets among the cheap shoes and clothes stores. In addition to these areas, **Liulichang** (see p.65), a street of imitation Qing buildings aimed especially at visitors, is a good spot to furnish yourself with lots of souvenirs, while **Jianguomenwai Dajie** is the place to head for clothes. The shopping experience is more exciting, and cheaper, in the city's many **markets**, even though they offer no guarantee of quality; you can – and should – **bargain** (aim to knock at least two thirds off the starting price).

Remember that China has a massive industry in **fakes** – nothing escapes the counterfeiters. You'll no doubt hear assurances to the contrary, but you can assume that all antiques and collectable stamps, coins and posters are replicas, the paintings are prints, and that Rolex watches will stop working as soon as you turn the corner. If you don't mind robbing artists of their livelihood, pirated CDs and DVDs are very cheap. Even more of a bargain are the widely available fake designer-label clothes and accessories.

Shops are generally open Monday to Saturday from 9am to 6pm, with the large shopping centres staying open till 9pm and opening on Sundays, too. Specific opening times in the listings below are given when these differ markedly. **Markets** don't have official opening times, but tend to trade from about 6am to 6pm. Phone numbers are given for shops that are particularly out of the way – head there in a taxi and ask the driver to call them for directions.

Antiques, curios and souvenirs

There's no shortage of **antique stores** and **markets** in the capital, offering opium pipes, jade statues, porcelain Mao figurines, mahjong sets, Red Guard alarm clocks, Fu Manchu glasses, and all manner of bric-a-brac – pretty much all of it fake. The jade is actually soapstone, inset jewels are glass, and that venerable painting is a print stained with tea. There are very few real antiques for sale in Beijing, and no bargains. **Liulichang**, south of Hepingmen subway stop, has the densest concentration of curio stores in town, with a huge selection of wares, particularly of art materials, porcelain and snuff boxes, though prices are steep. Chairman Mao's Little Red Book is ubiquitous (and only costs about ¥10), and the most popular memento is a soapstone **seal** for imprinting names in either Chinese characters or Roman letters (starting at around ¥40); to see ancient traditions meeting modern technology, go round the back and watch them laser-cut it.

For general goods, check out the city's **department stores**, which sell a little of everything, and give a general idea of current Chinese taste. A prime example is the Beijing Department Store at 255 Wangfujing Dajie. The newer Landao Store on Chaoyangmenwai Dajie is more impressive, as are the mega-malls on Xidan. All of these are aimed at the middle class; to see what the filthy rich fill their homes with, visit the Parkson Building on Fuxingmenwai Dajie or the Lufthansa Centre on Liangmaqiao Lu in the northeast of the city.

The new giant **malls** sell goods (clothes mostly) that cost as much as they do in the West, and also have supermarkets and food courts. The best ones to visit are Sun Dong'an and Oriental Plazas on Wangfujing Dajie, the China World Plaza in the World Trade Centre on Jianguomenwai Dajie, and the Japanese SOGO Store on Xuanwumenwai Dajie.

The **Friendship Store** on Jianguomenwai Dajie, built in the late 1970s, was the first modern department store in China; it was the only place in the city selling imported goods, and Chinese shoppers, barred from entering, would bribe foreigners to buy things for them. The store has since failed to reinvent itself, and is known for high prices and insouciant staff.

Good, widely available, inexpensive souvenirs include seals, kites, art materials, papercuts (images cut into thin card), tea sets, and ornamental chopsticks. For something a little unusual, you could get hold of a real jade bracelet (Weiwenshi Jewellery Store, 23 Qianmen Dajie); a mahjong set (any department store); a specialist tea blend (stores on Dazhalan); a stylish Serve the People T-shirt (*Serve the People* restaurant; p.144); a silver Tian'anmen tie clip (from the Police Museum; p.82); or a metal Chinese shop-sign character (Nanxinhua Jie, near Liulichang). If you're after something decidedly outré, you could buy a model ear marked with acupuncture points or some goat-penis aphrodisiac (Tongrentang pharmacy; p.65).

Beijing Curio City
北京古玩城
běijīng gǔwánchéng
21 Dongsanhuan Nan Lu, west of Huawei Bridge in the southeast of the city. Bus #300 from Guomao subway stop. A giant arcade of over 250 stalls, best visited on a Sunday, when other antique traders come and set up in the surrounding streets. Daily 9.30am–6.30pm.

Gongyi Meishu Fuwubu
gōngyì měishù fúwùbù
工艺美术服务部
200 Wangfujing Dajie. Bus #111 from Wangfujing subway stop. A huge and well-reputed store selling art supplies. Soft Chinese brushes (some with tips up to 15cm long) and decorated blocks of solid ink are good value. Daily 8am–6pm.

Hongqiao Department Store
红桥百货中心
hóngqiáo bǎihuò zhōngxīn
Northeast corner of Tiantan Park. Bus #41 from

Qianmen. The top floor of this giant mall is packed with stalls selling antiques and curios. One shop is given over solely to Cultural Revolution kitsch, such as alarm clocks with images of Red Guards on the face, porcelain Red Guards and Mao badges. The Socialist Realist posters are great (replicas, of course) though it's tough getting a sensible price for anything. The stalls are set up alongside a pearl and jewellery market. Clothes and fake bags are sold on the second floor; the first floor is the place to go for small electronic items, including such novelties as watches that speak the time in Russian when you whistle at them. Daily 9am–8pm.

Huaxia Arts and Crafts Store
华夏工艺品店
húaxià gōngyìpǐndiàn
293 Wangfujing Dajie. Stocks a decent selection of expensive objets d'art. The selection upstairs is better, with clocks, rugs and wood carvings. Mon–Sat 8.30am–8pm.

▲ Xidan shopping centre

Liangma Antique Market
亮马收藏品市场
liàngmǎ shōuchángpín shìchǎng
27 Liangmaqiao Lu. This market is small but
also less picked over than others, with
good carpet and furniture sections. One
for the serious collector, with time to root
around; you might even find the odd real
antique.

Panjiayuan Market
潘家园市场
pānjiāyuán shìchǎng
Panjiayuan Lu, one of the roads connecting the
southeastern sections of the second and third
ring roads, east of Longtan Park. Bus #300 from
Guomao subway stop or take a taxi. Also called
the "Dirt Market", this is Beijing's biggest
antique market, with a huge range of
souvenirs and secondhand goods on sale
(sometimes in advanced states of decay).
It's at its biggest and best at weekends
between 6am and 3pm, when the surrounding streets are packed with stalls,
worth a visit even if you're not buying. The
initial asking prices for souvenirs are more
reasonable than anywhere else.

Carpets and furniture

Created mainly in Xinjiang, Tibet and Tianjin, the beautiful handmade **carpets** on
sale in Beijing aren't cheap, but are nevertheless pretty good value. Tibetan carpets
are yellow and orange and usually have figurative mythological or religious motifs;
rugs from Xinjiang in the northwest are red and pink with abstract patterns, while
weaves from Tianjin are multicoloured. Check the colour for consistency at both
ends – sometimes, large carpets are hung up near a hot lamp, which causes fad-
ing.

As well as the places mentioned below, you can get carpets at the Friendship
Store (see opposite; bargain hard here), Yuanlong Silk Corporation (see p.163),
and on Liulichang.

There's a huge market for reproduction Oriental furniture.

Jianamani Tibetan Carpets
嘉纳玛尼
jiānàmǎní

6 Fangyuan Xi Lu. Bright, colourful pieces from Central Asia and Tibet, some of which will set you back millions of yuan. Daily 10am–10pm.

Linxia Flying Horse Carpet Shop
临夏飞马毛纺地毯市场
línxià fēimǎ máofǎngdìtan shìchǎng

66 Zhushikou Xi Dajie. Wool and silk hand-woven rugs from Gansu province, mostly with colourful *mandala*-like abstract designs.

Qianmen Carpet Shop
44 Xingfu Dajie, just north of the Tiantan Hotel. Bus #8 from Dongdan subway stop. A con-verted air-raid shelter selling carpets mostly from Xinjiang and Tibet; the silk carpets from Henan in central China are very popular. A typical 2m by 3m carpet can cost around ¥50,000, though the cheapest rugs start at around ¥2000. Mon–Fri 8.30am–5pm.

Zhaojia Chaowai Market
兆佳朝外市场
zhàojiā cháowaì shìchǎng

43 Huawei Bei Lu, off Dongsanhuan Lu, 100m north of Panjiayuan Junction. Some carpets and enormous quantities of reproduction traditional Chinese furniture in all sizes and styles, for those without enough lacquer in their life.

Books

Plenty of English-language **books** on Chinese culture – many hard to find in the West – are on sale in Beijing, ranging from giant coffee-table tomes celebrating new freeways in China to comic-book versions of Chinese classics. Even if you're not buying, Beijing's **bookshops** are pleasant environments in which to browse – Chinese customers spend hours reading the stock, sometimes bringing along their own stool and cushions to make themselves comfortable. Some bookshops have cafés and art galleries attached.

In addition to the outlets listed below, there's a bookshop within the Friendship Store (see p.160), selling foreign newspapers (¥50) – a few days out of date – as well as a wide variety of books on all aspects of Chinese culture, though rather over-priced. The *Bookworm* (see "Cafés", p.140) also functions as a library and bookshop.

Foreign Language Bookstore
外交书店
wàiwén shūdiàn

235 Wangfujing Dajie @www.bpiec.com.cn. The main store has the biggest selection of foreign-language books in mainland China. An information desk on the right as you go in sells listings magazines; opposite is a counter selling maps, including an enormous wall map of the city (¥80). The English books on offer downstairs include fiction, textbooks on Chinese medicine, and translations of Chinese classics. The upper floors, too, have more fiction in English, magazines, wall hangings, and Japanese *manga*. Sometimes, the same book is priced cheaper upstairs than downstairs. Mon–Sat 9am–8pm.

Haidian Book City
海淀图书城
hǎidiàn túshūchéng

31 Haidian Nan Lu. Bus #302 comes here from Dongsanhuan Bei Lu – you can pick it up oppo-site the Dazhong Temple.

A great resource, extensively used by foreign residents of the city, this giant complex of scholarly stores is full of books to help you learn Chinese, and also has a wide selection of English-language novels.

Timezone 8
现代书店
xiàndài shūdiàn

4 Jiuxianqiao, 798 Art District @www.tim-ezone8.com. This chic art bookstore with attached café is the most civilized venue in bobo (bohemian-bourgeois) playground, the 798 Art District. Tote a laptop to really fit in; free wi-fi. Daily 8.30am–9pm.

Tushu Daxia
图书大厦
túshū dàshà

Xichang'an Jie. Bus #22 from Qianmen. Beijing's biggest bookshop, with the commercial feel of a department store. English fiction is on the third floor. Mon–Sat 9am–7pm.

Clothes and fabrics

Clothes are a bargain in Beijing, but be sure to check the quality carefully. Head for Jianguomen Dajie, where the silk and cotton markets, the Friendship Store and the plazas offer something for every budget. If you're particularly tall or have especially large feet, you'll generally have difficulty finding clothes and shoes to fit you, though there's a reasonable chance of finding clothes in your size at the Silk Market.

Aliens Street Market
老番街
lǎofān jiē
Yabao Lu, south of the Fullink Plaza. This huge mall is where the Russian expats come, en masse. There's a vast range of goods, but it's particularly worth picking over for clothes and accessories.

Beijing Silk Shop
前门妇女服装店
qiánmén fūnǚ fúzhuāngdiàn
5 Zhubaoshi Jie, just west of Qianmen Dajie. Located just inside the first *hutong* to the west as you head south down Qianmen Dajie, this is the best place in Beijing to buy quality silk clothes in Chinese styles, with a wider selection and keener prices than any of the tourist stores. The ground floor sells silk fabrics, while clothes can be bought upstairs.

Dongwuyuan Wholesale Market
动物园服装批发市场
dóng wù yuán fúzhuāng pī fā shì chǎng
Xizhimenwai Daijie, south of the zoo. This giant indoor market is full of stalls selling very cheap clothes, shoes and accessories to locals in the know. You'll have to bargain, and there won't be anything in any large sizes, but it's possible to pick up a few cut-price outfits.

Five Colours Earth
五色土
wǔsètǔ
10 Dongzhimen Nan Dajie ⓦ www.fivecoloursearth.com. Interesting and unusual collections, often incorporating fragments of old embroidery, by a talented local designer. Not too expensive either; you can pick up a coat for ¥500.

Fou Clothing Company
85 Wangfujing Dajie. Designer *qipaos* – long, elegant dresses with a slit up the thigh – and bespoke tailoring.

Mingxing Clothing Store
明星中式服装店
míngxīng zhōngshì fúzhuāngdiàn
133 Wangfujing Dajie. Well-made Chinese-style garments, such as *cheongsams* and *qipaos*, with an on-site tailor.

Neiliansheng Shoes
内联升布鞋
nèiliánshēng bùxié
Western end of Dazhalan, Qianmen. Look out for the giant shoe in the window. All manner of handmade flat, slip-on shoes and slippers in traditional designs, starting from ¥100 or so – they make great gifts.

PLA Official Factory Outlet
Dongsanhuan Bei Lu, about 1km north of the World Trade Centre. Bus #300 from Guomao subway stop. As well as military outfits, they stock such oddments as wrist compasses, canteens, and police hats. There's also a huge selection of military footwear and chunky fur-lined coats.

Ruifuxiang Store
瑞蚨祥丝绸店
ruìfúxiáng sīchóudiàn
5 Dazhalan, off Qianmen Dajie; also at 190 Wangfujing Dajie. Silk and cotton fabrics and a good selection of shirts and dresses. Mon–Sat 8.30am–8pm.

Silk Market
秀水市场
xiùshùǐ shìchǎng
Xiushui Jie, off Jianguomenwai Dajie, very near Yong'anli subway stop. This huge six-storey mall for tourists has electronics, jewellery and souvenirs, but its main purpose is to profit through flouting international copyright laws, with hundreds of stalls selling fake designer labels. You'll need to haggle hard; you shouldn't pay more than ¥80 for a pair of jeans, or ¥70 for trainers. There are also a few tailors – pick out your material, then bargain, and can get a suit made in 24hrs for ¥800 or so. Vendors are tiresomely pushy.

Yuanlong Silk Corporation
元隆顾绣绸缎商场
yuánlóng gùxiù chóuduàn shānghán
15 Yongnei Dong Jie, 200m west of the south gate of the Temple of Heaven. A good selection of silk clothes. Mon–Sat 9am–6.30pm.

Yansha Outlets Mall
燕莎奥特莱斯购物中心
yànshān àotè lái sīgòuwù zhōngxīn
9 Dongsihuannan Jie, the southern end of

the eastern section of the fourth ring road
ⓣ010/67395678. A huge outlet for genuine designer clothes and bags, all old lines, at discounts of between thirty and fifty percent.

Yaxiu Clothing Market
雅秀服装市场
yǎxiù fúzhuāng shìchǎng
58 Gongrentiyuchang Bei Lu. A two-storey mall of stalls selling designer fakes. Not yet overrun with tourists, so the shopping

experience and the prices are better than at the Silk Market.

Yuexiu Clothing Market
越秀市场
yuèxiù shìchǎng
99 Chaoyangmennei Dajie. A new market with a little bit of everything and a great deal of fake clothes. It's much less well known than the Silk Market, so the shopping experience is considerably more pleasant.

CDs and DVDs

Pirated CDs and DVDs are sold by chancers who approach foreigners around the Friendship Store, on Dazhalan and in bars in Houhai and Sanlitun. The discs generally work, though sometimes the last few minutes are garbled. You can get DVDs for as little as ¥5, CDs for ¥4, though the asking price starts out at ¥15. Note that with DVDs of newly released films, you're likely to get a version shot illicitly in a cinema, with heads bobbing around at the bottom of the screen.

Otherwise, music shops selling legitimate CDs can be found throughout the city, with a particularly dense cluster around Xinjiekou Dajie in the northwest. Two of the best stores are listed below.

Fusheng
福声唱片店
fú shēng chàngpiàndiàn
Xinjiekou Dajie, 50m east of the Ping'anli intersection. Local rock and a few imports.

Hongyun
宏运音象中心
hóngyùnxiàng zhōngxīn
62 Xinjiekou Bei Dajie. A huge collection of legitimate CDs; Western imports, Mandopop and local rock.

Computer equipment

Computer **hardware** can be a bargain in China, though there's little after-sales support. Still, you can pick up memory chips, an MP3 player, a webcam or a medium-spec laptop for a fraction of what they cost at home, if you go for unglamorous Korean or Chinese brands such as Acer and Lenovo. Pirated **software**, though a steal in more ways than one, should be given a wide berth as it may well fail to work.

The main area for electronic goodies is **Zhongguancun** in northwest Beijng, nicknamed "Silicon Alley" for its plethora of computer shops and hi-tech businesses.

Hi-Tech Mall
百脑汇
bǎinǎohuì
Opposite the Dongyue Temple on Chaoyangmenwai Dajie. Convenient and orderly mall of stores, some of which will build you a PC for around ¥5000. Barter, but this isn't the Silk Market; you might get a third or so off.

Hailong Electronics Market
海龙大厦
hǎilóng dàshà
1 Zhongguancun Dajie, Haidian. A veritable bazaar, piled high with all manner of gadgetry. One of a few in the area, the biggest at five storeys.

13

Sports and fitness

2008 is the year of the **Olympics**, and athletic passion has become almost a patriotic duty. But the most visible forms of exercise are fairly timeless; head to any park in the morning and you'll see citizens going through all sorts of **martial arts** routines, as well as performing popular exercises deemed good for the *qi* (life force), such as walking backwards, chest slapping, and tree hugging. Plenty of people play **table tennis** (often with a line of bricks as a net) and **street badminton** (no net at all), while in the evening many public spaces (such as the square at the south end of Houhai Lake) become the venue for mass **ballroom dancing**.

Sadly though, facilities for organized sport are limited. Sport tends to be the first subject to be dropped by students in the high-pressure Chinese school system. The Chinese may claim to have invented football (an ancient game called *cuju* involved kicking a feather filled ball) but the only pitches are outside the third ring road. Still, the situation is improving and with luck, interest will linger beyond the last Olympic anthem.

Spectator sports

The Chinese excel at "small ball" games such as squash, badminton and particularly table tennis, at which they are world champions (you can see kids being

Olympic practicalities

The **Beijing Olympics** will take place from August 8, 2008 to August 24, 2008, with the opening ceremony beginning at 8.08pm and 08 seconds at the **National Olympic Stadium**. Some events, including football, sailing, and the new 10km swimming marathon, will be held in other Chinese cities such as Qingdao and Shanghai, while the equestrian events will take place in **Hong Kong.**

There are seven million **tickets**, including nearly three million for the opening and closing ceremonies. The most expensive cost ¥5000, but there are plenty of cheap seats at ¥200 or so. To get tickets, **book online** at ⊛www.tickets.beijing2008.cn or go to one of the thousand or so appointed branches of the Bank of China (call ☎8610 952008 for locations). Tickets will be delivered in May 2008.

As for **accommodation**, rooms are likely to be ten times more expensive than normal, and booked to capacity months in advance. You can rent apartments at ⊛www.homestaybeijing2008.com.

All **public transport** (see p.000) to the Olympic sites will be free. You can check out bus routes by calling 96166 and pressing 3 for English.

coached at the outdoor tables in Ritan Park), but admit room for improvement in the "big ball" games, such as football. Nevertheless, Chinese men follow soccer avidly, particularly foreign teams with Chinese players, such as (at the time of writing) Manchester City. English, Spanish and German league games are shown on CCTV5 and BTV. The domestic football league is improving, and decent wages have attracted a fair few foreign players and coaches. In season (mid-March to mid-Oct), **Guo'an**, Beijing's team, play at the Workers' Stadium on Sunday afternoons. Tickets cost ¥15 and can be bought on the day. The atmosphere at games is carnivalesque, and there's no trouble; no one sees the need to segregate fans, for example.

Basketball is almost as popular as football, and has thrown up the unlikely hero of Yao Ming, a 211-centimetre-tall (6' 11") Inner Mongolian who cuts a dash for the Houston Rockets in the USA's NBA. Chinese league teams, including Beijing's Shougang, play at the Workers' Stadium from October to March; tickets cost ¥30.

Gyms

Gyms are becoming as popular as they are in the West. Most large hotels have **gyms**; the *International Hotel* (see p.136) at 1 Jianguomen Dajie has a good one (☎010/65126688), as does the *China World Hotel* (see map on pp.80–81) in the China World Trade Centre on Jianguomenwai Dajie (☎010/65052266), though it's pricey. The best **private gym** is the Evolution Fitness Centre; there's one at Dabei-yao Centre, Sanhuan Dong Lu, behind the Motorola building (☎010/65670266; ¥100 for one visit, ¥1700/3 months membership, ¥4000/annual membership). A second branch is at the Blue Castle Centre, 3 Xidawang Lu, 300m north of Soho New Town (☎010/85997650). The Capital Gymnasium, at 5 Xizhimenwai Dajie (☎010/68335552), west of the zoo, is a **sports centre** offering badminton, basket-ball and climbing, at reasonable prices.

Hiking

Beijing Hikers (☎13910025516; ⓦwww.beijinghikers.com) is an expat-run group organizing frequent, imaginative **hikes** in the city's environs, to dilapidated sections of the Great Wall, caves and the like. Adults pay ¥200 and reservations are required. The Beijing Amblers (ⓦwww.chinesecultureclub.org) do fun short walks every weekend, to places of cultural or historical interest.

Ice skating

In winter, try Beida (see p.103), the Summer Palace (see p.104) or the Shicha Lakes for **ice skating**. Otherwise, there's Le Cool in Basement 2 of the China World Trade Centre (daily 10am–10pm except Tues & Thurs until 5.50pm, Sun until 8pm; ¥30/hr; see map on pp.80–81). You wouldn't want to visit any of these places as a novice, as Chinese skaters are very good and expect a certain degree of confidence.

Martial arts

There are **martial arts** classes at the Beijing Language and Culture Institute, 15 Xueyuan Lu, Haidian (℡010/62327531), and at the Beijing Milun School of Kung Fu (℡010/13910811934, ⓦwww.kungfuinchina.com). Lessons are held in Ditan Park (¥400/month) at the latter school; there are English-speaking instructors at both. You can study *tai ji* and *qi gong* in an English-speaking environment at the Chinese Culture Club at 29 Anjialou, Liangmaqiao Lu (℡010/64329341, ⓦwww.chinesecultureclub.org) for ¥70 a lesson; and Evolution Fitness Centre has kick-boxing classes (see "Gyms" on opposite). Serious martial artists should investigate the many courses at the Beijing Sport University on Zhongguancun Bei Dajie (℡010/62989341).

Skiing

Beijing has a number of decent new **ski resorts**; **Nanshan** (℡010/89091909; ⓦwww.nanshanski.com), northeast of the city, is the best, with thirteen 1500-metre long runs, two kickers, a mini pipe, and more than a dozen boxes and rails. Entrance is ¥20, and skiing costs ¥220 per day on Monday to Friday, ¥340 on Saturday and Sunday; gear rental is ¥30. To get there, take a bus from Dongzhimen bus station to Miyun Xidaqiao (¥10), then a taxi the rest of the way (¥10).

The city's longest trails are at the new **Shijinglong Resort** near Zhangshanying town in Yanqing County (℡010/69191617; ⓦwww.sjlski.com). Entrance is ¥20 and skiing costs ¥220 for a full day.

Snooker and pool

Pool and **snooker** are very popular; you can take on the local sharks at the Chengfeng Pool Hall, Olympic Stadium East Gate, 1 Anding Lu (℡010/64929199; snooker ¥36/hr, pool ¥20); Xuanlong Pool Hall, 179 Hepingli Xi Jie (℡010/84255566; snooker ¥25/hr, pool ¥16/hr).

Swimming

Avoid **swimming pools** at the weekend, when they're full of teenagers doing just about everything but swimming. Serious swimmers should check out the Olympic-size pool in the Asian Games Village, Anding Lu (daily 8am–9pm; ℡010/64910468; ¥40), which boasts some of the city's fiercest showers; it's on the route of trolleybus #108 from Chongwenmennei Dajie or Andingmen subway stop. The Dongdan Swimming Pool A Dahualu, (℡010/65231241; ¥30) is also impressive. The *China World, Great Wall Sheraton* and *Friendship* (see p.136) hotels all have pools open to non-guests, though you have to pay to use them, typically around ¥100.

Contexts

Contexts

A short history of Beijing

A centre of power for nearly a thousand years, Beijing is the creation of China's turbulent political history. Its pre-eminence dates back to the mid-thirteenth century, and the formation of **Mongol China** under **Genghis Khan**, and subsequently **Kublai Khan**. It was Kublai who took control of the city in 1264, and who properly established it as the capital, replacing the earlier power centres of Luoyang and Xi'an. **Marco Polo** visited him here and was clearly impressed with the city's sophistication: "So great a number of houses and of people, no man could tell the number…", he wrote. "I believe there is no place in the world to which so many merchants come, and dearer things, and of greater value and more strange, come into this town from all sides than to any city in the world…"

The wealth he depicted stemmed from Beijing's position at the start of the **Silk Road**, the trading route that stretched all the way to Central Asia: Marco Polo described "over a thousand carts loaded with silk" arriving in the city "almost each day". It allowed the Khans, who later proclaimed themselves emperors, to aspire to new heights of grandeur, with Kublai building himself a palace of astonishing proportions, walled on all sides and approached by great marble stairways; sadly, nothing remains of it now.

With the accession of the **Ming Dynasty**, who defeated the Mongols in 1368, the capital shifted temporarily to **Nanjing**. However, the second Ming emperor, Yongle, returned to Beijing, building around him prototypes of the city's two great monuments, the Forbidden City and the Temple of Heaven. It was during Yongle's reign, too, that the city's basic **layout** took shape, rigidly symmetrical, extending in squares and rectangles from the palace and inner-city grid to the suburbs, much as it is today. An inward-looking dynasty, the Ming also began constructing the **Great Wall** in earnest, in a grandiose but ultimately futile attempt to stem the incursions of northern Manchu tribes into China.

The Qing dynasty

The city's subsequent history is dominated by the rise and eventual collapse of the **Manchus** who, as the **Qing dynasty**, ruled China from Beijing from 1644 to the beginning of the twentieth century. Three outstanding Qing emperors brought an infusion of new blood and vigour to government early on. **Kangxi**, who began his 61-year reign in 1654 at the age of 6, was a great patron of the arts – as is borne out by the numerous scrolls and paintings blotted with his seals, indicating that he had viewed them. His fourth son, the Emperor **Yongzheng** (1678–1735), ruled over what is considered one of the most efficient and least corrupt administrations ever enjoyed by China. This was inherited by **Qianlong** (1711–99), whose reign saw China's frontiers greatly extended and the economy stimulated by peace and prosperity. In 1750, the capital was perhaps at its zenith, the centre of one of the strongest, wealthiest and most powerful countries in the world. It was at this time that the extraordinary **Summer Palace** was constructed. With two hundred pavilions, temples and palaces, and immense artificial lakes and hills, it was the world's most remarkable royal garden, a magnificent symbol of Chinese wealth and power, along with the Forbidden City.

China confronts European expansionism

In the late eighteenth century expansionist European nations were in Asia, looking for financial opportunities. China's rulers, immensely rich and powerful, and convinced of their own superiority, had no wish for direct dealings with foreigners. When a British envoy, **Lord Macartney**, arrived in Chengde in 1793 to propose a political and commercial alliance between King George III and the emperor, his mission was unsuccessful. This was partly because he refused to kowtow to the emperor, but also because the emperor totally rejected any idea of allying with one whom he felt was a subordinate. Macartney was impressed by the vast wealth and power of the Chinese court, but later wrote perceptively that the empire was "like an old crazy first-rate man-of-war which its officers have contrived to keep afloat to terrify by its appearance and bulk".

Foiled in their attempts at official negotiations with the Qing court, the British decided to take matters into their own hands and create a clandestine market in China for Western goods. Instead of silver, they began to pay for tea and silk with **opium**, cheaply imported from India. As the number of addicts – and demand for the drug – escalated during the early nineteenth century, China's trade surplus became a deficit, as silver drained out of the country to pay for the drug. The emperor suspended the traffic in 1840 by ordering the destruction of over twenty thousand chests of opium, an act that led to the outbreak of the first **Opium War**. This brought British and French troops to the walls of the capital, and the Summer Palace was first looted, then burned, more or less to the ground, by the British.

The fall of the Qing dynasty

While the imperial court lived apart, within the **Forbidden City**, conditions for the civilian population, in the capital's suburbs, were starkly different. Kang Youwei, a Cantonese visiting in 1895, described this dual world: "No matter where you look, the place is covered with beggars. The homeless and the old, the crippled and the sick, with no one to care for them, fall dead on the roads. This happens every day. And the coaches of the great officials rumble past them continuously."

The indifference spread from the top down. China was now run by the autocratic, out-of-touch **Cixi**, who could hardly have been less concerned with the fate of her people. She squandered money meant for the modernization of the navy on building a new Summer Palace of her own. Her project was really the last grand gesture of imperial architecture and patronage – and, like its predecessor, was badly burned by foreign troops, in another outbreak of the Opium War. By this time, in the face of successive waves of occupation by foreign troops, the empire and the city were near collapse. The **Manchus abdicated** in 1911, leaving the northern capital to be ruled by warlords.

A short-lived republic, under the idealistic **Sun Yatsen**, failed to unify the country, and the post-imperial period was initially characterized by chaos and factionalism. In 1928, Beijing came under the military dictatorship of **Chiang Kaishek**'s nationalist **Guomindang** party, who held the city until the Japanese seized it in 1939. At the end of World War II, Beijing was controlled by an alliance of Guomindang troops and American marines.

21C–16C BC	Xia dynasty
16C–11C BC	Shang dynasty
11C–771 BC	Zhou dynasty
770 BC–476 BC	Spring and Autumn Period – China fragments into city states and small kingdoms
457 BC–221 BC	Warring States – China's fragmentation continues
221 BC–207 BC	Qin dynasty
206 BC–220 AD	Han dynasty

The Three Kingdoms: China is divided into three competing territories

220–265	Wei kingdom
221–263	Shu Han kingdom
222–280	Wu kingdom
265–420	Jin dynasty
420–581	Southern dynasties and Northern dynasties – rapid succession of short-lived dynasties
581–618	Sui dynasty – China united for the first time since Han dynasty
618–907	Tang dynasty
907–960	Five dynasties – a period of discord and instability
960–1271	Song dynasty
1271–1368	Yuan dynasty
1368–1644	Ming dynasty
1644–1911	Qing dynasty
1911–45	Short-lived republic founded, its fall followed by civil war between Nationalists and Communists, and Japanese occupation
1945–49	Further period of civil conflict between Guomindang and the Communist People's Liberation Army
1949	Communists take power over all China; establishment of People's Republic

The Communist era

It wasn't until 1949, when **Mao Zedong**'s Communist People's Liberation Army defeated the Guomingdang, that the country was again united, and Beijing returned to its position as the centre of Chinese power. The city that Mao inherited for the Chinese people was in most ways primitive. Imperial laws had banned the construction of houses higher than the official buildings and palaces, so virtually nothing was more than one storey high. The roads, although straight and uniform, were narrow and congested, and there was scarcely any industry.

The rebuilding of the capital, and the erasing of symbols of the previous regimes, was an early priority for the Communists. The Communists wanted to retain the city's sense of ordered planning, with **Tian'anmen Square**, laid out in the 1950s, as its new heart. Initially, their inspiration was Soviet, with an emphasis on heavy industry and a series of poor-quality high-rise housing programmes. Most of the traditional courtyard houses, which were seen to encourage individualism, were destroyed. In their place went anonymous concrete buildings, often with inadequate sanitation and little running water. Much of the new social planning was misguided; after the destruction of all the capital's dogs – for reasons of hygiene

– in 1950, it was the turn of sparrows in 1956. This was a measure designed to preserve grain, but it only resulted in an increase in the insect population. To combat this, all the grass was pulled up, which in turn led to dust storms in the windy winter months.

In the zeal to be free of the past and create a modern, "people's capital", much of Beijing was destroyed or co-opted: the Temple of Cultivated Wisdom became a wire factory and the Temple of the God of Fire produced electric lightbulbs. In the 1940s, there were eight thousand temples and monuments in the city; by the 1960s, there were only around a hundred and fifty. Even the city walls and gates, relics mostly of the Ming era, were pulled down, their place taken by ring roads and avenues.

More destruction was to follow during the **Great Proletarian Cultural Revolution** – to give it its full title – that began in 1966. Under Mao's guidance, Beijing's students organized themselves into a political militia – the **Red Guards**, who were sent out to destroy the Four Olds: old ideas, old culture, old customs and old habits. The students attacked anything redolent of capitalism, the West or the Soviet Union; few of the capital's remaining ancient buildings escaped destruction.

The death of Mao

Mao's hold on power finally slipped in the 1970s, when his health began to decline. A new attitude of pragmatic reform prevailed, deriving from the moderate wing of the Communist Party, headed by Premier **Zhou Enlai** and his protégé, **Deng Xiaoping**.

In July 1976, a catastrophic earthquake in the northeast of the country killed half a million people. The Chinese hold that natural disasters always foreshadow great events, and no one was too surprised when Mao himself died on September 9. Deprived of their figurehead, and with memories of the Cultural Revolution clear in everyone's mind, Mao's supporters in the Party quickly lost ground to the right, and Deng was left running the country.

A degree of reform

The subsequent move away from Mao's policies was rapid: in 1978, anti-Maoist dissidents were allowed to display wall posters in Beijing, some of which actually criticized Mao by name. Though such public airing of political grievances was later forbidden, by 1980 Deng and the moderates were secure enough to officially sanction a cautious questioning of Mao's actions. In the capital, his once-ubiquitous portraits and statues began to come down. However, criticism of Mao was one thing – criticism of the Party was viewed quite differently. When demonstrators assembled in **Tian'anmen Square** in 1989, protesting at corruption and demanding more freedom, the regime dealt with them brutally, sending tanks and soldiers to fire on them.

Deng's "open door" policies of economic liberalization and welcoming to foreign influences brought about new social – rather than political – freedoms, and massive westernization. Western fast food, clothes and music, and Japanese motorbikes became (and remain) all the rage.

The present day

Deng stepped down in the early Nineties. His successors, **Jiang Zemin** and now **Hu Jintao**, are neither as popular, as secure, nor as charismatic as he was, and, although China did not implode with Deng's death in 1997, as many had feared, the nation today is living up to Sun Yatsen's description of Chinese society as a "bowl of sand" – unstable, shifting and hard to predict. Growth has been stellar – around ten percent a year – and the urban Chinese are much better off: in the 1970s, the "three big buys" – consumer goods that families could realistically aspire to – were a bicycle, a watch and a radio; in the 1980s, they were a washing machine, a TV and a refrigerator; now, like their counterparts in South Korea and Japan, the middle classes aim for a car and a laptop. But the **embrace of capitalism** has brought with it new problems: short-term gain has become the overriding factor in planning, with the result that the future is mortgaged for present wealth – Beijing's cultural heritage has vanished as *hutongs* are pulled down to clear space for badly made skyscrapers. As success is largely dependent on *guanxi* (personal connections), the potential for corruption is enormous; witness the men who stand outside Beijing subway stations, selling receipts so that cadres on junkets can pad their expense accounts. Not everyone has benefitted from the bonanza, and China's income disparities have become grotesque – eighty percent of the nation earns little more than a subsistence living, hard to imagine if you wander the new malls. Peasants, attracted by the big city's prospects, now flood to Beijing en masse – you'll see plenty outside Beijing Zhan, many of them finding the capital as novel as any foreigner does. The lucky ones end up working on building sites, though even they, far from home and un-unionized, are often exploited. Though the majority are family men who send the little money that they earn home, they are treated with suspicion by most city-dwellers – indicative of China's new class divisions, or the resurfacing of old resentments.

As the host to the **2008 Olympic games**, Beijing has become the recipient of a great deal of investment. Historic sites have been opened, renovated, or, it sometimes appears, invented. Though a ramshackle charm has been lost in the

▲ The modern shopping area of Xidan

Beijing's facelift

Modern Beijing has always been **image conscious** – anxious to portray a particular face to the world. When Mao took over, he wanted the feudal city of the emperors transformed into a "forest of chimneys"; he got his wish, and the capital became an ugly industrial powerhouse of socialism. In the 1980s, when the Party embraced capitalism "with Chinese characteristics", bland international style office blocks were erected with a pagoda-shaped "silly hat" on the roof as a concession to local taste.

Today Beijing is desperate to be viewed as a cool and **stylish** world city, and, with the Olympics as a spur, is undergoing the kind of urban transformation usually only seen after a war. The factories have been banished to the suburbs, six new subway lines are poised to open, a new terminal has been added to the airport, and some ten billion dollars has been spent on greening projects such as a tree belt around the city to control dust storms that whip in from the Gobi Desert.

Statement architecture – the kind of prestige project that not long ago would have been derided as bourgeois and decadent – is all the rage, designed by the world's hottest (and most expensive) architects. As well as the Olympic Park and environs, there's Paul Andreu's National Opera House (the "Egg"), and perhaps most striking of all, the new state television station (the "Twisted Doughnut") by Dutch architect Rem Koolhaas, which appears to defy gravity with its intersecting Z-shaped towers.

All this has been made possible by light planning laws, deregulation and the willingness of the government to allow developers to sweep homes away with desultory compensation to residents. Regrettably, very little of old Beijing has been preserved, with *hutong* neighbourhoods such as those around Qianmen levelled en masse. The city has been left with a disjointed feel; there's something arbitrary about the skyscrapers and single-use zones around them. Beijing looks modern, indisputedly, but it has a long way to go before you could call it beautiful.

wholescale redevelopment, on the whole the city has improved. It will never perhaps be memorable for attractiveness, but it's undeniably dynamic, new and exciting.

Books

D
on't expect too much variety of English-language reading in Beijing, though you will be able to find a good many cheap editions of the Chinese classics, published in English translation by two Beijing-based firms, Foreign Languages Press (FLP) and Panda Books (some of these titles are published outside China, too). In the reviews below, books that are especially recommended are marked ⚐, while o/p signifies out of print; the publisher is listed only if it's based in China or elsewhere in Asia.

History

⚐ **Peter Fleming** *The Siege at Peking*. A lively account of the events that led up to June 20, 1900, when the foreign legations in Beijing were attacked by the Boxers and Chinese imperial troops.

Harrison Salisbury *The New Emperors* (o/p). Highly readable account of the lives of China's twentieth-century "emperors", Mao Zedong and Deng Xiaoping, which tries to demonstrate that communist rule is no more than an extension of the old imperial Mandate of Heaven.

Arthur Waldron *The Great Wall of China* (o/p). More for the academic than the casual reader, this book traces the origins and history of the wall.

Justin Wintle *The Rough Guide History of China*. Pocket-sized but detailed chronicle of China's history, the key events and people put into context in a year-by-year format.

Jan Wong *Red China Blues*. Jan Wong, a Canadian of Chinese descent, went to China as an idealistic Maoist in 1972 at the height of the Cultural Revolution, and was one of only two Westerners permitted to enrol at Beijing University. She describes the six years she spent in China and her growing disillusionment, which led eventually to her repatriation. A touching, sometimes bizarre, inside account of the bad old days.

Culture and society

⚐ **Jasper Becker** *The Chinese*. Classic, weighty, erudite but very comprehensible introduction to Chinese society and culture.

Ian Buruma *Bad Elements: Chinese rebels from LA to Beijing*. Interviews with Chinese dissidents, both at home and in exile, make for a compelling, if inevitably rather jaundiced, view of the country.

Gordon G. Chang *The Coming Collapse of China*. This book theorizes that China's recent success is only skin deep, and that the country is about to

fall apart thanks largely to incompetent leadership. But people have been saying this for years, and it hasn't happened yet.

Roger Garside *Coming Alive: China after Mao*. Garside was a diplomat at the British Embassy in Beijing in 1968–70 and 1976–79. Here he describes the aftermath of the Cultural Revolution.

Marco Polo *The Travels*. Said to have inspired Columbus, *The Travels* is a fantastic read, full of amazing insights picked up during Marco Polo's 26 years of wandering in Asia between Venice and the Peking court of Kublai Khan. It's not, however, a coherent history, having been ghost-written by a romantic novelist from Marco Polo's notes.

Joe Studwell *The China Dream.* Subtitled "The Elusive Quest for the Greatest Untapped Market On Earth", this is mandatory reading for foreign business people in China. It's a cautionary tale, written in layman's terms, debunking the myth that there's easy money to be made from China's vast markets. A great read for anyone interested in business, politics or human greed.

Tiziano Terzani *Behind the Forbidden Door* (o/p). In 1980, Terzani was one of the first Western journalists to be allowed to live in China; he was kicked out four years later for the unacceptable honesty of his writing. There is no better evocation of the bad old pre-reform years than this collection of essays, on such varied subjects as the rebirth of kung fu, mass executions and the training of crickets.

Guides and reference books

Giles Beguin and Dominique Morel *The Forbidden City.* A good introduction to the complex, and to the history of the emperors who lived there, though the best thing about this pocket book (as with most books about the Forbidden City) is the illustrations.

Lin Xiang Zhu and Lin Cuifeng *Chinese Gastronomy* (o/p). A classic work, relatively short on recipes but strong on cooking methods and the underlying philosophy. Wavers in and out of print, sometimes under different titles – look for "Lin" as the author name. Essential reading for anyone serious about learning the finer details of Chinese cooking.

Jessica Rawson *Ancient China: Art and archaeology.* By the deputy keeper of Oriental antiquities at the British Museum, this scholarly introduction to Chinese art puts the subject in its historical context. Beginning its account in Neolithic times, the book explores the technology and social organization which shaped the development of Chinese culture up to the Han dynasty.

Mary Tregear *Chinese Art.* Authoritative summary of the main strands in Chinese art from Neolithic times, through the Bronze Age and up to the twentieth century. Clearly written and well illustrated.

Wang Wenqiao and Gang Wenbin *Chinese Vegetarian Cuisine* (New World Press, Beijing). Compendium of Chinese vegetarian cooking, from simple boiled beans with ginger to complex, imitation meat dishes such as sweet-and-sour "spare ribs". The straightforward recipes are derived from the famous *Gongdelin* restaurant in Beijing.

Religion and philosophy

Asiapac Comics Series (Asiapac, Singapore). Available at Beijing's Foreign Language Bookstore, this entertaining series of books presents ancient Chinese philosophy in cartoon format, making the subject accessible without losing too much complexity. They're all well written and well drawn; particularly good is the *Sayings of Confucius*. Unfortunately, they're not cheap, costing at least ¥80 each.

Confucius *The Analects* and *I Ching*.
Good, modern translation of this classic text, a collection of Confucius's teachings focusing on morality and the state. *I Ching*, also known as *The Book of Changes*: this classic volume teaches a form of divination. It includes coverage of some of the fundamental concepts of Chinese thought, such as the duality of *yin* and *yang*.

Lao Zi *Tao Te Ching*. This, the *Daodejing* in *pinyin*, is a collection of mystical thoughts and philosophical speculation that form the basis of Taoist philosophy. **Arthur Waley (trans)** *Three Ways of Thought in Ancient China*. Translated extracts from the writings of three of the early philosophers – Zhuang Zi, Mencius and Han Feizi. A useful introduction.

Biography and autobiography

E. Backhouse and J.O. Bland *China Under the Empress Dowager* (o/p).
Classic work on imperial life in late nineteenth-century China. It's based around the diary of a court eunuch, which is now generally accepted to have been forged (Backhouse was the prime suspect; see the review of *Hermit of Peking* by Hugh Trevor-Roper).
Jung Chang *Wild Swans* and *Mao: the untold story*. Enormously popular in the West, *Wild Swans* is a family saga covering three generations and chronicles the horrors of life in turbulent twentieth-century China. It serves as an excellent introduction to modern Chinese history, as well as being a good read. *Mao: the untold story* is a massive and well-researched character assassination; indeed, it's hard not to suspect that axes are being ground.
Rachel Dewoskin *Foreign Babes in Beijing*. Breezy account of an American girl's adventures among the city's artsy set in the Nineties. The most interesting parts concern the author's experiences working as an actress on a Chinese soap opera.
Pu Yi *From Emperor to Citizen* (FLP, Beijing). The autobiography of the last Qing emperor, Pu Yi, who lost his throne as a boy and was later briefly

installed as a puppet emperor during the Japanese occupation. He ended his life employed as a gardener.
Rius *Mao for Beginners*. Light-hearted, entertaining comic book about Mao Zedong and Maoism.
Jonathan Spence *Emperor of China: Self portrait of Kang Xi*. A magnificent portrait of the longest-reigning and greatest emperor of modern China.
Hugh Trevor-Roper *Hermit of Peking: the hidden life of Sir Edmund Backhouse*. Sparked by its subject's thoroughly obscene memoirs, *Hermit of Peking* uses external sources in an attempt to uncover the facts behind the extraordinary and convoluted life of Edmund Backhouse – Chinese scholar, eccentric recluse and phenomenal liar – who lived in Beijing from the late nineteenth century until his death in 1944.
Marina Warner *The Dragon Empress*. Exploration of the life of the Empress Dowager Cixi, one of only two female rulers of China. Warner lays bare the complex personality of a ruthless woman whose reign, marked by vanity and greed, culminated in the collapse of the imperial ruling house and the founding of the republic.

Chinese literature

Cyril Birch (ed) *Anthology of Chinese Literature from Earliest Times to the Fourteenth Century*. This survey spans three thousand years of Chinese literature, embracing poetry, philosophy, drama, biography and prose fiction. Interestingly, different translations of some extracts are included.

Cao Xueqing *Dream of Red Mansions* (available in a Penguin edition and from FLP, Beijing). Sometimes published under the English title *Dream of the Red Chamber*, this intricate eighteenth-century comedy of manners follows the fortunes of the Jia clan through the emotionally charged adolescent lives of Jia Baoyu and his two girl cousins, Lin Daiyu and Xue Baochai. The version published in the West by Penguin fills five paperbacks; the FLP edition, available in Beijing, is much simplified and abridged.

Chen Sue *Beijing Doll*. This rambling confessional concerns the teenage writer's adventures in the music scene. With plenty of sex and drugs, it caused quite a stir when it came out

and was, predictably, banned. The author, now on her fourth novel, is regarded as something of an icon of her generation – it helps that she's extremely attractive, of course.

Lao She *Rickshaw Boy* (FLP, Beijing). One of China's great modern writers, Lao She was driven to suicide during the Cultural Revolution. This story is a haunting account of a young rickshaw puller in pre-1949 Beijing.

Lu Xun *The True Story of Ah Q* (FLP, Beijing). Widely read in China today, Lu Xun is regarded as the father of modern Chinese writing. *Ah Q* is one of his best tales: short, allegorical and cynical, about a simpleton who is swept up in the 1911 revolution. (You can pick a copy up at Beijing's Lu Xun Museum.)

Luo Guanzhong *Romance of the Three Kingdoms* (various editions published in the West; also published by FLP, Beijing). One of the world's greatest historical novels. Though written 1200 years after the events it depicts, this vibrant tale vividly evokes the

▲ Red Guards reading from Chairman Mao's Little Red Book

battles, political schemings and myths surrounding China's turbulent Three Kingdoms period.

Ma Jian *Red Dust* and *The Noodle Maker*. Satirist Ma Jian is one of China's most insightful living writers, though most of his work is banned in China. *Red Dust* is a travelogue about an epic, beatnik-style jaunt around China in the Eighties, documenting a set of chaotic lives, not least the narrator's own; while *The Noodle Maker* is a dark novel concerning the friendship between a writer of propaganda and a professional blood donor.

Steven Owen *Anthology of Chinese Literature*. Unimaginably compendious, this colossal book contains delightfully translated excerpts and analyses from every era of Chinese literature up to 1911.

Wang Shuo *Playing For Thrills* and *Please Don't Call Me Human*. The bad boy of contemporary Chinese literature, Wang Shuo writes in colourful Beijing dialect about the city's seamy underbelly. These are his only novels translated into English: the first is a mystery story whose boorish narrator spends most of his time drinking, gambling and chasing girls; the second, banned in China, is a bitter satire portraying modern China as a place where pride is nothing and greed is everything, as a dignified martial artist is emasculated in order to win an Olympic gold medal.

Wu Cheng'en *Journey to the West* (FLP, Beijing). Absurd, lively rendering of the Buddhist monk Xuanzang's pilgrimage to India to collect sacred scriptures, aided by – according to popular myth – Sandy, Pigsy, and the irrepressible Sun Wu Kong, the monkey king. Arthur Waley's version, published in the West under the title *Monkey*, retains the tale's spirit while shortening the hundred-chapter opus to paperback length.

Language

Language

Chinese

A s the most widely spoken language on earth, Chinese is hard to overlook. **Mandarin Chinese**, derived from the language of Han officialdom in the Beijing area, has been systematically promoted over the past hundred years to be the official, unifying language of the Chinese people, much as modern French, for example, is based on the original Parisian dialect. It is known in mainland China as *putonghua*, "common language".

Chinese **grammar** is delightfully simple. There is no need to conjugate verbs, decline nouns or make adjectives agree – Chinese characters are immutable, so Chinese words simply cannot have different "endings". Instead, context and fairly rigid rules about word order are relied on to make those distinctions of time, number and gender that Indo-European languages are so concerned with. Instead of cumbersome tenses, the Chinese make use of words such as "yesterday" or "tomorrow" to indicate when things happen; instead of plural endings they simply state how many things there are. For English speakers, Chinese word order is very familiar, and you'll find that by simply stringing words together you'll be producing perfectly grammatical Chinese. Basic sentences follow the subject-verb-object format; adjectives, as well as all qualifying and describing phrases, precede nouns.

From the point of view of foreigners, the main thing that distinguishes Mandarin from familiar languages is that it's a tonal language. In order to pronounce a word correctly, it is necessary to know not only the sounds of its consonants and vowels but also its correct tone – though with the help of context, intelligent listeners should be able to work out what you are trying to say even if you don't get the tones quite right.

L

Pinyin

Back in the 1950s it was hoped eventually to replace Chinese characters with an alphabet of Roman letters, and to this end the **pinyin system**, a precise and exact means of representing all the sounds of Mandarin Chinese, was devised. It comprises all the Roman letters of the English alphabet (except "v"), with the four tones represented by diacritical marks, or accents, which appear above each syllable. The old aim of replacing Chinese characters with *pinyin* was abandoned long ago, but in the meantime *pinyin* has one very important function, that of helping foreigners pronounce Chinese words. However, there is the added complication that in *pinyin* the letters don't all have the sounds you would expect, and you'll need to spend an hour or two learning the correct sounds.

You'll often see *pinyin* in Beijing, on street signs and shop displays, but only well-educated locals know the system very well. The Chinese names in this book have been given both in characters and in *pinyin*; the pronunciation guide below is your first step to making yourself comprehensible. For more information, see the *Rough Guide Mandarin Chinese Phrasebook*, or *Pocket Interpreter* (FLP, Beijing; it's available at Beijing's Foreign Language Bookstore).

Pronunciation

There are four possible **tones** in Mandarin Chinese, and every syllable of every word is characterized by one of them, except for a few syllables, which are considered toneless. In English, to change the tone is to change the mood or the emphasis; in Chinese, to change the tone is to change the word itself. The tones are:

First or "high" ā ē ī ō ū. In English this level tone is used when mimicking robotic or very boring, flat voices.

Second or "rising" á é í ó ú. Used in English when asking a question showing surprise, for example "eh?"

Third or "falling-rising" ǎ ě ǐ ǒ ǔ. Used in English when echoing someone's words with a measure of incredulity. For example, "John's dead." "De-ad?!"

Fourth or "falling" à è ì ò ù. Often used in English when counting in a brusque manner – "One! Two! Three! Four!".

Toneless A few syllables do not have a tone accent. These are pronounced without emphasis, such as in the English **u**pon.

Note that when two words with the third tone occur consecutively, the first word is pronounced as though it carries the second tone. Thus *nǐ* (meaning "you") and *hǎo* ("well, good"), when combined, are pronounced *ní hǎo*, meaning "how are you?"

Consonants

Most consonants, as written in *pinyin*, are pronounced in a similar way to their English equivalents, with the following exceptions:

c as in ha**ts**

g is hard as in **g**od (except when preceded by "n", when it sounds like sa**ng**)

q as in **ch**eese

x has no direct equivalent in English, but you can make the sound by sliding from an "s" to an "sh" sound and stopping midway between the two

z as in su**ds**

zh as in fu**dge**

Vowels and diphthongs

As in most languages, the vowel sounds are rather harder to quantify than the consonants. The examples below give a rough description of the sound of each vowel as written in *pinyin*.

a usually somewhere between **fa**r and m**a**n

ai as in **eye**

ao as in c**ow**

e usually as in f**ur**

ei as in g**ay**

en as in hyph**en**

eng as in s**ung**

er as in b**ar** with a pronounced "r"

i usually as in b**ee**, except in zi, ci, si, ri, zhi, chi and shi, when i is a short, clipped sound, like the American military "**sir**".

ia as in **ya**k

ian as in **yen**

ie as in **yeah**

o as in s**aw**

ou as in sh**ow**

ü as in the German **ü** (make an "ee" sound and glide slowly into an "oo"; at the mid-point between the two sounds you should hit the ü-sound.

u usually as in **fool**, though whenever u follows j, q, x or y, it is always pronounced **ü**

ua as in s**ua**ve

uai as in **why**

ue as though contracting "you" and "air" together, **you'air**

ui as in **way**

uo as in **wo**re

Useful words and phrases

When writing or saying the name of a Chinese person, the surname is given first; thus Mao Zedong's family name is Mao.

Basics

I	我	wǒ
You (singular)	你	nǐ
He	他	tā
She	她	tā
We	我们	wǒmen
You (plural)	你们	nǐmen
They	他们	tāmen
I want...	我要	wǒ yào...
No, I don't want...	我不要	wǒ bú yào...
Is it possible...?	可不可以...	kě bù kěyǐ...?
It is (not) possible	(不)可以...	(bù)kěyǐ
Is there any/Have you got any...?	你有没有...	yǒu méi yǒu...?
There is/I have	有...	yǒu...
There isn't/I haven't	没有...	méi yǒu
Please help me	请帮我忙..	qǐng bāng wǒ máng
Mr...	...先生	xiānshēng
Mrs...	...太太	tàitai
Miss...	...小姐	xiǎojiě

Communicating

I don't speak Chinese	我不会说中文	wǒ búhuì shuō zhōngwén
Can you speak English?	你会说英语吗?	nǐ huì shuō yīngyǔ ma?
Can you get someone who speaks English?	请给我找一个会说英文的人?	qǐng gěiwǒ zhǎo yīgèhuìshuō yīngwén de rén?
Please speak slowly	请说得慢一点	qǐng shuōde màn yīdiǎn
Please say that again	请再说一遍	qǐng zài shuō yī biàn

I understand	我听得懂	wǒ tīngdedǒng
I don't understand	我听不懂	wǒ tīngbùdǒng
I can't read Chinese characters	我看不懂汉字	wǒ kànbùdǒng hànzì
What does this mean?	这是什么意思?	zhèshì shénme yìsi?
How do you pronounce this character?	这个字怎么念?	zhègè zì zěnme niàn?

Greetings and basic courtesies

Hello/How do you do/ How are you?	你好	nǐhǎo
I'm fine	我很好	wǒ hěnhǎo
Thank you	谢谢	xièxie
Don't mention it/ You're welcome	不客气	búkèqi
Sorry to bother you...	麻烦你	máfán nǐ
Sorry/I apologize	对不起	duìbùqǐ
It's not important/No problem	没关系	méiguānxì
Goodbye	再见	zàijiàn
Excuse me	不好意思	bùhǎoyìsi

Chit-chat

What country are you from?	你是哪个国家的?	nǐ shì nǎgè guójiā de?
Britain	英国	yīngguó
England	英国/英格兰	yīngguó/yīnggélán
Scotland	苏格兰	sūgélán
Wales	威尔士	wēi'ěrshì
Ireland	爱尔兰	ài'érlán
America	美国	měiguó
Canada	加拿大	jiānádà
Australia	澳大利亚	àodàlìyà
New Zealand	新西兰	xīnxīlán
South Africa	南非	nánfēi
China	中国	zhōngguó
Outside China	外国	wàiguó
What's your name?	你叫什么名字?	nǐ jiào shénme míngzi?
My name is...	我叫....	wǒ jiào...
Are you married?	你结婚了吗?	nǐ jiéhūn le ma?
I am (not) married	我(没有)结婚(了)	wǒ (méiyǒu) jiéhūn (le)
Have you got (children)?	你有没有孩子?	nǐ yǒu méiyǒu háizi?
Do you like...?	你喜不喜欢.....?	nǐ xǐ bù xǐhuān....?
I (don't) like...	我不喜欢....	wǒ (bù) xǐhuān...
What's your job?	你干什么工作?	nǐ gàn shénme gōngzuò?
I'm a foreign student	我是留学生	wǒ shì liúxuéshēng
I'm a teacher	我是老师	wǒ shì lǎoshī
I work in a company	我在一个公司工作	wǒ zài yígè gōngsī gōngzuò
I don't work	我不工作	wǒ bù gōngzuò
I'm retired	我退休了	wǒ tuìxiū le

Clean/dirty	干净/脏	gānjìng/zāng
Hot/cold	热/冷	rè/lěng
Fast/slow	快/慢	kuài/màn
Good/bad	好/坏	hǎo/huài
Big/Small	大/小	dà/xiǎo
Pretty	漂亮	piàoliang
Interesting	有意思	yǒuyìsi

Numbers

Zero	零	líng
One	一	yī
Two	二/两	èr/liǎng*
Three	三	sān
Four	四	sì
Five	五	wǔ
Six	六	liù
Seven	七	qī
Eight	八	bā
Nine	九	jiǔ
Ten	十	shí
Eleven	十一	shíyī
Twelve	十二	shíèr
Twenty	二十	èrshí
Twenty-one	二十一	èrshíyī
One hundred	一百	yìbǎi
Two hundred	二百	èrbǎi
One thousand	一千	yīqiān
Ten thousand	一万	yīwàn
One hundred thousand	十万	shíwàn
One million	一百万	yìbǎiwàn
One hundred million	一亿	yīyì
One billion	十亿	shíyì

* 两/liǎng is used when enumerating, for example "two people" liǎng gè rén. 二 /èr is used when counting.

Time

Now	现在	xiànzài
Today	今天	jīntiān
(In the) morning	早上	zǎoshàng
(In the) afternoon	下午	xiàwǔ
(In the) evening	晚上	wǎnshàng
Tomorrow	明天	míngtiān
The day after tomorrow	后天	hòutiān
Yesterday	昨天	zuótiān
Week/month/year	星期/月/年	xīngqī/yuè/nián

Next/last week/month/year	下/上 星期/月/年	xià/shàng xīngqī/yuè/nián
Monday	星期一	xīngqī yī
Tuesday	星期二	xīngqī èr
Wednesday	星期三	xīngqī sān
Thursday	星期四	xīngqī sì
Friday	星期五	xīngqī wǔ
Saturday	星期六	xīngqī liù
Sunday	星期天	xīngqī tiān
What's the time?	几点了?	jǐdiǎn le?
Morning	早上	zǎoshàng
Afternoon	中午	zhōngwǔ
10 o'clock	十点钟	shídiǎn zhōng
10.20	十点二十	shídiǎn èrshí
10.30	十点半	shídiǎn bàn

Travelling and getting around town

North	北	běi
South	南	nán
East	东	dōng
West	西	xī
Airport	机场	jīchǎng
Ferry dock	船码头	chuánmǎtóu
Left-luggage office	寄存处	jìcún chù
Ticket office	售票处	shòupiào chù
Ticket	票	piào
Can you sell me a ticket to...?	可不可以给我买到...的票?	kěbùkěyǐ gěi wǒ mǎi dào...de piào?
I want to go to...	我想到...去	wǒ xiǎng dào...qù
I want to leave at (8 o'clock)	我想(八点钟)离开	wǒ xiǎng (bādiǎnzhōng) líkāi
When does it leave?	什么时候出发?	shénme shíhòu chūfā?
When does it arrive?	什么时候到?	shénme shíhòu dào?
How long does it take?	路上得多长时间?	lùshàng děi duōcháng shíjiān?
CITS	中国国际旅行社	zhōngguó guójì lǚxíngshè
Train	火车	huǒchē
(Main) train station	主要火车站	(zhǔyào) huǒchēzhàn
Bus	公共汽车	gōnggòng qìchēzhàn
Bus station	汽车站	qìchēzhàn
Long-distance bus station	长途汽车站	chángtú qìchēzhàn
Express train/bus	特快车	tèkuài chē
Fast train/bus	快车	kuài chē
Ordinary train/bus	普通车	pǔtōng chē
Timetable	时间表	shíjiān biǎo
Map	地图	dìtú
Where is...?	...在 哪里?	...zài nǎlǐ?
Go straight on	往前走	wǎng qián zǒu

Turn right	往右走	wǎng yòu zǒu
Turn left	往左拐	wǎng zuǒ guǎi
Taxi	出租车	chūzū chē
Please use the meter	请打开记价器	qǐng dǎkāi jìjiàqì
Underground/subway station	地铁站	dìtiě zhàn
Bicycle	自行车	zìxíngchē
Can I borrow your bicycle?	能不能借你的自行车?	néngbùnéng jiè nǐdē zìxíngchē?
Bus	公共汽车	gōnggòngqìchē
Which bus goes to...?	几路车到...去?	jǐlùchē dào ... qù?
Number (10) bus	(十)路车	(shí) lù chē
Does this bus go to...?	这车到...去吗?	zhè chē dào ... qù ma?
When is the next bus?	下一班车几点开?	xiàyìbānchē jǐdiǎn kāi?
The first bus	头班车	tóubān chē
The last bus	末班车	mòbān chē
Please tell me where to get off	请告诉我在哪里下车	qǐng gàosù wǒ zàinǎlǐ xiàchē?
Museum	博物馆	bówùguǎn
Temple	寺庙	sìmiào
Church	教堂	jiàotáng

Accommodation

Accommodation	住宿	zhùsù
Hotel (upmarket)	宾馆	bīnguǎn
Hotel (cheap)	招待所,旅馆	zhāodàisuǒ, lǚguǎn
Hostel	旅社	lǚshè
Do you have a room available?	你们有房间吗?	nǐmen yǒu fángjiān ma?
Can I have a look at the room?	能不能看一下方向?	néngbùnéng kàn yíxià fángjiān?
I want the cheapest bed you've got	我要你这里最便宜的床位	wǒ yào nǐ zhèlǐ zuìpiányi de chuángwèi
Single room	单人房	dānrénfáng
Twin room	双人房	shuāngrénfáng
Double room with a big bed	双人房间带大床	shuāngrén fángjiān dài dàchuáng
Three-bed room	三人房	sānrénfáng
Dormitory	多人房	duōrénfáng
Suite	套房	tàofáng
(Large) bed	(大)床	(dà) chuáng
Passport	护照	hùzhào
Deposit	押金	yājīn
Key	钥匙	yàoshi
I want to change my room	我想换一个房间	wǒ xiǎng huàn yígè fángjiān

Shopping, money and the police

How much is it?	这是多少钱?	zhèshì duōshǎo qián?
That's too expensive	太贵了	tài guì le
I haven't got any cash	我没有现金	wǒ méiyǒu xiànjīn

Have you got anything cheaper?	有没有便宜一点的？	yǒu méiyǒu piányì yìdian de?
Do you accept credit cards?	可不可以用信用卡	kě bù kěyǐ yòng xìnyòngka?
Department store	百货商店	bǎihuò shāngdiàn
Market	市场	shìchǎng
¥1 (RMB)	一块（人民币）	yí kuài (rénmínbì)
US$1	一块美金	yí kuài měijīn
£1	一个英镑	yí gè yīngbàng
Change money	换钱	huàn qián
Bank	银行	yínháng
Travellers' cheques	旅行支票	lǚxíngzhīpiào
ATM	提款机	tíkuǎnjī
PSB	公安局	gōng'ān jú

Communications

Post office	邮电局	yóudiànjú
Envelope	信封	xìnfēng
Stamp	邮票	yóupiào
Airmail	航空信	hángkōngxìn
Surface mail	平信	píngxìn
Telephone	电话	diànhuà
Mobile phone	手机	shǒujī
SMS message	短信	duǎnxìn
International telephone call	国际电话	guójì diànhuà
Reverse charges/collect call	对方付钱电话	duìfāngfùqián diànhuà
Fax	传真	chuánzhēn
Telephone card	电话卡	diànhuàkǎ
I want to make a telephone call to (Britain)	我想给（英国）打电话	wǒ xiǎng gěi (yīngguó) dǎ diànhuà
I want to send an email to the US	我想发一个邮件到美国	wǒ xiǎng fā yīgè yóujiàn dào měiguó
Internet	网路	wǎngluò
Internet café/bar	网吧	wǎngbā
Email	电邮	diànzǐyóujiàn

Health

Hospital	医院	yīyuàn
Pharmacy	药店	yàodiàn
Medicine	药	yào
Chinese medicine	中药	zhōngyào
Diarrhoea	腹泻	fùxiè
Vomit	呕吐	ǒutù
Fever	发烧	fāshāo
I'm ill	我生病了	wǒ shēngbìng le
I've got flu	我感冒了	wǒ ganmào le
I'm (not) allergic to...	我对...(不)过敏	wǒ duì ... (bù) guòmǐn

Antibiotics	抗生素	kàngshēngsù
Condom	避孕套	bìyùntào
Tampons	卫生棉条	wèishēng miántiáo

A menu reader

General

Restaurant	餐厅	cāntīng
House speciality	拿手好菜	náshǒuhaocài
How much is that?	多少钱?	duōshǎo qián?
I don't eat (meat)	我不吃(肉)	wǒ bùchī (ròu)
I would like...	我想要...	wǒ xiǎng yào...
Local dishes	地方菜	dìfāng cài
Snacks	小吃	xiǎochī
Menu/set menu/English menu	菜单/套菜/英文菜单	càidān/tàocài/yīngwéncàidān
Small portion	少量	shǎoliàng
Chopsticks	筷子	kuàizi
Knife and fork	刀叉	dāochā
Spoon	勺子	sháozi
Waiter/waitress	服务员	fúwùyuán
Bill/cheque	买单	mǎidān
Cook these ingredients together	一快儿做	yíkuàir zuò
Not spicy/no chilli please	请不要辣椒	qǐng búyào làjiāo
Only a little spice/chilli	一点辣椒	yìdiǎn làjiāo
50 grams	两	liǎng
250 grams	半斤	bànjīn
500 grams	斤	jīn
1 kilo	公斤	gōngjīn

Drinks

Beer	啤酒	píjiǔ
Coffee	咖啡	kāfēi
Milk	牛奶	niúnǎi
(Mineral) water	(矿泉)水	(kuàngquán) shuǐ
Wine	葡萄酒	pútáojiǔ
Yoghurt	酸奶	suānnǎi
Tea	茶	chá
Black tea	红茶	hóng chá
Green tea	绿茶	lǜ chá
Jasmine tea	茉莉花茶	mòlìhuā chá

Staple foods

Aubergine	笋子	qiézi
Bamboo shoots	笋尖	sǔn
Bean sprouts	豆芽	dòuyá
Beans	豆子	dòuzi
Beef	牛肉	niúròu
Bitter gourd	葫芦	húlu
Black bean sauce	黑豆豉	hēidòuchǐ
Bread	面包	miànbāo
Buns (filled)	包子	bāozi
Buns (plain)	馒头	mántou
Carrot	胡萝卜	húluóbo
Cashew nuts	腰果	yāoguǒ
Cauliflower	菜花	càihuā
Chicken	鸡	jī
Chilli	辣椒	làjiāo
Chocolate	巧克力	qiǎokèlì
Coriander (leaves)	香菜	xiāngcài
Crab	蟹	xiè
Cucumber	黄瓜	huángguā
Duck	鸭	yā
Eel	鳝鱼	shànyú
Eggs (fried)	煎鸡蛋	jiānjīdàn
Fish	鱼	yú
Fried dough stick	油条	yóutiáo
Garlic	大蒜	dàsuàn
Ginger	姜	jiāng
Green pepper (capsicum)	青椒	qīngjiāo
Green vegetables	绿叶蔬菜	lǜyè shūcài
Jiaozi (ravioli, steamed or boiled)	饺子	jiǎozi
Lamb	羊肉	yángròu
Lotus root	莲心	liánxīn
MSG	味精	wèijīng
Mushrooms	蘑菇	mógū
Noodles	面条	miàntiáo
Omelette	摊鸡蛋	tānjīdàn
Onions	洋葱	yángcōng
Oyster sauce	蚝油	háoyóu
Pancake	摊饼	tānbǐng
Peanut	花生	huāshēng
Pork	猪肉	zhūròu
Potato (stir-fried)	(炒)土豆	(chǎo) tǔdòu
Prawns	虾	xiā
Preserved egg	皮蛋	pídàn
Rice noodles	河粉	héfěn

Rice porridge (aka "congee")	粥	zhōu
Rice, boiled	白饭	báifàn
Rice, fried	炒饭	chǎofàn
Salt	盐	yán
Sesame oil	芝麻油	zhīma yóu
Shuijiao (ravioli in soup)	水铰	shuǐjiǎo
Sichuan pepper	四川辣椒	sìchuān làjiāo
Snake	蛇肉	shéròu
Soup	汤	tāng
Soy sauce	酱油	jiàngyóu
Squid	鱿鱼	yóuyú
Straw mushrooms	草菇	cǎogū
Sugar	糖	táng
Tofu	豆腐	dòufu
Tomato	蕃茄	fānqié
Vinegar	醋	cù
Water chestnuts	马蹄	mǎtí
White radish	白萝卜	báiluóbo
Wood ear fungus	木耳	mùěr
Yam	芋头	yùtóu

Cooking methods

Boiled	煮	zhǔ
Casseroled (see also "Claypot")	焙	bèi
Deep-fried	油煎	yóujiān
Fried	炒	chǎo
Poached	白煮	báizhǔ
Red-cooked (stewed in soy sauce)	红烧	hóngshāo
Roast	烤	kǎo
Steamed	蒸	zhēng
Stir-fried	清炒	qīngchǎo

Everyday dishes

Braised duck with vegetables	蔬菜炖鸭	shūcài dùn yā
Cabbage rolls (stuffed with meat or vegetables)	菜卷	càijuǎn
Chicken and sweetcorn soup	玉米鸡丝汤	yùmǐ jīsī tā ng
Chicken with bamboo shoots and babycorn	笋尖嫩玉米炒鸡片	sǔnjiān nènyùmǐ chǎojipiàn
Chicken with cashew nuts	腰果鸡片	yāoguǒjīpiàn
Claypot/sandpot (casserole)	砂锅	shāguō
Crispy aromatic duck	香酥鸭	xiāngsūyā
Egg flower soup with tomato	蕃茄蛋汤	fānqiédàntāng
Egg fried rice	蛋炒饭	dànchǎofàn

Fish ball soup with white radish	萝卜鱼蛋汤	luóbo yúdàn tāng
Fish casserole	砂锅鱼	shāguōyú
Fried shredded pork with garlic and chilli	大蒜辣椒炒肉片	dàsuànlàjiāo chǎo ròupiàn
Hotpot	火锅	huǒguō
Kebab	串肉	chuànròu
Noodle soup	汤面	tāngmiàn
Pork and mustard greens	芥菜叶炒猪肉	jiè càiyè chǎo zhūròu
Pork and water chestnut	马蹄猪肉	mǎtízhūròu
Prawn with garlic sauce	蒜汁虾	suànzhīxiā
"Pulled" noodles	拉面	lā miàn
Roast duck	烤鸭	kǎoyā
Scrambled egg with pork on rice	滑蛋猪肉饭	huádàn zhūròufàn
Sliced pork with yellow bean sauce	黄豆肉片	huángdòu ròupiàn
Squid with green pepper and black beans	豆豉青椒炒鱿鱼	dòuchǐ qīngjiāo chǎo yóuyú
Steamed eel with black beans	豆豉蒸鳝	dòuchǐ zhēng shàn
Steamed rice packets wrapped in lotus leaves	荷叶蒸饭	héyè zhēngfàn
Stewed pork belly with vegetables	回锅肉	huíguōròu
Stir-fried chicken and bamboo shoots	笋尖炒鸡片	sǔnjiān chǎo jīpiàn
Stuffed bean-curd soup	豆腐汤	dòufu tāng
Sweet and sour spare ribs	糖醋排骨	tángcù páigǔ
Sweet bean paste pancakes	赤豆摊饼	chìdòu tānbǐng
White radish soup	白萝卜汤	báiluóbo tāng
Wonton soup	馄饨汤	húntun tāng

Vegetables and eggs

Aubergine with chilli and garlic sauce	大蒜辣椒炒茄子	dàsuàn làjiāo chǎo qiézi
Aubergine with sesame sauce	芝麻酱拌茄子	zhīmájiàng bàn qiézi
Bean curd and spinach soup	菠菜豆腐汤	bōcài dòufu tāng
Bean-curd slivers	豆腐花	dòufuhuā
Bean curd with chestnuts	栗子豆腐	lìzi dòufu
Pressed bean curd cabbage	白菜豆腐	báicài dòufu
Egg fried with tomatoes	蕃茄炒蛋	fānqié chǎo dàn
Fried bean curd with vegetables	豆腐炒蔬菜	dòufu chǎo shūcài
Fried bean sprouts	炒豆芽	chǎodòuyá
Spicy braised aubergine	炖香辣茄子条	dùn xiānglà qiézitiáo
Stir-fried bamboo shoots	炒冬笋	chǎodōngsǔn

| Stir-fried mushrooms | 炒鲜菇 | chǎo xiāngū |
| Vegetable soup | 素菜汤 | shūcài tāng |

Regional dishes

Northern

Aromatic fried lamb	炒羊肉	chǎoyángròu
Fish with ham and vegetables	火腿蔬菜鱼片	huǒtuǐ shūcài yúpiàn
Fried prawn balls	炒虾球	chǎoxiāqiú
Mongolian hotpot	蒙古火锅	ménggǔ huǒguō
Beijing (Peking) duck	北京烤鸭	běijīng kǎoyā
Red-cooked lamb	红烧羊肉	hóngshāo yángròu
Lion's head (pork rissoles casseroled with greens)	狮子头	shīzitóu

Sichuan and western China

Boiled beef slices (spicy)	水煮牛肉	shuǐzhǔ niúròu
Crackling-rice with pork	爆米肉片	bàomǐ ròupiàn
Crossing-the-bridge noodles	过桥米线	guòqiáo mǐxiàn
Carry-pole noodles (with a chilli-vinegar-sesame sauce)	担担面	dàndànmiàn
Deep-fried green beans with garlic	大蒜煸四季豆	dàsuàn biǎn sìjìdòu
Dong'an chicken (poached in spicy sauce)	东安鸡子	dōng'ā n jīzi
Doubled-cooked pork	回锅肉	huíguōròu
Dry-fried pork shreds	油炸肉丝	yóuzhà ròusi
Fish-flavoured aubergine	鱼香茄子	yúxiāng qiézi
Gongbao chicken (with chillies and peanuts)	公保鸡丁	gōngbǎo jīdīng
Green pepper with spring onion and black bean sauce	豆豉洋葱炒青椒	dòuchǐ yángcōng chǎo qīngjiāo
Hot and sour soup (flavoured with vinegar and white pepper)	酸辣汤	suānlà tāng
Hot-spiced bean curd	麻婆豆腐	mápódòufu
Rice-flour balls, stuffed with sweet paste	汤圆	tāngyuán
Smoked duck	熏鸭	xūnyā
Strange flavoured chicken (with sesame-garlic-chilli)	怪味鸡	guàiwèijī
Stuffed aubergine slices	馅茄子	xiànqiézi
Tangerine chicken	桔子鸡	júzijī
"Tiger-skin" peppers (pan-fried with salt)	虎皮炒椒	hǔpí qīngjiāo
Wind-cured ham	扎肉	zhāròu

Southern Chinese/Cantonese

Baked crab with chilli and black beans	辣椒豆豉焙蟹	làjiāo dòuchǐ bèi xiè
Barbecued pork ("char siew")	叉烧	chāshāo
Casseroled bean curd stuffed with pork mince	豆腐碎肉煲	dòufu suìròu bǎo
Claypot rice with sweet sausage	香肠饭	xiāngchángfàn
Crisp-skinned pork on rice	脆皮肉饭	cuìpíròufàn
Fish-head casserole	焙鱼头	bèiyútóu
Fish steamed with ginger and spring onion	清蒸鱼	qīngzhēngyú
Fried chicken with yam	芋头炒鸡片	yùtóu chǎo jīpiàn
Honey-roast pork	叉烧	chāshāo
Lemon chicken	柠檬鸡	níngméngjī
Litchi (lychee) pork	荔枝肉片	lìzhiròupiàn
Salt-baked chicken	盐鸡	yánshuǐjī

Dim sum

Dim sum	点心	diǎnxīn
Barbecued pork bun	叉烧包	chāshāobāo
Crab and prawn dumpling	蟹肉虾饺	xièròu xiā jiǎo
Custard tart	蛋挞	dàntà
Doughnut	油炸圈饼	yóuzhà quānbǐng
Pork and prawn dumpling	烧麦	shāomài
Fried taro and mince dumpling	蕃薯糊饺	fānshǔ hújiǎo
Lotus paste bun	莲蓉糕	liánrónggāo
Moon cake (sweet bean paste in flaky pastry)	月饼	yuèbǐng
Paper-wrapped prawns	纸包虾	zhǐbāoxiā
Prawn crackers	虾片	xiā piàn
Prawn dumpling	虾饺	xiā jiǎo
Spring roll	春卷	chūnjuǎn
Steamed spare ribs and chilli	辣椒蒸排骨	làjiāo zhēng páigǔ
Stuffed rice-flour roll	肠粉	chángfěn
Stuffed green peppers with black bean sauce	豆豉馅青椒	dòuchǐ xiàn qīngjiāo
Sweet sesame balls	芝麻球	zhīmá qiú

Fruit

Fruit	水果	shuǐguǒ
Apple	苹果	píngguǒ
Banana	香蕉	xiāngjiāo
Grape	葡萄	pútáo
Honeydew melon	哈密瓜	hāmìguā
Longan	龙眼	lóngyǎn
Lychee	荔枝	lìzhī

Mandarin orange	橘子	júzi
Mango	芒果	mángguǒ
Orange	橙子	chéngzi
Peach	桃子	táozi
Pear	梨	lí
Persimmon	柿子	shìzi
Plum	李子	lǐzi
Pomegranate	石榴	shíliú
Pomelo	柚子	yòuzi
Watermelon	西瓜	xīguā

Glossary

General terms

Arhat Buddhist saint.

Bei North.

Binguan Hotel; generally a large one, for tourists.

Bodhisattva A follower of Buddhism who has attained enlightenment, but has chosen to stay on earth to teach rather than enter nirvana; Buddhist god or goddess.

Boxers The name given to an anti-foreign organization that originated in Shandong in 1898. Encouraged by the Qing Empress Dowager Cixi, they roamed China attacking westernized Chinese and foreigners in what became known as the Boxer Movement.

Canting Restaurant

Cheongsam Long, narrow dress slit up the thigh.

CITS China International Travel Service. Tourist organization primarily interested in selling tours, though they can help with obtaining train tickets.

CTS China Travel Service. Tourist organization similar to CITS.

Cultural Revolution Ten-year period beginning in 1966 and characterized by destruction, persecution and fanatical devotion to Mao.

Dagoba Another name for a *stupa*.

Dong East.

Fandian Restaurant or hotel.

Fen Smallest denomination of Chinese currency – there are one hundred fen to the yuan.

Feng Peak.

Feng shui A system of geomancy used to determine the positioning of buildings.

Gong Palace.

Guanxi Literally "connections": the reciprocal favours inherent in the process of official appointments and transactions.

Guanyin The ubiquitous Buddhist Goddess of Mercy, who postponed her entry into paradise in order to help ease human misery. Derived from the Indian deity Avalokiteshvara, she is often depicted with up to a thousand arms.

Gulou Drum tower; traditionally marking the centre of a town, this was where a drum was beaten at nightfall and in times of need.

Guomindang (GMD) The Nationalist Peoples' Party. Under Chiang Kaishek, the GMD fought Communist forces for 25 years before being defeated and moving to Taiwan in 1949, where it remains a major political party.

Han Chinese The main body of the Chinese people, as distinct from other ethnic groups such as Uigur, Miao, Hui or Tibetan.

Hui Muslims; officially a minority, China's Hui are, in fact, ethnically indistinguishable from Han Chinese.

Hutong A narrow alleyway.

Immortal Taoist saint.

Jiao (or mao) Ten fen.

Jie Street.

Jiuba Bar or pub.

Lamaism The esoteric Tibetan and Mongolian branch of Buddhism, influenced by local shamanist and animist beliefs.

Ling Tomb.

Little Red Book A selection of "Quotations from Chairman Mao Zedong", produced in 1966 as a philosophical treatise for Red Guards during the Cultural Revolution.

Lu Street.

Luohan Buddhist disciple.

Maitreya Buddha The Buddha of the future, at present awaiting rebirth.

Mandala Mystic diagram which forms an important part of Buddhist iconography, especially in Tibet; *mandalas* usually depict deities and are stared at as an aid to meditation.

Men Gate/door.

Miao Temple.

Middle Kingdom A literal translation of the Chinese words for China.

Nan South.

Palanquin A covered sedan chair, used by the emperor.

Peking The old English term for Beijing.

PLA The People's Liberation Army, the official name of the Communist military forces since 1949.

PSB Public Security Bureau, the branch of China's police force which deals directly with foreigners.

Pagoda Tower with distinctively tapering structure.

Pinyin The official system of transliterating Chinese script into Roman characters.

Putonghua Mandarin Chinese; literally "Common Language".

Qiao Bridge.

Qiapo Another word for a *cheongsam* (see opposite).

RMB Renminbi. Another name for Chinese currency literally meaning "the people's money".

Red Guards The unruly factional forces unleashed by Mao during the Cultural Revolution to find and destroy brutally any "reactionaries" among the populace.

Renmin The people.

Si Temple, usually Buddhist.

Siheyuan Traditional courtyard house.

Spirit wall Wall behind the main gateway to a house, designed to thwart evil spirits, which, it was believed, could move only in straight lines.

Spirit Way The straight road leading to a tomb, lined with guardian figures.

Stele Freestanding stone tablet carved with text.

Stupa Multi-tiered tower associated with Buddhist temples that usually contains sacred objects.

Ta Tower or pagoda.

Tai ji A discipline of physical exercise, characterized by slow, deliberate, balletic movements.

Tian Heaven or the sky.

Uigur Substantial minority of Turkic people, living mainly in Xinjiang.

Waiguoren Foreigner.

Xi West.

Yuan China's unit of currency. Also a courtyard or garden (and the name of the Mongol dynasty).

Zhan Station.

Zhong Middle; China is referred to as *zhongguo*, the Middle Kingdom.

Zhonglou Bell tower, usually twinned with a *gulou*. The bell it contained was rung at dawn and in emergencies.

Zhuang Villa or manor.

Travel
store

Avoid Guilt Trips

Buy fair trade coffee + bananas ✓

Save energy - use low energy bulbs ✓

- don't leave tv on standby ✓

Offset carbon emissions from flight to Madrid ✓

Send goat to Africa ✓

Join Tourism Concern today ✓

Slowly, the world is changing.
Together we can, and will, make a difference.

Tourism Concern is the only UK registered charity fighting exploitation in one of the largest industries on earth: people forced from their homes in order that holiday resorts can be built, sweatshop labour conditions in hotels and destruction of the environment are just some of the issues that we tackle.

Sending people on a guilt trip is not something we do. We know as well as anyone that holidays are precious. But you can help us to ensure that tourism always benefits the local communities involved.

Call 020 7133 3330
or visit **tourismconcern.org.uk** to find out how.

A year's membership of Tourism Concern costs just £20 (£12 unwaged)
- that's 38 pence a week, less than the cost of a pint of milk, organic of course.

Fighting Exploitation in Tourism

TourismConcern

UK & Ireland
Britain
Devon & Cornwall
Dublin **D**
Edinburgh **D**
England
Ireland
The Lake District
London
London **D**
London Mini Guide
Scotland
Scottish Highlands
  & Islands
Wales

Europe
Algarve **D**
Amsterdam
Amsterdam **D**
Andalucía
Athens **D**
Austria
Baltic States
Barcelona
Barcelona **D**
Belgium &
  Luxembourg
Berlin
Brittany & Normandy
Bruges **D**
Brussels
Budapest
Bulgaria
Copenhagen
Corfu
Corsica
Costa Brava **D**
Crete
Croatia
Cyprus
Czech & Slovak
  Republics
Denmark
Dodecanese & East
  Aegean Islands
Dordogne & The Lot
Europe
Florence & Siena
Florence **D**
France
Germany
Gran Canaria **D**
Greece
Greek Islands

Hungary
Ibiza & Formentera **D**
Iceland
Ionian Islands
Italy
The Italian Lakes
Languedoc &
  Roussillon
Lanzarote &
  Fuerteventura **D**
Lisbon **D**
The Loire Valley
Madeira **D**
Madrid **D**
Mallorca **D**
Mallorca & Menorca
Malta & Gozo **D**
Menorca
Moscow
The Netherlands
Norway
Paris
Paris **D**
Paris Mini Guide
Poland
Portugal
Prague
Prague **D**
Provence
  & the Côte D'Azur
Pyrenees
Romania
Rome
Rome **D**
Sardinia
Scandinavia
Sicily
Slovenia
Spain
St Petersburg
Sweden
Switzerland
Tenerife &
  La Gomera **D**
Turkey
Tuscany & Umbria
Venice & The Veneto
Venice **D**
Vienna

Asia
Bali & Lombok
Bangkok
Beijing

Cambodia
China
Goa
Hong Kong & Macau
Hong Kong
  & Macau **D**
India
Indonesia
Japan
Kerala
Laos
Malaysia, Singapore
  & Brunei
Nepal
The Philippines
Rajasthan, Dehli
  & Agra
Singapore
Singapore **D**
South India
Southeast Asia
Sri Lanka
Taiwan
Thailand
Thailand's Beaches
  & Islands
Tokyo
Vietnam

Australasia
Australia
Melbourne
New Zealand
Sydney

North America
Alaska
Baja California
Boston
California
Canada
Chicago
Colorado
Florida
The Grand Canyon
Hawaii
Honolulu **D**
Las Vegas **D**
Los Angeles
Maui **D**
Miami & South Florida
Montréal
New England
New Orleans **D**
New York City

New York City **D**
New York City Mini
  Guide
Orlando & Walt
  Disney World® **D**
Pacific Northwest
San Francisco
San Francisco **D**
Seattle
Southwest USA
Toronto
USA
Vancouver
Washington DC
Washington DC **D**
Yellowstone & The
  Grand Tetons
Yosemite

**Caribbean
& Latin America**
Antigua & Barbuda **D**
Argentina
Bahamas
Barbados **D**
Belize
Bolivia
Brazil
Cancùn & Cozumel **D**
Caribbean
Central America
Chile
Costa Rica
Cuba
Dominican Republic
Dominican Republic **D**
Ecuador
Guatemala
Jamaica
Mexico
Peru
St Lucia **D**
South America
Trinidad & Tobago
Yúcatan

Africa & Middle East
Cape Town & the
  Garden Route
Dubai **D**
Egypt
Gambia
Jordan

D: Rough Guide
DIRECTIONS for
short breaks

Available from all good bookstores

NOTES

Small print and
Index

A Rough Guide to Rough Guides

Published in 1982, the first Rough Guide – to Greece – was a student scheme that became a publishing phenomenon. Mark Ellingham, a recent graduate in English from Bristol University, had been travelling in Greece the previous summer and couldn't find the right guidebook. With a small group of friends he wrote his own guide, combining a highly contemporary, journalistic style with a thoroughly practical approach to travellers' needs.

The immediate success of the book spawned a series that rapidly covered dozens of destinations. And, in addition to impecunious backpackers, Rough Guides soon acquired a much broader and older readership that relished the guides' wit and inquisitiveness as much as their enthusiastic, critical approach and value-for-money ethos.

These days, Rough Guides include recommendations from shoestring to luxury and cover more than 200 destinations around the globe, including almost every country in the Americas and Europe, more than half of Africa and most of Asia and Australasia. Our ever-growing team of authors and photographers is spread all over the world, particularly in Europe, the USA and Australia.

In the early 1990s, Rough Guides branched out of travel, with the publication of Rough Guides to World Music, Classical Music and the Internet. All three have become benchmark titles in their fields, spearheading the publication of a wide range of books under the Rough Guide name.

Including the travel series, Rough Guides now number more than 350 titles, covering: phrasebooks, waterproof maps, music guides from Opera to Heavy Metal, reference works as diverse as Conspiracy Theories and Shakespeare, and popular culture books from iPods to Poker. Rough Guides also produce a series of more than 120 World Music CDs in partnership with World Music Network.

Visit www.roughguides.com to see our latest publications.

Rough Guide travel images are available for commercial licensing at www.roughguidespictures.com

SMALL PRINT

Rough Guide credits

Text editor: Lucy White
Layout: Dan May
Cartography: Amod Singh
Picture editor: Sarah Cummins
Production: Rebecca Short
Proofreader: Adam Smith
Cover design: Chloë Roberts
Photographer: Tim Draper
Editorial: **London** Claire Saunders, Ruth
Blackmore, Alison Murchie, Karoline Densley,
Andy Turner, Keith Drew, Edward Aves, Alice
Park, Jo Kirby, James Smart, Natasha Foges,
Róisín Cameron, Emma Traynor, Emma Gibbs,
James Rice, Kathryn Lane, Christina Valhouli,
Joe Staines, Peter Buckley, Matthew Milton,
Tracy Hopkins, Ruth Tidball; **New York** Andrew
Rosenberg, Steven Horak, AnneLise Sorensen,
April Isaacs, Ella Steim, Anna Owens, Sean
Mahoney; **Delhi** Madhavi Singh, Karen D'Souza
Design & Pictures: **London** Scott Stickland, Dan
May, Diana Jarvis, Mark Thomas, Chloë Roberts,
Nicole Newman, Sarah Cummins, Emily Taylor;
Delhi Umesh Aggarwal, Ajay Verma, Jessica

Subramanian, Ankur Guha, Pradeep Thapliyal,
Sachin Tanwar, Anita Singh, Nikhil Agarwal
Production: Rebecca Short, Vicky Baldwin
Cartography: **London** Maxine Repath, Ed
Wright, Katie Lloyd-Jones; **Delhi** Jai Prakash
Mishra, Rajesh Chhibber, Ashutosh Bharti, Rajesh
Mishra, Animesh Pathak, Jasbir Sandhu, Karobi
Gogoi, Amod Singh, Alakananda Bhattacharya,
Swati Handoo
Online: Narender Kumar, Rakesh Kumar,
Amit Verma, Rahul Kumar, Ganesh Sharma,
Debojit Borah, Saurabh Sati
Marketing & Publicity: **London** Liz Statham,
Niki Hanmer, Louise Maher, Jess Carter, Vanessa
Godden, Vivienne Watton, Anna Paynton, Rachel
Sprackett; **New York** Geoff Colquitt, Megan
Kennedy, Katy Ball; **Delhi** Ragini Govind
Manager India: Punita Singh
Reference Director: Andrew Lockett
Publishing Coordinator: Helen Phillips
Publishing Director: Martin Dunford
Commercial Manager: Gino Magnotta
Managing Director: John Duhigg

Publishing information

This third edition published March 2008 by
Rough Guides Ltd,
80 Strand, London WC2R 0RL
345 Hudson St, 4th Floor,
New York, NY 10014, USA
14 Local Shopping Centre, Panchsheel Park,
New Delhi 110017, India
Distributed by the Penguin Group
Penguin Books Ltd,
80 Strand, London WC2R 0RL
Penguin Group (USA)
375 Hudson Street, NY 10014, USA
Penguin Group (Australia)
250 Camberwell Road, Camberwell,
Victoria 3124, Australia
Penguin Books Canada Ltd,
10 Alcorn Avenue, Toronto, Ontario,
Canada M4V 1E4
Penguin Group (NZ)
67 Apollo Drive, Mairangi Bay, Auckland 1310,
New Zealand

Cover concept by Peter Dyer.
Typeset in Bembo and Helvetica to an original
design by Henry Iles.
Printed in Italy by LegoPrint S.p.A.
© Simon Lewis/Rough Guides, 2008
No part of this book may be reproduced in any
form without permission from the publisher except
for the quotation of brief passages in reviews.
236pp includes index
A catalogue record for this book is available from
the British Library
ISBN: 978-1-84353-907-0
The publishers and authors have done their best
to ensure the accuracy and currency of all the
information in **The Rough Guide to Beijing**,
however, they can accept no responsibility for
any loss, injury, or inconvenience sustained by
any traveller as a result of information or advice
contained in the guide.

1   3   5   7   9   8   6   4   2

Help us update

We've gone to a lot of effort to ensure that the
third edition of **The Rough Guide to Beijing** is
accurate and up to date. However, things change
– places get "discovered", opening hours are
notoriously fickle, restaurants and rooms raise
prices or lower standards. If you feel we've got it
wrong or left something out, we'd like to know,
and if you can remember the address, the price,
the hours, the phone number, so much the better.

Please send your comments with the subject
line "**Rough Guide Beijing Update**" to ©mail@
roughguides.com. We'll credit all contributions
and send a copy of the next edition (or any other
Rough Guide if you prefer) for the very best
emails.
Have your questions answered and tell others
about your trip at
Ⓦcommunity.roughguides.com

Acknowledgements

Simon would like to thank: Du, Tim, Tie Ying, Noe, Shen Ye, Joyce, Summer and Elena and the rest of the Lamas, Xiao Song and Kat.

Readers' letters

Thanks to all the readers who have taken the time to write in with comments and suggestions (and apologies if we've inadvertently omitted or misspelt anyone's name):

Simon Allen, Edithe Aussedat, Matthew Chance, Mary Durran, Nigel Gayner, Ben Krempel and Kerry Lynch, Barbara Martin Leung, Sarah Pritchard, Tom Shortland, Christian Williams, Nan Wu, Winnie Wong.

SMALL PRINT

Photo credits

All photos © Rough Guides except the following:

Title page
Night scene of CBD Beijing © Panorama Media Ltd/Alamy

Full page
Newspaper stand, Qianmen Dajie © Keith Drew

Introduction
Chinese fish painting © Keith Drew
Children playing football in Jingshang Park © Kevin Foy/Alamy
Bronze bird statue outside hall of Supreme Harmony, Forbidden City © Wendy Connett/Alamy
Chinese Instruction worksheet for learning the printed language © Aron Hsiao/Alamy

Things not to miss
01 Great Wall © Keith Drew
09 Forbidden City © Keith Drew
13 Tiananmen Square © Image State/Alamy
16 Mao's Mausoleum © Zhang jie/Imagine China

Black and whites
p.139 Wonton soup © Photolibrary
p.180 China's Red Guard read from Mao's Little Red Book © Popperfoto/Alamy

Temples colour section
Temple Guardian in the Fragrant Hills © Rochaphoto/Alamy
Worshippers toss metal discs at bell at the White Cloud temple © Dbimages/Alamy
Buddhist monks © Dk/Alamy
Lions dance at Temple Fair © Panorama Media Ltd/Alamy

Capital cuisine colour section
Donghuamen Night food market © Andrew McConnell/Alamy
Chinese Bird's nest soup © Panorama Media Ltd/Alamy
Market Beijing © Tim Hall/Axiom

SMALL PRINT

Index

Map entries are in colour.

INDEX

🅘

I

INDEX

221

INDEX

Map symbols

maps are listed in the full index using coloured text

- - - - Chapter division boundary
━ ━ ・・ Province boundary
═══ Road
━━━ Railway
------ Path
········ River
▪▪▪▪▪ Wall
⊠—⊠ Gate
‿ Bridge
▲ Hill
✕ Airport
◉ Metro station
⊛ Bus stop/station
◆ Point of interest
@ Internet cafe
(i) Tourist office

(C) Telephone office
⊠ Post office
⊞ Hospital
[E] Embassy/consulate
⌂ Observatory
▣ Restaurant
♀ Museum
🛕 Temple
⊥ Dagoba
🕌 Mosque
☐ Market
▬ Building
⊞ Church
◯ Stadium
▦ Park

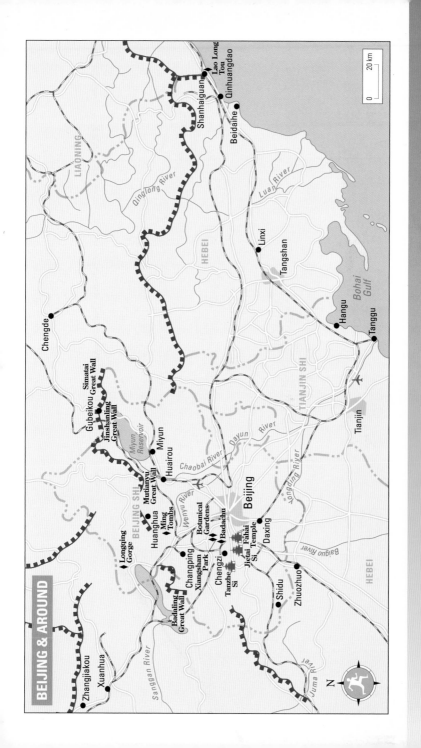

BEIJING & AROUND

0   20 km

N

LIAONING

HEBEI

Zhangjiakou

Xuanhua

Sangan River

Badaling Great Wall

Longqing Gorge

Huanghua

Changping

Xiangshan Park

Chengzi

Tanzhe Si

Jietai Si

Fahai Temple

BEIJING SHI

Ming Tombs

Botanical Gardens

Badachu

Daxing

Shidu

Zhuozhuo

Juma River

Baigou River

HEBEI

Beijing

Wenyu River

Chaobai River

Huairou

Miyun

Miyun Reservoir

Mutianyu Great Wall

Gubeikou

Jinshanling Great Wall

Simatai Great Wall

Chengde

Qinglong River

Dayun River

Longding River

Luan River

TIANJIN SHI

Tianjin

Tanggu

Hangu

Bohai Gulf

Tangshan

Linxi

Beidaihe

Qinhuangdao

Shanhaiguan

Lao Long Tou

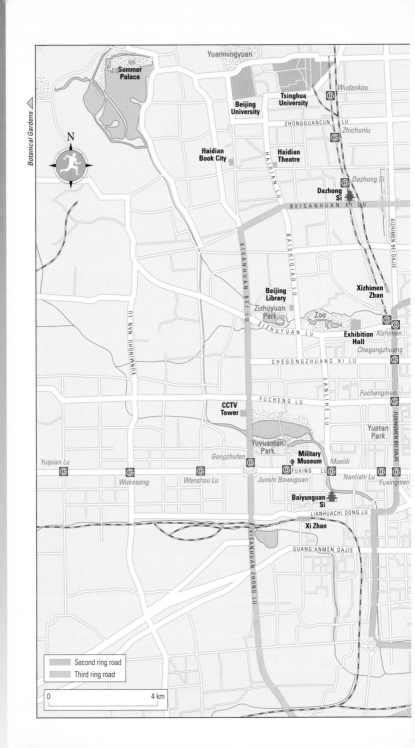

Olympic Forest Park & National Stadium

BEIJING

798 Art District, Holiday Inn Lido & Airport

Olympic Park

National Olympic Sports Centre

BEISIHUAN ZHONG LU

HUIXINGDONG JIE

JINGSHUN LU

BEISANHUAN ZHONG LU

DESHENGMENNEI DAJIE

ANDINGMENNEI DAJIE

HEPINGLI DONG JIE

BEISANHUAN DONG LU

Liufang

Hepingli Zhan

Sino Japanese Youth Centre & Century Theatre

2 Kolegas

XUEYUAN

XINJIEKOU DAJIE

Liangma Antique Mkt

LIANGMAHE LU

Deshengmen Bus station

Gulou

ANDINGMEN XI DAJIE

Ditan Park

Yonghegong

SANLITUN LU

DONGSANHUAN BEI LU

Lufthansa Centre

Jishuitan

Andingmen

YONGHEGONG DAJIE

Yonghe Gong

Dongzhimen Bus station

Chaoyang Park West Gate

Chaoyang Park

XISI BEI DAJIE

DI'ANMEN XI DAJIE

Dongzhimen

DONGZHIMENWAI DAJIE

Dongsi Shitiao

GONGRENTIYU CHANG BEI LU

Workers' stadium

DONGDAN BEI DAJIE

WANGFUJING DAJIE

Chaoyangmen

Jingguang Centre

Chaoyang Theatre

XIDAN BEI DAJIE

Forbidden City

Ritan Park

CHAOYANGMENWAI DAJIE

CHAOYANG LU

World Trade Centre

Wangfujing

Dongdan

Jianguomen

Yong'anli

Tian'anmen Dong

XICHANG'AN JIE

DONGCHANG'AN JIE

JIANGUOMENWAI DAJIE

Xidan

Tian'anmen Xi

Tian'anmen Square

Beijing Zhan

Guomao

Changchun Jie

Hepingmen

QIANMEN XI DAJIE

QIANMEN DONG DAJIE

Beijing Zhan

DONGSANHUAN NAN LU

Xuanwumen

Qianmen

Chongwenmen

QIANMEN DAJIE

CHONGWENMENWAI DAJIE

GUANQUMENWAI DAJIE

GUANQU LU

NIU JIE

Friendship Hospital

Natural History Museum

Majuan Bus station

Tiantan Park

TIYUGUAN LU

Longtan Park

Zhaojia Chaowai Market

Temple of Heaven

Panjiayuan Market

Taoranting Park

Capital Library

YONGDINGMENNEI

YONGDINGMEN XI JIE

YONGDINGMENWAI DAJIE

CHONGWENMENWAI DAJIE

YONGDINGMEN DONG JIE

Yongdingmen Train & Bus station

Haihutun Bus station

NANSANHUAN DONG LU

Zhaogongkou Bus station

NANSANHUAN ZHONG LU

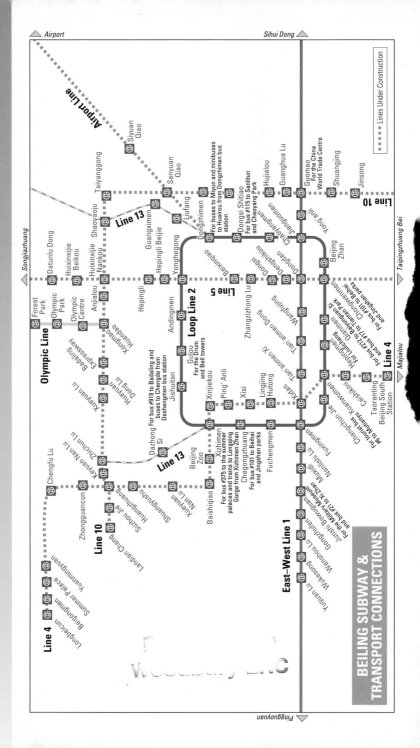

BEIJING SUBWAY & TRANSPORT CONNECTIONS

Lines Under Construction